PARACHUTE RIFLE COMPANY

PARACHUTE RIFLE COMPANY

A Living Historian's Introduction to
the Organization, Equipment, Tactics and Techniques
of the U.S. Army's Elite Airborne Troops in Combat
on the Western Front in World War II

Written and Edited by Robert Todd Ross
Author of The Supercommandos, and U.S. Army Rangers

Schiffer Military History
Atglen, PA

Acknowledgments

The author wishes to thank in particular Kirk B. Ross for his contributions toward the completion of this book. It is with pleasure that I take a moment here to suggest that all with an interest in the history of U.S. Airborne forces in World War II, make a special effort to read his book, *The Sky Men, A Parachute Rifle Company's Story of the Battle of Bulge and the Jump Across the Rhine*, Schiffer Publishing, Ltd., Atglen, 2000, that is, according to Clayton Laurie, Ph.D., U.S. Army Center of Military History, "The most comprehensive small unit history of World War II ever written." I concur.

Others whose help also deserve mention are Luther Hanson of the U.S. Army Quartermaster Museum, Charles E. Nesbitt, Bruce Waters, and Bob Biondi of Schiffer Publishing, Ltd.

Author's note: All photographs in this book feature battle recreations by living historians; there are no representations beyond this on the part of the author or the living historians. Throughout, the author refers to the living historians as if they are actual World War II-era paratroopers participating in actual historic events. This is done solely to heighten the dramatic effect of the photographs, and to convey more effectively the kind of story telling that is the nature and purpose of this hobby.

Original Maps, Charts and Graphic Design, and Photographs by Robert Todd Ross.

For Jane and Emma

and to

Charles Cram
506th Parachute Infantry Regiment,
101st Airborne Division

Book design by Robert Biondi.

Printed in China.
ISBN: 978-0-7643-3511-2

We are always looking for people to write books on new and related subjects. If you have an idea for a book, please contact us at the address below.

Published by Schiffer Publishing Ltd. 4880 Lower Valley Road Atglen, PA 19310 Phone: (610) 593-1777 FAX: (610) 593-2002 E-mail: Info@schifferbooks.com. Visit our web site at: www.schifferbooks.com Please write for a free catalog. This book may be purchased from the publisher. Please include $5.00 postage. Try your bookstore first.	In Europe, Schiffer books are distributed by: Bushwood Books 6 Marksbury Ave. Kew Gardens, Surrey TW9 4JF England Phone: 44 (0)20 8392-8585 FAX: 44 (0)20 8392-9876 E-mail: info@bushwoodbooks.co.uk www.bushwoodbooks.co.uk

CONTENTS

DOCUMENTS AND MONOGRAPHS

GRAPHIC PLATES

Color Coded

Authentically Styled Document for Tactical Battle Recreations

APPENDICES

1600 hours, 19 September 1944. The lieutenant leading 2nd Platoon entered the trees with his men in one rush, overrunning the German positions as they moved. Caught off guard by the suddenness and ferocity of the assault (some light machine gun crews even fired from the hip), most of the startled defenders surrendered immediately or fled, not willing to face the 'troopers in close quarters combat. A small group of die-hard SS men huddling in their foxhole were finished off with a white phosphorous hand grenade; their final shrieks rising above the din of small arms fire. As the attack punched though the deepest part of the woods, the lieutenant could see 1st platoon and the rest of the company cleaning out the enemy bunkers on the eastern side of the contested thicket. Soon, the first enemy prisoners were being prodded to the rear. The cry of "medic" went up, and they came, picking their way through the fallen to do what they could.[1]

As the smoke clears, the lieutenant slumps against a nearby tree and slides exhaustedly down its trunk until he is kneeling on the ground, breathing hard. He is soaked with sweat after the exertion of having dashed from cover and across an open thicket that they had all crossed to reach the wood line. Collecting himself, he has a moment of reflection. *He has traveled thousands of miles and has fought many battles in the months since leaving his home. His training and preparation have served him well so far, but there are many battles left to fight in this unfinished war.* He picks himself up calls for his platoon sergeant, and prepares for what is to come next.

How did we get to this point? The events described above could have happened during World War II. Certainly, similar occurrences did. But these are more recent. On any given weekend, throughout the United States, and indeed across other parts of the world, too, one will find numbers of men, outfitted as GIs battling similarly garbed Axis troops in mock combat, manning static or 'living history' displays for the public, or engaged as individuals, or in groups, in researching or practicing their hobby. This hobby is World War II reenacting. This volume, part historical reference and part living historian's guide book, is focused on arguably the most popular impression in this hobby today: that of the members of a U.S. Army Parachute Rifle Company in combat on the Western Front.

PROLOGUE

Arrayed in line abreast, members of A/508 advance on German-held positions atop Hill 75.9 known as Teufels Berg (or Devils Hill), in the vicinity of Nijmegen, Holland, 19 September 1944. They succeeded in recapturing the position, sending the surviving enemy fleeing in all directions.

"Like other young people, he wished to be able, in the winter nights of old age, to recount to those around him what he has heard and learned of the heroic age preceding his birth, and which of the Argonauts, particularly, he was in time to have seen ..." – Thomas Jefferson[1]

Awakening to the past. For anyone who ever wondered what it would be like to walk in the shoes of an American parachute infantryman during World War II, reenacting may hold the key. Most of us experience the past through our imaginations as piqued by books, or even movies and film documentaries. While sometimes very evocative, books and movies can take us only so far. Instead of reading about men on a march with heavy field packs and wondering how they must have felt, one can *know* this for himself. That is just what reenacting provides, a personal knowledge of what the past was like.

After the war, many combat veterans generally talked little of their battle experiences; and when they did it was often only to each other. This reluctance to speak about the fighting has, over the years, been misrepresented as a sign of this generation's modesty and humbleness. However, what in fact prompts their silence is that these men do not want to awaken the demons that haunt their minds.

Reenacting is, all told, an enjoyable experience, far from the harsh realities of actual combat. As such, and justifiably so, the threshold for knowledge through personal experience has its limits. This hobby thankfully does not provide a means for reenactors to really know the mind-crippling terror, or the debilitating deprivation that the war inflicted on our forebears. For living historians, testimony as to these hardships, offered by actual combat veterans must be proof alone.

When I was about ten years old, my parents took my twin brother and me to an airshow in Baltimore, Maryland. There, in a hanger, I saw for the first time living historians portraying World War II infantrymen. Looking back, I can hardly remember the aircraft, but I do remember how impressed I was with those 'GIs'. They were arrayed as members of the U.S. 29th Infantry Division, the old 'Blue and Gray' Division that assaulted Omaha Beach on D-Day, the one to which – specifically to that division's K Company, 115th Infantry – many of the men in the county where I grew up had belonged. As of the time of this writing, the war is more than six decades in the past. The veteran soldiers who are still with us today were themselves little more than boys at the time.

As a youngster, I was captivated by all things World War II. This interest was fed by frequent trips to the Army surplus stores in my area, and by movies, but moreover by books, such as Cornelius Ryan's *The Longest Day*, and *A Bridge Too Far*, that I eagerly devoured before my teens. There, too, were the early awkward conversations with the veterans themselves. In point of fact, it was only after immersing myself in research for my first book, *The Supercommandos*, that I felt adequately equipped to discuss in detail with World War II veterans their wartime experiences. Not having experienced combat – nor having served in the military at all for that matter – I will forever remain an outsider to that ordeal. Yet, this does not prevent me from feeling pride in, and gratitude for, those who shouldered that terrible responsibility. And while I am not envious of their experience, I do marvel at their strength. They will live long in my memory.

I started kicking around ideas for this book in 2000. I observed that men, and women, too, from all walks of life, from every ethnic and socioeconomic background have taken up this hobby. I speculated as to what motivates individuals to participate in World War II reenacting, where the vast majority of participants portray American GIs on the Western Front. Of the many possible reasons, certain are plain: An overwhelmingly enthusiastic interest in history, and a desire to know a little bit more about what 'it' must have been like. But what is it about this time in our history that moves people so?

In World War II reenacting, it is the spirit of the U.S. soldier that draws one in. For the American fighting man of World War II was not dispatched to foreign shores as a conqueror. Rather, he was a liberator, on a most noble and great mission. It was with dread, loathing, humor, humanity, compassion, but above all with resignation that the Armies of freedom waged a relentless war against cruel Axis oppressors. And luckily, for the world, freedom prevailed. If it sounds as if I am being something of a cheerleader, it is only because I am. However, the American combat soldier of the Second World War must not be overly simplified.

Taking the good with the bad. There are pitfalls in attempting to assume the persona of our past heroes, not the least of which is the penchant on the part of many, moved by want for nostalgic icons, to 'interpret' only *some* of the facts while ignoring others. In the absence of strict objectivity, one may do, however unintentionally, a disservice to history and those who made it by casting light on only the positive aspects of the World War II GIs' character. It must be pointed out that these were a group of men who, at their core, were not so dissimilar to any group that might today be gathered for a similar purpose, rendering their accomplishments on the battlefield all the more tangible, relevant and meaningful. For it is in the understanding of those who came before us that we may better understand ourselves.

As Michael C.C. Adams points out in his wryly-titled and acerbic book, *The Best War Ever*, many combat infantrymen near or at the front used an abundance of profanity, were commonly drunk, they looted, they often malingered, many engaged in promiscuous sexual activity, many suffered from combat fatigue (neurosis), and some mistreated or even brutalized and killed enemy prisoners. In extreme cases, some troops even shot their own officers and NCOs who they deemed too reckless. Furthermore, S.L.A. Marshall charges in his controversial study, *Men Against Fire*, that only a small percentage of infantrymen actually fired their weapons in battle, even among the Army's so-called elite units.[2]

Adams, speaking on the war in general, cautions: "… when nostalgia drives us to depict a war as a golden age in our cultural development, a time of cheerful production, team spirit, prosperity, and patriotism, we trivialize the event by slighting the real suffering that took place; we make it into a carnival. And we loose sight of the fact that war is inherently destructive – wasteful of human and natural resources, disruptive of normal social development. We risk initiating human catastrophes in the questionable belief that history shows that war will cure our social problems and make us feel strong again."[3]

The root word is actor. Whether identified as a Reenactor, or as a Living History Interpreter, the goal of all such individuals is essentially the same: to, by careful analysis of the historical record, and through personal performance, effectively explain and portray a true and lifelike account of a character from the past; in this case, the World War II parachute infantryman on the Western Front during 1944 and 1945. Role playing and performance, as if an actor in a drama, with all the appropriate affectations, garb and accouterments is an integral part of this form of story telling.

As reenacting, or more simply put, 'acting', is but one facet of this pursuit, it may be more acceptable to most in this hobby to be referred to by the latter of the two aforementioned labels: Living History Interpreters, implying that individuals have acquired a requisite dose of accurate and detailed historical knowledge through meaningful and painstaking study. But, herein the terms are considered interchangeable and are attributed equal weight.

Good relations and serendipitous saviors. Fearing that World War II reenacting will suffocate from over-applied or misdirected political correctness, it is natural that reenactors should seek to portray themselves – through their impressions – in the most positive possible light and avoid negative scrutiny. But, trying to look good has to some degree become more important than actually being good – that is, being accurate. This is not wholly unjustifiable. Especially given the fact that this hobby must rely – at least in part, if not wholly – on the good will of the public for its very survival. For the general public views the subject of reenacting and reenactors with a mix of curiosity and trepidation.

Partly to blame is the inescapable fact that the reenacting community is an exclusive subculture, and the subject matter is itself esoteric. Nevertheless, the hobby appears to be growing. Vendors of World War II militaria and reproduction uniforms and equipment report their businesses are growing as a result. And, happily, as a byproduct of their interest in the subject, the World War II reenacting community has, by coincidence, become both a savior and a custodian of the history of the period. And the public does benefit from reenactors. At airshows, parades, and similar events, reenactors invite everyone to share the experience, to touch and to feel history.

No easy task. *Parachute Rifle Company* may be called a first stab at introducing a literature into the hobby of the World War II reenacting. In essence, it is a distillation of pertinent World War II-period infantry doctrine and history into an unfettered, reenactor-friendly guide offering an approach on how to effectively adapt wartime doctrine to the reenacting environment. In order to maintain and convey the feel of period documents, much of the text is taken verbatim from Army manuals of the day. While focusing squarely on U.S. Army parachute infantryman afoot on the Western Front between 1944 and 1945, this book presents themes – among them the supreme value of diligent research and an open mind – that are universally beneficial to reenacting soldiers in other theaters of war, and even of other armies and other wars altogether.

We have all heard the old expression: "There's a right way, and a wrong way, and then there is the Army way." The purpose of *Parachute Rifle Company* is not to foist upon readers the notion that in reenacting there is simply a right or wrong way of doing things. I am, herein, as much as adaptation may allow, conveying to readers the "*Army way!*" Because World War II was an event of unbelievably monumental complexity and importance, to be good at what they do, reenactors must acquire the tools to master the detailed knowledge of a very specific facet of that history, while at the same time the perspective to demonstrate its relevance. Each must be a skilled historian, a conscientious teacher and a deft performer, as well as bit of a politician. This is no easy task. The information presented herein is drawn from my experience in compiling my two previous books, *The Supercommandos: First Special Service Force 1942-1944*, and *U.S. Army Rangers & Special Forces of World War II*; from consulting on The History Channel film documentary, *The Black Devils*; from information gathered reading countless books, accounts, manuals, and documents; from long-time collecting of period memorabilia; and from interviews with reenactors and with combat veterans. I can safely say that I know at least a little about how to conduct valid research.

From detailed and frank conversations with my twin brother, Kirk, I gained much insight into what may be the high points and the low points of battle recreations and living history events; Kirk, the author of the highly-regarded, *The Sky Men*, learned first hand by organizing two greatly successful large-scale events in the mid-1990s. And from participating in both tactical and living history events myself, I bring my own first hand experiences and opinions to bear. *Parachute Rifle Company* challenges a number of ideas and practices prevalent in the hobby today, while embracing others. It is meant to bring the reenacting community together and to instill in it a spirit of mutual support and cooperation. In no way is this book intended to be any sort of exposé. Rather, I hope that readers will find its contents objective, balanced, and ultimately useful to their enjoyment of history, and this hobby.

In the wake of retaking Teufels Berg, a platoon leader, in this case a second lieutenant, rests alongside his RTO, who is speaking into the platoon's SCR536 radio. The lieutenant is armed with a U.S. .30 MI rifle, preferring this robust weapon and its stopping power to that of the .30 MI carbine most often carried by officers.

"The trouble with the world is not that people know too little, but that they know so many things that ain't so." – Mark Twain

The origins of parachute infantry. In 1787 Benjamin Franklin, inspired by his contemporary Montgolfier's success with the hot air balloon, first proposed the use of an airborne assault in warfare when he stated: "Where is the Prince who can afford so to cover his country with troops for its defense, as that ten thousand men descending from the clouds, might not, in many places, do an infinite amount of mischief before a force could be brought together to repel them?" By the time the Wright Brothers first flew at Kitty Hawk in 1903, the parachute was already six centuries old, but it was not until the First World War that the first serious suggestions for the military application of the parachute for airborne forces arose.

Brigadier General Billy Mitchell, commander of American Air Service in France during World War I, suggested the first airborne assault in October 1918. Envisioned to support the anticipated Spring 1919 offensive, General Mitchell proposed to deploy the better part of the 1st U.S. Infantry Division by parachute behind the German lines around Metz. The 'Airdoughs,' armed with a large number of automatic weapons, would be dropped from heavy bombers, protected by an umbrella of fighter aircraft, and resupplied by air. Though the operation was seriously considered, the armistice arrived before it became a reality. It is an interesting footnote, however, that working out the details of Mitchell's "wild" proposal was "a young Air Service staff officer," Lewis H. Brereton, "the future commander of the First Allied Airborne Army in 1944-1945."

After the First World War, several European nations, including France, Italy, and Great Britain, began experimenting with the concept of airborne operations. However, it was Nazi Germany and the Soviet Union that undertook the most serious study of this new kind of warfare. The Soviets were the first to apply airborne concepts when, during the Red Army maneuvers near Moscow in 1930, they landed a lieutenant and eight men by parachute. By 1935 the Soviets had organized an Airlanding Corps capable of transporting an entire division. The following year the Russians jumped two battalions of infantry, one thousand men, supported by sixteen artillery pieces and one hundred fifty machine-guns in less than eight minutes during tactical exercises near Kiev. The force assembled and rapidly occupied a town that was their objective. An additional four thousand reinforcements were air-landed and joined the paratroopers.

The exercises made a mixed impression on most of the foreign observers, but in Germany the Airborne concept was enthusiastically embraced. Germany may have also been impressed by the remark made by Red Air Force Marshal Michal Schtscherbakov to "French Marshal Petain during a tour of the Maginot Line: Fortresses like this may well be superfluous in the future if your potential adversary … parachutes over them." The Germans began the rapid development of an airborne arm within the Luftwaffe with the activation of the *1st Jäger Battalion, Regiment "Herman Göring"* in January 1936. A second battalion was formed by the army that same month. By the time of the invasion of Poland, the Germans had organized most of the *7.Flieger-Division*. Though these men did not participate in the Polish campaign, Hitler promised their commander, *General der Flieger* Kurt Student that they would see action in the west.

And so they did. The arrival of parachute troops in Norway, Holland, and Belgium, in advance of the Germans' main forces, paved "the way for the capture of airfields and reduction of fortifications in 1940 [and] startled anew a world not yet recovered from the accounts of air-ground blitzkrieg in Poland and Scandinavia. Spearheading the German drive through the low countries in May, a small force of five hundred parachutists captured the crossings of the Albert Canal intact. Two officers and seventy-eight men arrived by glider atop the broad roof of the great Belgian fort, Eben Emael, and held the garrison at bay until mechanized infantry arrived the next day. In April 1941 Germans used gliderborne troops in the seizure of Corinth. Less than a month later they offered their final demonstration that airborne troops were "here to stay" – the parachute, glider, and air-landing assault on Crete. The capture of that strategic island in the Mediterranean left "a lasting impression on the Allied armies" and the dramatic display of German airborne power served to spur on the United States Army's fledgling Airborne Effort.

Despite the fact that the United States had developed emergency parachutes for its aviators as early as 1918, the Army did not begin experimenting with parachutes for the deployment of airborne forces until 1928. On 29 April, General Billy Mitchell watched as three volunteers from the 2nd Infantry Division jumped at Kelly Field near San Antonio, Texas. The three men assembled and fired a machine-gun as part of the exercise. Unfortunately, no further experiments were conducted until May 1939, when the Chief of Infantry again raised the question of "air infantry." By 2 January 1940, it had been ordered that a test platoon be formed under the Infantry Board. The cooperation of the Air Corps was ordered as well and what was to become known as the Airborne Effort had begun. The German achievements in the Low Countries provided urgency to the program and "proved the [airborne] concept valid."

The pioneer days of American airborne began on 25 June 1940 under the red clay bluffs of Fort Benning, Georgia, the home of the Infantry School, with the activation of the Parachute Test Platoon. "Thus," wrote General James M. Gavin, the famed commander of the 82nd Airborne Division, "it is a historical fact that airborne warfare, at least in a modern sense, was originated by the Russians and developed to a state of combat effectiveness by the Germans. But it is also a historical fact that the American Army took this new instrument of warfare and, with the British, refined and improved it and unleashed upon our enemies airborne forces of such power and perfection as even they had not dreamed of." Of the two hundred men from the 29th Infantry Regiment who volunteered, forty-eight men were selected. Training began right away with the first jumps being made on 16 August and a mass jump being made on the twenty-ninth. While these men worked, the services vied over the control of the new arm.

For more than a year there had been a debate within the Army over who would control the airborne troops. After the Air Corps was approached regarding air transportation for "air infantry" they suggested that airborne forces be brought under their control and be named "Air Grenadiers." Even the Corps of Engineers suggested that, in light of Airborne's role as saboteurs operating behind enemy lines, they be placed under their command. It was not until mid-1940 that the Army's Deputy Chief of Staff finally directed that airborne forces, whose primary mission was ground combat, remain under the Chief of Infantry and train at Fort Benning. Things then began to heat up.

On 16 September 1940, the 501st Parachute Infantry Battalion was activated, absorbing the members of the original test platoon. The following summer saw the creation of the 502nd Parachute Battalion which drew on the 501st for cadre. New training areas and additional drop zones were created to cope with the growing needs of the Airborne Effort. By the end of 1941, two more parachute infantry battalions would be formed, the 503rd and the 504th. The growth of the Airborne program had occurred not a moment too soon as war was declared on 8 December 1941, the day after the surprise Japanese attack of the American Naval Base at Pearl Harbor, Hawaii.

Throughout 1942, the Airborne Effort intensified. On 21 March, the Provisional Parachute Group was redesignated Airborne Command and all existing airborne units were placed under its authority. Airborne Command served to coordinate all aspects of the Airborne Effort including the activation of the various formations, training of personnel, and coordination of air transportation with the Army Air Forces. Parachute field artillery and other formations were soon to follow. At the same time, the role these men were to play was also being discussed.

In May 1942, the mission of airborne forces was put forth in Field Manual 31-30, *Tactics and Techniques of Air-borne Troops*: parachute troops were considered "the spearhead of a vertical envelopment or the advance and guard element of airlanding troops or other forces." The concept of airborne warfare generally was one which envisioned the seizure of suitable landing areas by parachute troops, and then their reinforcement by troops arriving by glider or airplane. Accompanying this was listed a whole series of possible objectives for airborne troops: "river and canal crossings, defiles, establishing bridgeheads; attack of defended positions by landing on flank or in rear, or within the perimeter; destruction of enemy supply and communication installations; consolidation and holding of ground taken by armored forces until the arrival of other ground units; and assistance to ground offensives by vertical envelopment."

War Department Training Circular No.113, *The Employment of Airborne and Troop Carrier Forces*, of 9 October 1943, further detailed the use of the new arm. It stated that these forces would be deployed in mass, but went on to say that: "Airborne troops should not be employed unless they can be supported by other ground or naval forces within approximately 3 days, or unless they can be withdrawn after their mission has been accomplished. This was later proven by operations to be sound doctrine. The circular also stated: "[airborne forces presented] a constant threat by their mere presence in the theater of operations thereby causing the enemy to disperse his forces over a wide area in order to protect his vital installations." The new airborne arm, therefore, provided the Army with the means to apply the naval concept of "Fleet in Being" and, as a footnote, espoused Benjamin Franklin's vision of mighty armies descending from the clouds. As Airborne Command worked out the details that would put these ideas into practice, new volunteers were being trained to fill the ranks of the ever increasing airborne arm.[1]

Answering the call. In the wake of the attack on the U.S. naval station at Pearl Harbor, Hawaii, on that fateful morning of December 7, 1941, Americans by the millions clamored to *join up*, to join the war effort. Fathers and sons, young and old, rich and poor. Nearly 16 million American men and women entered military service during World War II; nearly 1 in 10 Americans. From September 1940, the Selective Training and Service Act proscribed, "all men between the ages of 21 and 35 to register with their local draft boards". By 16 October 1940, the deadline for registration, more than 16 million men had registered, and by the end of the war the number swelled to nearly 50 million. Later in the war, the age limit was expanded to include ages 18 through 65, though only men up to age 36 were in fact drafted. Those who registered, and were by means of a questionnaire deemed qualified, submitted to a physical examination. Each would-be soldier whose physical fitness was judged 1-A – "available for military service" – by the three members of his local draft board, was notified by letter, given 10 days to get his personal affairs in order, and "told … when and where to report." The numbers are staggering. More remarkable still, nearly 100,000 convicted felons joined the armed services straight from Federal penitentiaries.[2]

There were, of course, a number of legitimate reasons for which able-bodied potential draftees could secure deferment from military service, chief among them fatherhood. However by the end of 1944 more than 7 million fathers were drafted. "Until 1943 the Army was the only branch to rely on draftees, and it deliberately set its physical requirements at rock bottom. The minimum height for draftees was five feet and the minimum weight 105 pounds. The selectees had to have correctable vision and at least half of their natural teeth; they must not have flat feet, hernia or venereal disease."[3]

Once in the Army, soldiers ceased being civilians, and were no longer subject to civil law; their conduct was now subject to the Articles of War. And, like the men who entered the service during the war, those new to reenacting the GI combat soldier in Europe must become acclimated and blend into their new set of standards, too. But unlike the Army of yesteryear, reenactors are largely on their own when it comes to this task. One must purchase appropriate uniforms and appropriate insignia. He must provide himself with his own field equipment, weapon(s) and blank ammunition. And he may want even to outfit himself with some personal paraphernalia that is apropos to the period. Army courtesies and customs, as well as soldiering skills must be studied and practiced – marching, saluting, and the manual of arms. There is even a new lexicon to learn. "Hurry up and wait," "on the double," "chow," and so on.[4]

Brash and Unruly. "America's citizen-soldiers, like their ancestors in the Civil War and the Revolution, were a brash and unruly lot. They chafed under regimentation and lived for the day when they could chuck the military life and go home."[5] There is no reason, then, to think that regimentation would not grate on reenactors, too. After all, reenacting is a hobby. And reenactors participate in this hobby as a form of escapism, just as some folks collect stamps, and others participate in sports. As such, the 'so-close-and-yet-so-far'-nature of reenacting is demonstrated by the fact that on one hand, some degree of military regimentation is unavoidable and indeed necessary, while on the other, reenactors often have a tendency to disregard military hierarchy as a form of personal convenience.

Pride and Prejudice. "He found a home in the Army" was the saying that described any man – especially one who had become down-and-out during the depression – who had joined up, not out of any feelings of patriotism, but to get a roof over his head, clothes on his back and three meals a day. Once America entered the war, the man in uniform suddenly became the object of respect and admiration, replacing pre-war derision.[6] More than simply being a costume, the wearing of a Yank's uniform is an expression of pride felt by reenactors for their forebears.

Many of the discomforts faced by white servicemen were mild compared with those faced by so-called colored soldiers – particularly those of African-American or Nisei extraction. The U.S. Army of World War II was segregated, and colored troops found that the bigotry and discrimination that so many suffered in civilian life was just as prevalent in the service. "In the training camps, blacks were relegated to separate eating and recreational facilities. Army units were segregated by race from the battalion to the divisional level and, in any unit, no black officer could outrank a white one."[7]

Beginning in February 1942, some 127,000 Japanese-Americans were resettled from the West Coast to interment camps in the interior of the United States by order of a federal government that gave in to the ground swell of public uncertainty, fear, prejudice and hostility following the Japanese attack on Pearl Harbor. While many Japanese-Americans – Nisei – volunteered for the service in an attempt to show their patriotism and loyalty, many were drafted right out of what President Roosevelt, himself, called concentration camps.[8] What outrage "colored" soldiers must have felt at the hypocrisy of fighting and dying for the cause of freedom overseas, while at home their families and they themselves were not accorded the same rights and freedoms as the majority of Americans.

Combat outpost of the 82nd Airborne Division, built into a standing type double foxhole, and camouflaged with deadfall and foliage. The officer at left leans on the parapet of the foxhole as he scans the fields to his front with a pair of M3 binoculars, while the Browning automatic rifleman stands ready to deliver fire upon whatever target may be designated.

Volunteers All. In some ways, one might liken his entry into World War II reenacting to how young men volunteered for service in World War II. Moved by some voice, and after weighing the pros and cons of the various branches of the military and each of their arms and services, one marches up to his local recruiter and states: "I want to join the U.S. Army; give me Airborne!, and I want combat!" To some extent, you never had a choice; the wings of the reenactor Army Air Corps are decidedly clipped. And the Navy? What Navy? Then there are the Marines. But that bunch are destined to force a landing on some strange, malarial jungle-island whose name one cannot even pronounce. Forget it. Army it's gonna be! And one notable similarity in the reenacting Airborne: it is all volunteer!

Taking the place of recruiters in the reenacting context are, to some degree, the many already established reenacting units whose websites may be found on the Internet. Links abound, especially on the websites of the more high-profile dealers of reproduction uniforms and equipment. The websites of these units are a source of information – each unit's creed, uniform standards, abbreviated histories, upcoming events, links – for their current members, and act as 'shingles' hung out to attract new prospects. Making up the largest portion of the established American reenactment units are the combat infantry types, including groups portraying – some generically, and some more specifically – elements of infantry divisions, airborne divisions, Ranger infantry battalions, and special units such as the First Special Service Force.

It is not compulsory that one join an already established unit. However, the current tide in reenacting dictates that individuals join units, many of which are further aligned with regional or national reenacting societies or organizations. The wisdom of this is that members of established units conform to approved authenticity and safety standards for displays and events, and that some modicum of control, organization and accountability may be more easily effected.

Beginning the journey. As hobbies go, World War II reenacting might be compared with sports, particularly with team sports. This is a fair comparison as the military experience is replete with references to various types of teams: combined arms team, mortar teams, light machine gun teams, and so forth. In the field, cohesion and teamwork is crucial not only to the success of the military mission, but to one's very existence. However, it is as an individual that one will most often enter into this hobby.

Upon launching oneself into reenacting, he will have to define his interests, allocate time, conduct research, set goals, determine a budget, and purchase supplies including clothing, equipment, weapons, props, and so on.

History in the flesh. As a would-be living historian, one of the first things that one will need do is establish his first-person impression. To render a first-person impression, one simply assumes the persona of an historical character – in this case a parachute infantryman. This alter ego may be maintained throughout the duration of a living history event, whether it be a public display or a tactical reenactment. Whereas home-grown U.S. reenactors who portray foreign soldiers – Russians, French, Germans, and so on – must carry out a substantial amount of research in order to craft a credible impression, those who seek to portray a U.S. parachute infantryman have only to look at their own personal histories for a basis.

Some of the basic elements of one's first-person impression are his name, age and birthday, his home town, details about his family background and social class, and some information about his life before the war. Was he drafted or did he enlist? What are his hobbies, if any? While one may fabricate any of these details, it is much easier to simply 'date' these details in order to fit in with the time period in question. Some older reenactors may even want to fashion their first-person impression as having served in World War I.

To demonstrate how this works, we will use as an example a fictitious reenactor, John S. Doe, who, as of the time of this writing, is 34 years old. As a 34-year-old in 1944, John Doe's birthday is, for the sake of argument, April 1, 1910 – April Fool's Day. Due to his age, reenactor Doe enjoys attending events as *Captain John S. Doe, AUS.* Patterned after Doe's own early life, *Captain Doe* was born and raised in Maryland, the youngest of three children with a brother and a sister. His mother is a homemaker, and his father is an engineer retained by a firm near Baltimore, involved in Government contract work. Doe had a comfortable childhood and, growing up on a large farm, he learned how to handle firearms at an early age and was an avid hunter who was taught field craft by his father. He went to grade school and high school locally. He attended college – *from this point the remaining details of his life are altered to give credibility to his first-person impression* – on an ROTC scholarship and upon graduation in 1932, with a BA in History, took a commission in the Regular Army as a second lieutenant. Doe enjoyed Army life. In 1933, he attended the Infantry School at Fort Benning, Georgia, where he demonstrated to his instructors a natural talent for planning and tactics, and was soon promoted to First Lieutenant. Doe was married in 1936. While promotion came slow during the inter-war years, after Pearl Harbor, and with the expansion of the Regular Army, need of his skills brought about his transfer to the staff of the Provisional Parachute Group in March 1941. And the rest, as they say, is history.

One might consider his first-person impression as a character in an historical fiction novel. Developing a first-person impression is a creative and fun way to learn more about the historical time period at hand, and it is a great way to share history with fellow living historians and the public alike. In order to sound and act like a soldier, one need not reinvent himself. By swaggering or taking on the style of a martinet, barking curt orders

Paratroopers peer around the corner of a factory building in Normandy, June 1944. This study reveals a variety of uniform variations including field expedient camouflage paint applied to the jackets, trousers and helmets, various helmet nets, a cross-section of company-level weapons and associated equipment.

at fellow reenactors or deluging them with profanity, one's behavior is over-the-top and only succeeds in effecting a rude caricature of an enlisted man or officer. In other words, one becomes in the lexicon of the day, "chicken-shit." One need not alter his real-life demeanor to play the part of a soldier well. People of the 1940s are much the same as we are today. Simply showing courtesy and respect – military or otherwise – to one's fellow reenactors is all that is required.

Question everything. "Believe only half of what you see and nothing that you hear."[9] In other words, conduct research! But where may one turn to find reliable information, and how will one know that it is in fact reliable? Because history is largely a collection of stories about the past handed down, one may, at best, only hope to gather a reasonably accurate record. Though not common, and nearly always unintentional, blunders are sometimes made. For many different reasons: personal motives, lack of diligent research, laziness, by simple mistake, or in some cases simply by not caring, historians have falsified, omitted, embellished, distorted, or invented facts. The following paragraphs describe a few such 'blunders', and though the points are minor, they illustrate well the question at hand.

In his book *Fatal Decision: Anzio and the Battle for Rome*, author Carlo D'Este describes members of the First Special Service Force as being "Outfitted with red berets and needle-sharp sheathknives …"[10] D'Este cites the book *The Devil's Brigade* as the source for this information. However, this book mentions nothing of red berets (and rightly so as the First Special Service Force was, in fact, never issued any such item). Only in the 1968 movie, *The Devil's Brigade*, was the Force ever previously portrayed as having worn red berets. D'Este obviously used a Hollywood film as the basis for his comment about the Force. Does anyone see something wrong with this picture? Little by little, like water, inaccuracies trickle into the history and begin to mix with the facts, sometimes supplanting facts themselves.[11]

D'Este goes on to state: "Frederick also devised a nasty calling card in the form of paper stickers containing the symbol of the Special Service Force (two crossed lightning bolts with a dagger pointing upward through the middle) and a phrase in German that translated into: 'The worst is yet to come.' Whenever a German was killed behind their lines, one of these stickers would be left on his helmet or forehead. Other calling cards in the form of red stickers emblazoned with the Force spearhead symbol were left on buildings and fenceposts behind German lines."[12]

For the passage above, D'Este cites Lt. Colonel Robert D. Burhans' *The First Special Service Force*, page 194. On page 194, Burhans states: "Psychological warfare also supplied the Force with red spearhead stickers to slap on fenceposts and doors during raids into the enemy line, a sort of Force calling card." While one cannot be sure from where D'Este got his information regarding the 'symbol' of the Special Service Force, one is sure from where he did not, namely from Burhans' book. The Force's arm of service insignia was a pair of crossed arrows. The modern U.S. Army Special Forces' insignia incorporates a pair of crossed arrows with a dagger pointing upwards in the middle.

The foregoing is not an attempt to besmirch the name of an otherwise highly-respected author. Yet, here is a case where a trusted historian – himself, given to fallibility on occasion like everyone else – has become responsible for the spread of incorrect information. And one could bet that he is not the only one. Only diligent and careful research may be the cornerstone for both understanding the historical backdrop in question, and for fielding a meaningful impression of the U.S. parachute infantryman. In one's research one must be wary as secondary source material is riddled with erroneous information. The time and effort one spends in research will mean the difference between a simple, clumsy impression painted with broad strokes, or a more interesting one with finely polished details and great character.

Turning one's scrutiny to television and movies, the special feature "Field Guide, Chain of Command" in the television series *Band of Brothers'* offers information concerning rank structure for non-commissioned officers and enlisted men more suited to the Vietnam time-period than World War II. This TV show's special feature includes a "sergeant first class" (not of the time-period) when the corresponding insignia (three chevrons and two rockers) denotes a technical sergeant. There are a number of other mistakes, too, in this

special feature. For correct World War II U.S. Army ranks and insignia, please refer to the color plate, *Rank Insignia* in this guide. It is beyond me to understand why, in a television production of this quality, that mistakes like this happen, that the facts are so easily overlooked.

A picture is worth a thousand words? Photo histories are wonderful sources for images of, in this case, paratroops. Where most of these books fall short is that they give only superficial details about the subject. That is to say that they most often point out details that are already quite apparent, such as mentioning the kind of kit a soldier is wearing. Identifying items is all well and fine, but to know the meaning of such objects, and their place in the overall history is what is important. It is all too often that the trappings of the paratroopers are celebrated far more than the skills and tactics of the men themselves. This book strives to turn one's attention to the latter.

Soldier's of Colonel James Coutts' 513th Parachute Infantry enjoy a 'smoke' in Germany a few days following the commencement of Operation Varsity, the 24 March 1945 airborne assault across the Rhine River at Wesel, Germany. The 507th PIR had also participated in the Varsity assault as part of the U.S. 17th Airborne Division.

Primary sources. Primary source material is that which is original, which, in the context of military history, would include personal letters and diaries, original documents and after action reports, period sketches, maps and photographs, transcriptions of interviews with actual battle participants, unpublished monographs and personal accounts, and wartime field manuals, technical manuals, and publications. Secondary source describes historical material derived from primary sources, most often books.

The single greatest source of first-hand information are the various government and military archives, and to a lesser degree museums, most located on the East Coast of the United States. While access to many of the collections of these archives may now be obtained online, the resources of some may still be only fully appreciated by personal visit, but the effort may be handsomely rewarded. The wealth of information, much of it largely untapped, can be overwhelming and may take some time, and indeed numerous trips, to become familiar with. Patience and meticulous organization, and sometimes an appointment with a staff archivist/librarian, are keys to fruitful searches. The top six archives for research (ranked in order of ease of access and weight of material) are as follows.

The National Archives II
8601 Adelphia Road
College Park, Maryland 20740
Website: http://www.archives.gov/index.html

The Infantry School
Donovan Research Library
Fort Benning, Georgia
Website: https://www.infantry.army.mil/donovan/
Monograph Collection Online: https://www.benning.army.mil/monographs/

U.S. Army Heritage and Information Center
Military History Institute
Ridgway Hall
Carlisle Barracks
Carlisle, Pennsylvania
Website: http://www.carlisle.army.mil/usamhi/

National Personnel Records Center
Military Personnel Records
9700 Page Avenue
St. Louis, Missouri
Website: http://www.archives.gov/st-louis/military-personnel/

U.S. Army Center of Military History
Fort Lesley J. McNair
Washington, DC
Website: http://www.army.mil/cmh-pg/

U.S. Army Command and General Staff College
Fort Leavenworth, Kansas
Combat Studies Institute
Combined Arms Research Library
Center for Army Lessons Learned
Website: http://usacac.army.mil/cac2/cgsc/

PERSONAL EXPERIENCE MONOGRAPHS

One of the greatest resources for detailed information and for inspiration in creating tactical event scenarios (which will be discussed later in this book) is the Donovan Library's Monograph Collection at the Infantry School, Fort Benning, Georgia. These monographs – concise, detailed narratives of personal combat experiences with accompanying maps and supporting documents – were written shortly after the war by officers who were students in the Advanced Infantry Officers Course. The following are among the Airborne-related titles on hand:

Operations of the 101st Airborne Division East of Ste. Mere Eglise, France, 5-6 June 1944, Normandy Campaign, Personal Experience of an Assistant G-3. Captain John A. Kindig. Airborne division spearheading the invasion of fortified coast.

Operations of a Mixed Group from Units of the 507th Parachute Infantry, 82nd Airborne Division, In the Invasion of France, 5-7 June 1944, Normandy Campaign, Personal Experience of a Company Commander. Major Roy E. Creek. Mixed unit of a parachute infantry attacking in flat, swampy terrain.

Plans and Operations of the 506th Parachute Infantry, 101st Airborne Division, In the Invasion of Normandy, 5-30 June 1944, Normandy Campaign, Personal Experience of a Company Commander, 3rd Battalion, 5-7 June 1944. Major John T. McKnight. Plans and operations of a parachute infantry regiment.

Operations of a Regimental Pathfinder Unit, 507th Parachute Infantry Regiment, 82nd Airborne Division, In Normandy, 6 June 1944, Normandy Campaign, Personal Experience of a Regimental Pathfinder Leader. Captain John T. Joseph. Pathfinder operation.

Operations of the 1st Battalion, 506th Parachute Infantry, 101st Airborne Division, In the Vicinity of Carentan, 6-8 June 1944, Normandy Campaign, Personal Experience of a Company Commander. Major Knut H. Raudstein. Parachute infantry battalion attacking in the enlargement of a beachhead.

Operations of the 1st Platoon, Company I, 507th Parachute Infantry Regiment, 82nd Airborne Division, At the Forcing of the Merderet River Causeway At Lafiere, France, 9 June 1944, Normandy Campaign, Personal Experience of a Platoon Leader. 1st Lieutenant Donald C. O'Rourke. Platoon in the attack.

Operations of the 2nd Platoon, Company D, 506th Parachute Infantry, 101st Airborne Division, In the Vicinity of Carentan, France, 11-13 June 1944, Normandy Campaign, Personal Experience of a Rifle Platoon Leader. Captain Ronald M. Speirs. Airborne infantry platoon attacking in hedgerow country.

Operations of the 550th Airborne Infantry Battalion, First Airborne Task Force, In the Airborne Invasion of Southern France, 13-16 August 1944, Southern France Campaign, Personal Experience of a Battalion Executive Officer. Major James M. Wilson. Airborne battalion in the attack.

Operations of Company C, 509th Parachute Infantry Battalion at St. Tropez, Southern France, 15-16 August 1944, Southern France Campaign, Personal Experience of a Platoon Leader. 1st Lieutenant Raymond F. Ruffelaere. Parachute infantry company in an airborne assault landing.

Operations of the First Airborne Task Force In the Invasion of Southern France, 15-20 August 1944, Southern France Campaign, Personal Experience of an Assistant G-2. Captain Harris W. Hollis. Airborne assault in conjunction with an amphibious landing.

Operations of Company E, 517th Parachute Infantry Combat Team, In a River Crossing and Attack at La Roquette, France, 27-28 August 1944, Southern France Campaign. Captain Walter G. Irwin.

Operations of the 101st Airborne Division In the Airborne Invasion of the Netherlands, 17 September - 27 September 1944. Major Robert R. Kemm.

Operations of the 3rd Battalion, 506th Parachute Infantry Regiment, 101st Airborne Division at the Marshalling Area In England and Holland, 14-19 September 1944, Personal Experience of a Battalion Intelligence Officer. Captain William D. Cann, Jr. Airborne infantry battalion in an airborne invasion.

Supply Operations of the 508th Parachute Infantry Regiment, 82nd Airborne Division, In the Invasion of Holland, Arnhem Operation, 15-19 September 1944, Rhineland Campaign. Captain Kenneth L. Johnson.

Operations of the 1st Battalion, 508th Parachute Infantry Regiment, 82nd Airborne Division, In the Holland Invasion, 15-24 September 1944, Rhineland Campaign, Personal Experience of a Battalion Executive Officer. Major B.F. Dolamater. Parachute battalion in an airborne invasion.

Operation of Company D, 2nd Battalion, 508th Parachute Infantry Regiment, 82nd Airborne Division, at Nijmegen, Holland, 17-18 September 1944, Rhineland Campaign, Personal Experience of a Platoon Leader. Captain Robert L. Sickler. A parachute infantry company scouring and holding a glider-landing zone.

Operations of Company H, 504th Parachute Infantry Regiment, 82nd Airborne Division, In the Invasion of Holland, 17-21 September 1944, Rhineland Campaign, Personal Experience of a Rifle Company Commander. Captain Carl W. Kappel. Parachute rifle company dropped to secure key terrain to expedite the advance of friendly troops.

Operations of the 505th Parachute Infantry Regiment, 82nd Airborne Division, In the Airborne Landing and Battle of Groseboek and Nijmegen, Holland, 17-23 September 1944, Rhineland Campaign, Personal Experience of a Company Commander. Captain Jack Tallerday.

Operations of the 506th Parachute Infantry Regiment, 101st Airborne Division, In Holland, 17 September - 9 October 1944, Rhineland Campaign, Personal Experience of an Assistant Regimental Operations Officer. Captain Lloyd E. Wills. Regiment in an airborne invasion.

Operations of Company G, 327th Glider Infantry Regiment, 101st Airborne Division, In Holland, 18 September - 15 October 1944, Rhineland Campaign, Personal Experience of a Company Commander. Captain Robert H. Evans. Glider infantry company in the defense and attack.

Operations of the 3rd Platoon, Company E, 505th Parachute Infantry Regiment, 82nd Airborne Division, In the Seizure of the Nijmegen Bridge, 19-20 September 1944, Rhineland Campaign, Operations of the First Allied Airborne Army In the Invasion of Holland, Personal Experience of a Platoon Leader. Captain John D. Phillips, Jr. Seizure of a bridge.

Operations of 1st Battalion, 325th Glider Infantry Regiment, 82nd Airborne Division, At Mook, Holland, 1-3 October 1944, Rhineland Campaign, Personal Experience of a Battalion Headquarters Company Commander. Captain Robert H. Ward. Airborne infantry battalion in the attack.

Supply Operations In the 1st Battalion, 501st Parachute Infantry Regiment, 101st Airborne Division, In the Battle of Bastogne, 18-26 December 1944, Ardennes-Alsace Campaign, Personal Experience of a Battalion S-4. Captain Joseph E. Jenkins. Supply operations under adverse conditions.

Operations of the 2nd Battalion, 504th Parachute Infantry Regiment, 82nd Airborne Division, In the German Counteroffensive, 18 December 1944 - 10 January 1945, Ardennes-Alsace Campaign, Personal Experience of a Battalion S-3. Captain Victor W. Campana. Reduction of a salient.

Operations of the 501st Parachute Infantry Regiment, 101st Airborne Division, At Bastogne, Belgium, 19-20 December 1944, Ardennes-Alsace Campaign, Personal Experience of a Regimental S-3. Major Elvy B. Roberts. Regiment in a meeting engagement and reinforced regiment in defense.

Operations of Company F, 325th Glider Infantry Regiment, 101st Airborne Division, In the Defense of Bastogne, Belgium, 19-26 December 1944, Ardennes-Alsace Campaign, Personal Experience of a Company Commander. Captain James F. Adams. Company in defense.

Operations of the 2nd Battalion, 327th Glider Infantry Regiment, 101st Airborne Division, In the Defense of Bastogne, Belgium, 20-26 December 1944, Ardennes-Alsace Campaign, Personal Experience of a Battalion Commanding Officer. Major Robert B. Galbreaith. Battalion in the defense.

Operations of the 81mm Mortar Platoon, Headquarters Company, 1st Battalion, 517th Parachute Infantry Regimental Combat Team, At Soy, Belgium, 21-26 December 1944, Ardennes-Alsace Campaign, Personal Experience of an 81mm Mortar Platoon Leader. Captain James M. Townsend. 81mm mortar platoon supporting the attack of a battalion to relieve a surrounded garrison and establish a main line of resistance.

Operations of the 1st Battalion, 517th Parachute Infantry Regiment, At Soy, Belgium, 22-24 December 1944, Ardennes-Alsace Campaign, Personal Experience of a Battalion Liaison Officer. Captain Sidney M. Marks. A battalion attacking to seize and secure critical terrain and to establish a main line of resistance.

Operations of the 1st Battalion, 508th Parachute Infantry Regiment, 82nd Airborne Division, Near Rencheux, Belgium, 22-25 December 1944, Ardennes-Alsace Campaign, Personal Experience of a Company Commander. Major Jonathan E. Adams, Jr. Company in defense and withdrawal.

Operations of the 2nd Battalion, 508th Parachute Infantry Regiment, 82nd Airborne Division, In the Withdrawal From and Recapture of Thier-du-Mont Ridge, Belgium, 22 December 1944 - 7 January 1945, Ardennes-Alsace Campaign, Personal Experience of a Battalion Operations Officer. Captain Henry E. Le Febvre. A parachute infantry battalion withdrawing from and attacking a ridge.

Operations of the 502nd Parachute Infantry Regiment, 101st Airborne Division, In the defense of Bastogne, Belgium, 24-25 December 1944, Ardennes-Alsace Campaign, Personal Experience of a Regimental Commanding Officer. Major Ivan G. Phillips. Regiment in the defense.

Operations of the 1st Battalion, 502nd Parachute Infantry Regiment, 101st Airborne Division at Champs, Belgium, 25 December 1944, Ardennes-Alsace Campaign, Personal Experience of a Company Commander. Captain Clarence A. Thompson, Jr. Reserve Battalion in reduction of penetration.

Operations of the 1st Platoon, Company B, 401st Glider Infantry Regiment, 101st Airborne Division, In the Battle of Bastogne, Belgium, 25 December 1944, Ardennes-Alsace Campaign, Personal Experience of a Platoon Leader. Captain John T. O'Halloran. Infantry rifle platoon attacking enemy entrenched buildings.

Operations of 3rd Platoon, Company G, 505th Parachute Infantry Regiment, 82nd Airborne Division, On the Salm River In the Vicinity of Halleux, Belgium, 25 December 1944, Ardennes-Alsace Campaign, Personal Experience of a Platoon Leader. Captain Francis J. Meyers, Jr. Platoon in the defense, platoon in the covering force.

Operations of the 3rd Battalion, 513th Parachute Infantry Regiment, 17th Airborne Division, In the Battle of the Bulge, 25 December 1944 - 9 January 1945, Ardennes-Alsace Campaign, Personal Experience of a Battalion S-3. Captain Wilbur S. Hilton. Battalion in the attack.

Operations of the 551st Parachute Infantry Battalion, Attached to the 82nd Airborne Division and the 517th Parachute Infantry Regiment, In the Attack, In the Vicinity of Trois Ponts, Belgium, 2-7 January 1945, Ardennes-Alsace Campaign, Personal Experience of a Headquarters Company Commander. Captain Bill G. Smith. Parachute infantry battalion in a continuous attack in woods and during a period of extreme cold.

Operations of the 3rd Battalion, 507th Parachute Infantry Regiment, 17th Airborne Division, The Battle of Dead Man's Ridge, Vicinity of Laval-Chisogne, Belgium, 7-8 January 1945, Ardennes-Alsace Campaign, Personal Experience of a Battalion Liaison Officer. Major Murray L. Harvey. Parachute infantry battalion attacking and occupying a hill position.

Operations of Company B, 504th Parachute Infantry Regiment, 82nd Airborne Division, In Piercing the Siegfried Line Near Losheimergraben, Germany, 2-4 February 1945, Rhineland Campaign, Personal Experience of a Platoon Leader. Captain Edward F. Shaifer, Jr. Parachute rifle company in a normal ground role assaulting permanent fortifications.

Attack of the 3rd Battalion, 517th Parachute Infantry Regimental Combat Team (Separate) in the vicinity of Bergstein, Germany, 4-8 February 1945, Rhineland Campaign, Personal Experience of a Battalion Communications Officer (Without Emphasis On Communications). Ronald L. Gohmert. A parachute infantry battalion in the attack of a fortified position.

Operations of the 17th Airborne Division In the Crossing of the Rhine River, 24 March 1945, Operation Varsity, Central Europe Campaign, Personal Experience of the Aide-de-Camp of the Commanding General. Captain James P. Lyke. Airborne assault behind a river line.

Operations of Company B, 507th Parachute Infantry Regiment, 17th Airborne Division, In the Airborne Assault Crossing of the Rhine River, 24 March 1945, Central Europe Campaign, Personal Experience of a Company Commander. Captain John W. Marr. Parachute infantry rifle company seizing an objective by airborne assault.

Operations of the 507th Parachute Infantry Regiment, 17th Airborne Division, In Germany, 24 March - 5 May 1945, Central Europe Campaign, Personal Experience of a Company Commander. Captain Howard A. Stephens.

Many of the above-listed monographs are digitized in PDF format and appear online. Others may be obtained by contacting the Donovan Library. "Donovan Research Library is currently in the midst of transitioning its massive 10,000+ collection of student papers to digital format. This collection includes after action reports, command diaries, case studies, battle accounts and first hand experiences from U.S. Army personnel during World War

I, World War II, the Korean War, the Vietnam War and other conflicts following 1980. It represents the intellectual talent of research and education that soldiers receive from the faculty and staff at the U.S. Army Infantry School and its divisions. Prior to this effort these materials were only accessible through on-site visits. Phase I will consist of text in PDF format only. Phase II will include the digitization of accompanying maps. Maps needed prior to Phase II will be done by request only. Contact library staff at: DonovanRefDesk@ benning.army.mil."

COMBAT INTERVIEWS

Another tremendous source for primary source information on airborne operations is found at the United States National Archives II, at College Park, Maryland, in the *List of the European Theater of Operations Combat Interviews 1944-1945*. Not only interview transcripts, these files in many cases contain, as well, one or more of the following: maps, narratives, overlays, photographs, and sketches.

Box	Folder	Unit	Dates/Operation	Additional Material
24029	65	17th A/B Div.	24 December 1944 - 20 January 1945 Ardennes	Interviews and Overlays
24029	66	17th A/B Div.	2-13 January 1945 Ardennes Campaign	Narrative and Overlays
24030	67	17th A/B Div.	24-31 March 1945 Wesel Airborne Operation	Narrative
24030	68	17th A/B Div.	24 March - 1 May 1945 Rhine-Ruhr-Elbe Operation	Interviews, Narratives, And Maps
24057	170	82nd A/B Div.	June 1944, Operation Neptune	Interviews, Narrative, And Overlay
24057	171	82nd A/B Div.	17-26 September 1944 Holland	Interviews
24058	172	82nd A/B Div.	18 December 1944 - 9 February 1945 Ardennes (The Battle of the Bulge)	Interviews, Maps, And Overlays
24058	173	82nd A/B Div.	18 December 1944 - 9 February 1945 Houffalize to the Roer River	Interviews, Maps, Narratives and Overlays
24058	174	82nd A/B Div.	5-19 August 1944, Brittany	Interviews, Overlay, And Photograph
24058	175	82nd A/B Div.	10 - 15 December 1944 Roer River (Vic. Duren)	Interviews, Narrative, Maps and Overlay
24072	222	101st A/B Div.	6 - 10 June 1944, Cotentin Peninsula	Interviews, Narrative, Maps, Overlays, Photographs and Sketches
24072	223	101st A/B Div.	6 - 10 June 1944, The Fight at the Lock/ The Carentan Causeway Fight	Narrative, Maps, And Sketches
24073	224	101st A/B Div.	6 - 10 June 1944	

Box	Folder	Unit	Dates/Operation	Additional Material
24073	225	101st A/B Div.	6 - 10 June 1944 The Carentan Causeway Fight	Narrative
24073	226	101st A/B Div.	September - October 1944 Operation Market (Holland)	Interview, Narrative Overlays and Sketches
24073	226a	101st A/B Div.	September - October 1944 Operation Market (Holland)	Narrative and Sketch
24074	227	101st A/B Div.	18 December 1944 - 2 January 1945 The Siege of Bastogne	Interview and Overlay
24074	228	101st A/B Div.	18 December 1944 - 2 January 1945 The Battle of the Bulge	Narrative, Photographs Of Drawings
24075	229	101st A/B Div.	18 December 1944 - 2 January 1945 The Battle of the Bulge	Interviews, Narrative And Overlays
2405	230	101st A/B Div.	19 - 27 December 1944 The Battle of the Bulge	Narratives and Overlays

And for anyone willing to put in the time to sift through the reams of documents, the United States Army's List of Awards and Decorations, grouped by Army and Corps, will provide an inspiring collection of citation documents, filed chronologically as the awards were issued (rather than chronologically with the actual event or action for which the award was given).

War Movies: Any resemblance to actual persons or events is purely coincidental. There is no doubt that many of our first impressions of what it was to be an American soldier in World War II Europe, were drawn from the images presented in movies. With film releases commencing before the end of the war, and continuing right up until present, Hollywood war movies offer vivid and rousing – if not wholly accurate – portrayals of men in combat. It is only natural to be drawn in by the heroic deeds, the grandeur of the events, and the inspiring themes of bravery, sacrifice, and honor. Some of the most recent Hollywood efforts – showcases of special effects wizardry – have brought home the sights and sounds of battle with a remarkably visceral quality, in a way never before possible. Modern filmmakers, competing for the business of an ever more demanding public that is virtually bathed in media imagery, have gone to great lengths to assure that their war stories are wrapped in a veneer of visual authenticity. However, it is imperative to bear in mind that Hollywood war movies are just that – *Hollywood* – works of fiction. The overriding consideration governing their production is whether or not they will have enough box office appeal to generate the revenue necessary to repay their tremendous production costs, and then to show a profit. Historical facts are not altered only if they do not get in the way of telling a "good story." Too often the plots of war movies are superficial, or even farcical, and most only succeed as being restatements of previous work.

Ironically, three of the finest movies about GI's – not specifically paratroops – at war in Europe, released in the immediate wake of its conclusion, were *The Story of GI Joe* (1945), *A Walk in the Sun* (1945), and *Battleground* (1949). The overall feel of each of these movies is sober and low key – almost documentary in style – and the individual performances are both subtle and eloquent. Each of these films gives the audience a view into the world of infantrymen at war, which in the case of *The Story of GI Joe*, a film based on the news stories of legendary war correspondent Ernie Pyle, is "a small, uncomfortable world full of rain and mud, short tempers, sudden, unexpected violence, whimsical humor, and a lot of boredom." Director William A. Wellman used a mix of actors and real-life

GIs off the battle fronts of North Africa, Sicily and Italy to craft a gritty, and realistic portrayal of men in combat. (Among the technical advisors for Wellman's film were none other than Lt.Col. Roy A. Murray, Jr., Major Walter Nye, and Captain Charles Shunstrom, veterans of Darby's 1st and 4th Ranger Battalions, and survivors of some of the fiercest fighting of the war). Similarly, *A Walk in the Sun*, a film depicting a rifle platoon of the U.S. 36th Infantry Division during the invasion of Italy, at Salerno, offers "no propaganda statements, no expressions of patriotic fervor." *Battleground*, while subtly voicing an anti-Communist message, eschews contrived heroics while following another rifle platoon – in this case, glider men of the U.S. 101st Airborne Division – as they wage "a series of bitter contests for short stretches of snowy ground" during the Battle of the Bulge. *Battleground*, as do the other two films, shows GIs simply for what they are: "Ordinary men far from where they want to be."[13]

The written word: While movies allow us to get in a "quick fix" of World War II action, reenactors must seek out critical accounts of the war and non-traditional accounts such as personal letters, diaries, et cetera, that may offer more detail or may even run counter to official accounts. These are vitally important to one's overall understanding of the war and the individuals who participated in it. Furthermore, many reenactment units could benefit from starting book clubs among their own membership, or posting recommended reading on their unit websites.

At the end of this book is a list of suggested titles for further reading. Included are two of the great classics of World War II literature: *Up Front*, by Bill Mauldin, and *Brave Men*, by Ernie Pyle. Both books, published before the end of the war, convey the true feeling and emotional impact felt by the fighting troops, and should be viewed as required reading for all reenactors seeking to perfect their impression. Another classic of its type is Leinbaugh's and Campbell's, *The Men of Company K*, that set the standard for World War II oral histories. While these are not specifically about paratroops, they do provide a 'baseline' for authenticity.

Included with the Combat Chronicles section of this book is a note on each airborne division's unit history, most published just after the war. These are typically highly detailed accounts of the campaigns, battles, and stand-out individuals of each of these units.

General Subjects Section
ACADEMIC DEPARTMENT
THE INFANTRY SCHOOL
Fort Benning, Georgia

ADVANCED INFANTRY OFFICERS COURSE
1948 - 1949

THE OPERATIONS OF THE 2D PLATOON
D COMPANY, 506 PARACHUTE INFANTRY
(101ST AIRBORNE DIVISION)
IN THE VICINITY OF CARENTAN, FRANCE
11-13 JUNE 1944
(NORMANDY CAMPAIGN)
(Personal Experience of a Rifle Platoon Leader)

Type of Operation described: AIRBORNE INFANTRY
PLATOON ATTACKING IN HEDGEROW COUNTRY

Captain Ronald C Speirs, Infantry
ADVANCED INFANTRY OFFICERS CLASS NO. II

TABLE OF CONTENTS

Map A - Omaha and Utah Beachheads.

Map B - Attack on Carentan.

Map C - German Counterattack.

Map D - Second Platoon Defense.

BIBLIOGRAPHY

A-1   Crusade in Europe
By General of the Army, Dwight D. Eisenhower
(TIS Library)

A-2   Utah Beach to Cherbourg (6 June-27 June 1944)
Historical Division, Department of the Army
(TIS Library)

A-3   Normandy To The Baltic
By Field Marshal Montgomery
21st Army Group (TIS Library)

A-4   Rendezvous with Destiny
A History of the 101st Airborne Division
By Leonard Rapport and Alfred Northwood Jr.
Infantry Journal Press, 1948

A-5   Airborne Warfare
By Major General James M Gavin
Infantry Journal Press, 1947
(TIS Library)

A-6   Four Stars of Hell
By L Critchell, 1947
(TIS Library)

A-7   History of the 508th Parachute Infantry
By William G. Lord II
Infantry Journal Press, 1948
(TIS Library)

A-8   Summary of Operations of 101st Airborne Division
Army Ground Forces Report No. O-116 (5 June-30 June 1944)
(TIS Library)

A-9   The Carentan Causeway Fight
USA ETO Historical Section
(TIS Library)

A-10   506 Parachute Infantry Regiment in Normandy Drop
USA ETO Historical Section (TIS Library)

A-11   Currahee
Scrapbook of 506th Parachute Infantry Regiment
(20 July 1942-4 July 1945)
(Personal possession of author)

A-12   Omaha Beachhead (6 June-13 June 1944)
American Forces in Action Series
Historical Division, WD (TIS Library)

A-13   Statement of Major Richard D. Winters, 8 December 1948,
then Commander of E Company, 506 Parachute Infantry,
101st Airborne Division in letter to the author.
(Personal possession of the author)

A-14   Statement of Captain F. T. Heyliger, 19 December 1948,
        former 81 mm Mortar Platoon Leader, 2d Battalion, 506
        Parachute Infantry, 101st Airborne Division in letter
        to the author. (Personal possession of the author)

A-15   Statement of Captain Lewis Nixon Jr, 8 December 1948,
        former S2, 2d Battalion, 506 Parachute Infantry, 101st
        Airborne Division, in letter to the author.

A-16   Statement of Captain Joe F. McMillan, 17 December 1948,
        former D Company Commander, 506 Parachute Infantry,
        101st Airborne Division. (Personal possession of author)

A-17   Small Unit Actions
        Pointe du Hoe (2d Ranger Battalion)
        Historical Division, WD, 4 April 1946
        (TIS Library)

A-18   82d Airborne Division
        Action in Normandy France 6 June-8 July 1944
        Published by 82d Airborne Division
        (Personal Possession of Author)

A-19   Report by the Supreme Commander to The Combined Chiefs
        of Staff on the Operations in Europe of the Allied
        Expeditionary Force, 6 June 1944-8 May 1945
        (TIS Library)

A-20 Operations of the 506th Parachute Infantry in the Invasion
        of Western Europe, Report of Lt Col Hannah, Regimental S3,
        506 PIR, 6 June 1944-8 July 1944
        (Personal possession of Major K.H.Raudstein)

3

THE OPERATIONS OF THE 2D PLATOON, D COMPANY
506 PARACHUTE INFANTRY, (101ST AIRBORNE DIVISION)
IN THE VICINITY OF CARENTAN, FRANCE
11-13 JUNE 1944
(NORMANDY CAMPAIGN)
(Personal Experience of a Rifle Platoon Leader)

INTRODUCTION

This monograph covers the operations of the 2d Platoon, D Company, 506 Parachute Infantry, 101st Airborne Division, in the battle for Carentan, 11-13 June 1944, during the invasion of Normandy.

The Allied invasion of Northern Europe took place on 6 June 1944. The initial landings were made by 21st Army Group, commanded by General Sir Bernard L. Montgomery. VII Corps, commanded by Major General J. Lawton Collins, landed at Utah Beach and V Corps landed at Omaha Beach, both under the First US Army commanded by Lt General Omar N. Bradley. To the east of the Americans, the Second British Army landed, commanded by Lt General Miles C. Dempsey.

Three hours before dawn on 6 June 1944, the 101st Airborne Division landed by parachute on the Cotentin peninsula. 432 C-47 type airplanes were used for the division, carrying 6600 paratroopers. Three hours later, 51 troop-carrier gliders came in and at dusk on D-day an additional 32 gliders landed. The Glider Regiment of the division came in with the seaborne forces and joined after the airborne-beachhead linkup. As was to be expected in an airborne assault of a heavily defended area, losses in men and equipment were heavy.(1) When the German resistance on the exits to the beaches was broken, the division turned and drove toward the city of Carentan. All along the beachheads the Americans, British and Canadians attacked on a 60-mile front. (2)

(1) A-2, p.14; (2) A-1, p.243.

4

THE GENERAL SITUATION

On 11 June the 101st Airborne Division, after six days of bitter fighting against a determined enemy, had accomplished all its assigned objectives and was in a defensive position on the high ground north of the city of Carentan. The defensive line followed the Douve river and extended from Chef-du-Pont on the west to the east where the Douve river joins the Atlantic.(3)(Map A)

The 4th Division, 12 miles to the north on the right flank of the beachhead, was engaged in heavy fighting in their attempts to reach the high ground northeast of Montebourg.(4)

The 82d Airborne Division to the northwest was in defensive positions along the line of the Merderet river, with a bridgehead established in the area of La Fiere. The 90th Infantry Division, coming up from the beach, attacked through the 82d Airborne on the 10th and 11th, and on the evening of the 11th had cleared Amfreville, but was meeting violent resistance in its efforts to capture Pont L'Abbe. (5)

To the east, Omaha Beach extended for a depth of 12 miles. The 1st Infantry Division was preparing to attack toward Caumont, and the 2d Infantry and 29th Infantry Divisions were moving to the south of Cerisy Forest and the Elle river. (6) The 2d Armored Division was in the process of landing on the beachhead, and those units of the division which had landed were in Corps reserve. The 29th captured Isigny on the 9th, and on the 10th the 327 Glider Infantry made contact with Company K, 175th Infantry, 29th Division near Catz. (7) The main attacks of the 29th were to the south, keeping east of the Vire river, and the link-up between VII Corps and V Corps was not strong and solid as should be the case.
(8)

(3) A-2, p.78; (4) A-2, p.108; (5) A-2, p.128; (6) A-12, p.150;
(7) A-8, p. 5; (8) A-12, p. 157.

At this time the Corps boundary ran just to the east of Carentan along the line of the Douve river, but on the next day it was moved east to the Vire river. (9) This change was to affect the 101st Airborne, as it was directed by General Bradley to seize this area. *INDEFINITE* The original missions of the division had been accomplished with the capture of the three bridges north of Carentan. (10)

In the British sector to the east of Omaha Beach, the 6th Airborne Division was defending its bridgehead across the Orne river, secured in their initial airborne drop by glider and parachute. The Commandos were attacking toward Cabourg, but with no success. There was savage fighting in the Caen area, where the British infantry divisions were attempting to capture the city against strong enemy resistance. The Canadians and British armor and infantry were attacking in the Tilly-sur-Seulles area, with the British 7th Armored Division preparing to attack the next day in conjunction with the US 1st Division on its right. (11)

THE PLAN OF ATTACK

The plan of Corps and Army on the 11th of June was to effect a solid junction of the Omaha and Utah beachheads by capturing the city of Carentan. These orders had come directly from General Eisenhower. The mission was given to the 101st Airborne Division. At the same time, V Corps was to attack from Isigny toward Carentan. (12) (See map A)

101st Airborne Division activated these plans on the 10th of June by sending the 3d Battalion, 502 Parachute Infantry across the bridges on the road from St Come-du-Mont, passing (See map B)

(9) A-12, p.158; (10) A-2, Map No.II; (11) A-12, p.143; (12) A-2, p. 77; A-19, p. 26.

through the outposts of the 506 Parachute Infantry on the bridges. The battalion had a murderous fight to move 500 yards past the last bridge, and the 1st Battalion of the 502 Regiment was brought to assist. Neither battalion was able to advance, taking very heavy casualties because of the strong enemy resistance and good defensive positions. The flooded fields to either flank made it impossible to flank the defenders. Simultaneously the 327 Glider Infantry crossed the Douve river three miles to the east and, after heavy fighting on the 10th and 11th, was in possession of the bridges to the south. *INDEFINITE* The glider troops were unable to advance into the city because of the canals which barred their way and the heavy fire being encountered. (13)

The division plan on the evening of the 11th was a move to encircle the city with the 506 Parachute Infantry closing around from the west through the battered 502 Regiment while the 501 Parachute Infantry Regiment was to swing south, then west of the 327th. Both regiments were to join on the high ground south of the city. *HILL 30?* Concurrently, the 327 Glider Infantry was to attack from their present positions directly into the city. (Map B) The importance of the attack can be measured by the presence of Lt General Courtney H. Hodges while the division order was issued. Brigadier General McAuliffe was in command of the attacking force. (14)

Colonel R. F. Sink, commander of the 506 Infantry issued his order to the assembled company commanders and staff at 2200 hours. The 1st and 2d Battalions were to move out immediately in that order, while the 3d Battalion remained in position in division *where?* reserve. (15)

(13) A-2, p.78-89; (14) A-2, p. 89; (15) A-13, p.2.

7

THE ENEMY SITUATION

The German High Command was well aware of the importance of Carentan to them, preventing as it did a junction between the American Omaha and Utah beachheads. Field Marshal Erwin Rommel, Army Group Commander, personally stated that Carentan must be held. (16) The troops charged with this mission were the 6th Parachute Regiment, which had arrived in Normandy in June from the fighting in Russia. (17)

The platoon leader and his men were well aware of the German paratroopers fighting capabilities because the Germans had defended St Come-du-Mont and Vierville in the earlier fighting to the north. They attacked strongly when ordered, and were armed with a high percentage of automatic weapons. They wore special camouflage suits and paratroop helmets. Their morale seemed good. (18) This was possibly because fighting the Americans was preferable to fighting both Russians and cold weather. The German High Command did not share the American opinion of the 6th Parachute. Their War Diary for this period states, "The 6th Parachute Regiment has been fighting far better than expected."

The 17 SS Panzer Grenadier Division was being rushed up from the south of France. Elements of this division, along with the 6th Parachute Regiment, were the forces that struck Carentan on 12-13 June. The platoon leader and his men were also aware that there was armor in the vicinity of Carentan. While outposting a bridge on the St Come-du-Mont--Carentan road a few days previously, the platoon was fired upon by a German armored car

(16) A-12, p. 147 & 149; A-4, p.166; (17) A-12, p.112;
(18) Personal knowledge.

8

coming from the direction of Carentan. One man of the platoon was killed. The car then withdrew to the city. (19)

The 17 SS Panzer Grenadier Division had been delayed and its tanks unloaded far behind the front lines because of the overwhelming Allied air attacks on the railroads and communications system. These delays had caused German Seventh Army to push an engineer battalion to Carentan, presumably to bolster the defenses by fighting as infantry. (20) The 17 SS Panzer Grenadier Div was said to consist of good, tough troops, and had in addition to its organic artillery regiment, another battalion of artillery, a heavy howitzer battery, and another artillery group. (21)

THE TERRAIN

Carentan, a city with a population of 4000 people, is located 10 miles along the Douve river from where it enters the Atlantic. The city is connected with the Douve by a short stretch of canal. The buildings in the town are all very old and strongly built of stone. There is an excellent road and railroad net in the area, running directly through the city. Several paved highways intersect the city, including the main road to Cherbourg in the north. (22) The entire area, with the exception of the city, and to the southwest, was swampy and intersected with drainage ditches, streams, and canals. Nowhere does the terrain rise above 30 meters.

The drainage areas around the city, feeding into the rivers and canals, had been flooded, restricting movement to the roads, except to the southwest, where the terrain was dry and intersected with high Normandy hedgerows and deeply cut farm roads and paths.

(19) Personal knowledge; (20) A-12; p 148 & 149; (21) A-4, p.234 & 235; (22) A-4, p. 166; personal knowledge.

The highest point in this area is Hill 30, just outside the town to the south. (23)

THE PLATOON PRIOR TO THE ATTACK

The 2d Platoon of D Company, on the evening of 11 June, had been through six days of violent fighting, after a parachute drop which scattered the platoon over a large area. The platoon was very low in strength because of the many casualties suffered and the men missing from the parachute drop. (See Chart A) *Page 12*

The strength of the platoon at this time was one officer and 14 men. Each parachute infantry platoon was authorized two officers due to the expected casualty rate. My assistant platoon leader, Lt Watkins, was wounded by mortar fire a few days previously, and evacuated. He returned to the division later, and was killed in the fighting in Holland. (24)

The remainder of D Company was in bad shape also. The executive officer was killed on the parachute jump, and the company commander was killed by artillery fire a few days later. One entire planeload of men of the 1st Platoon was ditched in the English Channel, with the assistant platoon leader aboard. Lt McMillan, 1st Platoon Leader, took over the company, leaving no officers in his platoon. Both 3d Platoon officers were evacuated. The strength of the company was approximately 75 men.(25)

During the long night airplane flight into Normandy and the six days fighting which followed, the platoon had only one full night of sleep, and the men were physically and mentally affected. Our food consisted of K rations with which we had jumped, and a resupply of the same after contact with the beachhead was made.

(23) A-4, p.169; (24) Platoon rosters, casualty reports (Personal possession of the author); (25) Personal knowledge.

The Tables of Organization for an airborne unit at that time were different from the infantry. Some basic differences are the following:

(a) Three identical rifle companies and a Battalion Head-
      quarters Company in the battalion. In place of a
      Heavy Weapons Company were the 81 mm Mortar Platoon
      and Light Machine Gun Platoon in Battalion Headquarters
      Company.

(b) D Company was a rifle company in the 2d Battalion,
      the others being E and F, and Battalion Headquarters
      Company. This point is emphasized because of the fact
      that D Company in the regular Infantry T/O is a heavy
      weapons company, while in the parachute troops it was
      a rifle company.

(c) The rifle companies had three identical rifle platoons
      and a Company Headquarters, but no weapons platoon.
      Instead, each rifle platoon had only two rifle squads
      and a 60 mm mortar squad. Each 12-man rifle squad had
      a light machine gun team organic to it.

The 2d Platoon 60 mm mortar had been lost on the parachute jump, but no loss resulted because our depleted strength would not have allowed the platoon to operate it. Riflemen were needed much more than mortarmen. Only one light machine gun was carried because the platoon leader felt that riflemen were more valuable during the constant attacking in which we had been engaged. Our light machine guns during the Normandy Campaign were not provided with the bipod, but only a tripod, which was not satisfactory while attacking in hedgerow country. (26)

(26) Personal knowledge.

11

<u>CHART A</u>

<u>PARACHUTE INFANTRY RIFLE PLATOON</u>

<u>Platoon Headquarters</u>

Platoon Commander
~~Asst Platoon Commander~~
~~Platoon Sergeant~~
Messenger
~~Messenger~~
~~Radio Operator~~

<u>Rifle Squad</u>

~~Squad Leader~~
Assistant Squad Leader
Machine Gunner, Justice
~~Asst Machine Gunner~~
~~Ammunition Bearer~~
Scout
Scout
~~Rifleman~~
Rifleman
Rifleman
Rifleman
Rifleman

<u>Rifle Squad</u>

~~Squad Leader~~
~~Asst Squad Leader~~
Machine Gunner
~~Asst Machine Gunner~~
~~Ammunition Bearer~~
~~Scout~~
~~Scout~~
~~Rifleman~~
~~Rifleman~~
Rifleman
~~Rifleman~~
~~Rifleman~~

<u>60 mm Mortar Squad</u>

~~Squad Leader~~
~~Mortar Gunner~~
Asst Mortar Gunner
Ammunition Bearer
~~Ammunition Bearer~~
Ammunition Bearer

<u>LEGEND</u>

——— KIA
━━ Missing on Parachute Jump
▬▬ WIA During Previous Fighting

<u>CHART A</u>

NIGHT MARCH TO HILL 30

The battalion moved out in a column of companies with F
Company leading, then E, Headquarters Company, and D. Previously,
each company had been given a horse and cart to carry equipment
and ammunition. Being airborne, we had no organic transportation.
These carts were kept to the rear of the column to eliminate
noise.(27) Headquarters Company was having trouble keeping up
with the rest of the battalion because of their heavy loads of
mortars, machine guns, and rocket launchers. A provisional antitank platoon in the company was armed with 2.36" rocket launchers.

The men moved slowly down the causeway in single file across
the four bridges which span the river and canals. Up ahead, fires
could be seen in Carentan, and the booming of the naval gunfire
could be heard. The city was given a heavy shelling by the US
Navy and other friendly weapons as we moved in. (28)

At the farmhouse where the 502 Parachute Infantry had the
fierce battle with the German defenders during the day, the
battalion left the road. The column moved across country keeping to the west of the town. The terrain began to rise gently
and there were a great many fences to climb. At one gate there
was a dead paratrooper, and every man in the long column stepped
on him in the dark. The necessity for maintaining silence and
keeping contact with the man ahead in the murk left no time for
flank security. Headquarters Company ahead was having trouble
with their loads, and D Company helped out. At this time the
column was stopping and starting as the 1st Battalion up ahead
probed their way through the dark, silent hedgerows. No enemy
contact had been made as yet. (29)

(27) A-13, p. 1 & 2; (28) A-2, p. 89; (29) Personal knowledge.

13

Lt Winters, commanding E Company, upon reaching the front of his column found that contact had been lost with F Company ahead. He led his men on until reaching the railroad, and by sending scouts out was able to regain contact at 2400 hours. The two companies in the rear were the next to lose contact. Contact was regained and our slow uncertain progress resumed. Some firing was heard up ahead when the 1st Battalion struck a German outpost, but was able to push on. (30) The slow movement caused the tired men to doze off to sleep when the column stopped, and the officers in the companies had to wake men up and urge them forward. At 0100 hours the 1st Battalion reached Hill 30, the assigned objective, and the 2d Battalion stopped astride the Baupte road. (See Map B) D Company sent out security to the right and left along the road.

At 0230 hours the company commanders were called to the command post to receive the order for the attack for the next day. There was no sign of enemy activity, and the men slept where they dropped. There was much discussion at the battalion command post and the order was finally issued. The battalion S3, Capt Hester, gave out the order under a raincoat to the company commanders and staff. The 2d Battalion was to attack Carentan, while the 1st Battalion stayed at Hill 30. E Company was to be on the right and F Company on the left. The plan was to drive into town and join the glider troops attacking from the other side of town. D Company was to follow on the road to the right. (The nights were very short in Normandy at this time of year, but just before dawn F Company shot a 1st Battalion man who had strayed into their area. Dawn broke at 0400 hours.) At 0530 hours the

(30) A-13, p. 4.

14

company commanders were called back to the command post and given the time of attack, which was 0600 hours. As Lt Winters moved to the command post he was shot at twice by a sniper, without success. (31)

THE MOVE INTO CARENTAN (See map 5)

The regimental command post group, during the night movement, had strayed too close to town, and at the time of the dawn attack was actually closer to town than either of the battalions. Their situation was not realized until daylight, when they were fired upon from the town. The 1st Battalion was ordered by radio to send one company toward the firing and extricate the command post from its predicament. This was very quickly done. (32) The desirability of getting into town quickly caused the 2d battalion to move straight down the main road in a column of companies. F Company was leading, E, Headquarters, and D following in that order. The battalion light machine gun platoon was given the mission of covering the open fields to the north of the roads to protect the flank of the battalion. F Company crossed the LD about 20 minutes late, but was able to move into town without too much trouble. E Company following, however, was caught at the main intersection just outside of town, and had 10 serious casualties from mortar and rifle grenade fire. There was quite a bit of long-range machine gun fire coming down the road also, and the E Company commander, Lt Winters, was struck in the leg. He was not evacuated, however, and in spite of a stiff and painful leg, stayed until the end of the campaign.

The battalion was now being fired on from the houses east of the road to Carentan. Major Horton, battalion executive officer, ordered E Company to clear this area. This was done by

(31) A-13, p.5; A-16, p.1; (32) A-4, p. 229.

moving into a house on the west side of the road and firing rifle grenades and a light machine gun from the upper floor. The rifle grenadier put a direct hit on the German machine gun and soon the enemy withdrew. The machine gun was fired at the retreating enemy from the same position. (33)

By 0830 hours the battalion sector was quiet, although firing could still be heard towards the center of Carentan. Shortly before, F Company had met the glidermen attacking through town from the opposite direction. D Company was ordered to move into the city and did so, stopping just across the railroad at the intersection of the two main roads from the northwest and southwest. Carentan had suffered heavily from the pre-attack shelling; whole blocks were ablaze, while many buildings were in ruins. (34)

The 501 Parachute Infantry had difficulty with the flooded area to the east, but was able to swing around the town. Their final assault up the *what hill? against what opposition?* hill was aided by 4.2" mortars and artillery, enabling the two regiments to join forces at Hill 30. (35) (Map B)

ATTACK WEST FROM CARENTAN *(see map c)*

Orders were issued from 101st Airborne Division Headquarters that afternoon for the 501 and 506 Parachute Infantry to attack south and west from the town. The objective of the 506th was Baupte, and of the 501st was Sainteny. When Lt McMillan, D Company commander returned from a battalion meeting with this order, he was heard with amazement by the platoon leaders. He agreed that the plan, to say the least, was an ambitious one. Four phase lines had been designated, but the platoon leaders, Lt Speirs, S/Sgt Long, and Sgt Rice, felt the company would be fortunate to reach the first. But the attack was necessary.

Phase lines not shown on map c

(33) A-13, p. 9; (34) Personal knowledge; (35) A-4, p 232.

16

Otherwise, a German counterattack *could* ~~would~~ pin the Division in the city with the enemy in control of the high ground to the south-west. (36)

The 506 Parachute Infantry moved out with the 2d Battalion on the right of the Baupte road and the 1st Battalion on the left. The 2d Battalion was responsible for the road. The strength of the 1st Battalion at this time was 150 enlisted men. In the 2d Battalion the formation was D on the right from the flooded area to include the Le Hay du Puits railroad which ran due west along our advance. F Company was on the left and E Company in reserve. (37)

Within D Company the 2d Platoon was on the right, 3d on the left, and the 1st Platoon followed the 3d in support. The initial mission assigned the 2d Platoon was to clear the village of Pommenauque of enemy, while the 3d Platoon was to move astride the railroad embankment, keeping contact with F Company. (38)

As the company commander moved out with the left platoon, he met a lone French civilian coming from the direction of the enemy. Sgt Westphal, who had a smattering of French, interrogated the man, who said there were 1000 Germans back up the railroad. This was unhappy news to battered D Company but the company pressed on. (39)

The 2d Platoon found no enemy in the village; only a few frightened civilians. One Frenchman had been badly wounded by shellfire and the platoon leader advised him to go to the aid stations in Carentan. As the platoon moved out of the village to rejoin the company, it was brought under fire by long-range machine guns from the west. By infiltrating the men in rushes

(36) Personal knowledge; A-4, p.236; (37) A-16, p.1; Statement of Major K. H. Raudstein, 15 Dec 1948; (38) Personal knowledge; A-16, p. 1; (39) A-16, p.1

17

across the open fields, the platoon reached the shelter of the railroad embankment with no casualties. In the meantime, the 3d Platoon, about 500 yards down the railroad, had struck the enemy. A German machine gun, cleverly dug in between the railroad ties, opened up, killing the lead scout of the platoon. The 3d Platoon moved ahead by rushes until the volume of machine gun and rifle fire pinned them down. The terrain in the immediate area was extremely flat, with only small ditches and low hedgerows. To the left of the railroad were open fields to the woods, where the bursts of fire indicated F Company had met the enemy. The machine gun on the railroad continued to fire and was joined by other weapons. The 2d Platoon came up behind the 3d Platoon and extended the flank along the hedgerow to the flooded ground, but no progress was made. Lt McMillan was in touch with battalion by SCR 300 radio, and informed them of the situation. Battalion requested that he adjust fire for the airborne artillery pack howitzers with which they had contact. Lt McMillan could see this fire and he adjusted it on the woods and railroad to our front. Battalion called on the SCR 300 and ordered that the company was to hold in position and not attempt to advance. (40)

F Company, now at the village of Douville, was heavily engaged with the enemy. E Company stopped and dug in to strengthen the line to the rear. German rifle and machine gun fire was intense all along the line and the battalion was unable to advance in any part of the zone. The 1st Battalion, 506 Parachute Infantry, and the 501 Parachute Infantry, had struck the same enemy positions to the south and were unable to advance. 88 mm

(40)A-16, p.2; personal knowledge.

cannon fire was heard, and mortar fire began to strike our positions all along the line. Lt Winters saw that the gun crews of two attached 57 mm antitank guns were down in the ditches and making no attempt to set up. He ordered them to take the machine guns off their gun-towing ¼-ton trucks and start firing. This was done, but the firing was not accurate. (41)

The 81 mm mortar platoon of the Battalion moved into position at this time and began firing. The platoon was equipped with four mortars and was at about 75% strength. The platoon leader's order from the Headquarters Company commander was: "Set up anywhere and start firing!" Lt Heyliger set up on the forward slope of the hill behind the battalion command post. His guns were protected by the high hedgerow to the front, and were dug in. He commenced firing in 10 minutes and improved his positions later. The mortar platoon leader had his ammunition supply in horse-drawn carts, and these he sent to the rear along the road. The carts were 100 yards to the rear of the guns and also were protected by the hedgerows along the road. (42)

The machine gun platoon of the battalion was attached to the three rifle companies, one section per company. The platoon had suffered numerous casualties during the previous fighting and was able to man only six light machine guns. (43)

Just as it was growing dark, D Company had a call on the SCR 300 radio from battalion. The order was to pull back along the railroad and rejoin the battalion which had decided to consolidate for the night. This move brought D Company through E Company, and up on the right of F Company. The boundary between

(41) A-13, p.12; (42)(43) A-14, p.1.

GERMAN COUNTERATTACK ON CARENTAN

Just before dawn 13 June the 81 mm mortar platoon commenced firing at the house which the platoon was to attack. They fired a heavy concentration, causing the roof of the house to be set ablaze. The platoon leader lined his men along the hedgerow facing down a gentle slope. At the bottom of the slope, seen through the orchard, was the house. The platoon was the size of a large squad but had for automatic weapons both an automatic rifle and a light machine gun. The platoon looked anxiously toward the house as dawn began to break, but no enemy could be seen. (48)

The platoon crossed the hedgerow "as skirmishers" and moved down through the regularly spaced trees. At that moment a heavy mortar and artillery concentration landed in the area. One of the platoon riflemen was struck by this fire and lay moaning on the ground. Back at the road where the company commander was calling battalion and notifying them that the platoon had moved out, the same barrage killed the radio operator and wounded another man. (49)

The platoon reached the stone wall surrounding the house at the bottom of the hill, vaulted the wall, and found the courtyard empty. As the platoon leader crossed the waist-high wall, he looked back up the hill and saw German soldiers running along the hedgerow he had just left.(Map D)

The machine gun was quickly mounted, firing through a gate in the stone wall. The automatic rifle was placed on the wall and heavy fire was rained on this threat. Screams of pain were heard, and many casualties inflicted on this unit of the enemy. The enemy returned fire but the stone wall protected the platoon.

(48)(49) Personal knowledge.

22

The platoon leader sent four riflemen to the other portion of the wall which faced directly toward the enemy-held west. They faced an open field except at the left where the orchard joined a hedge-row. At this moment a shower of grenades was received from the west where the hedgerow blocked our observation. The automatic rifleman was killed and the platoon leader struck by small frag- ments. A machine gun began firing from the hill at the machine gunner as he lay exposed behind the gate. The platoon machine gunner was killed and the machine gun rendered useless. (50)

Back up the road, Lt McMillan had called battalion and noti- fied them that the 2d Platoon was cut off, and his other platoon was being fiercely pressed from the front. Major Horton, battal- ion executive officer, told the company commander to fall back. Lt McMillan could see a field piece being dragged up behind the next hedgerow by the enemy. (51) D Company slowly fell back, leaving the 2d Platoon isolated.

On the left of the battalion, F Company was thrown back by a savage tank-infantry attack, which drove them back to the battalion reserve line. Here E Company had deployed along the road which crossed the battalion area. The F Company line joined E Company at the battalion command post house, which was now on the front lines. It was converted to an aid station by the battalion sur- geon, Captain Neville, who was doing a marvelous job with the casualties that were pouring in. The battalion command post moved back down the road about 40 yards into the ditch and stayed there throughout the action. (52)

The attack of the 506 Parachute Infantry at dawn exactly coincided with the attack of the 17 SS Panzer Grenadiers and the

(50) Personal knowledge; (51) A-16, p.3; (52) Personal knowledge.

23

6th Parachute Regiment. The attack stopped the American regiment in its tracks. The German intention was to recapture Carentan. The Berlin radio boasted that evening to all of Europe that the attack was successful and Carentan was again in German hands. (53)

The 1st Battalion was being attacked heavily to our left, and the 3d Battalion of the Regiment which had been in Division reserve was moved up to strengthen the 1st Battalion line. The 501 Parachute Infantry to the south was heavily engaged, but losing no ground. (54)

To the front of the 2d Battalion, the 2d Platoon of D Company was running low on ammunition. It was not possible to replenish the supply because E Company was firing on the courtyard from the rear. There was good cover behind the stone walls from flat trajectory fire, but a few hand grenades began to strike inside the courtyard, coming from the Germans to our front. Most of these were the small egg grenade type which can be thrown for long distances. The burst of a grenade caught another rifleman squarely, stretching him kicking and screaming on the stones of the courtyard. The platoon leader was able to do nothing for him because at that moment a squad of enemy soldiers burst out of the trees to our direct front. They were paratroopers, recognized by their distinctive helmets and uniforms. They were about 25 yards away and firing as they came. The platoon from behind the wall cut them down with aimed rifle fire and killed them all before any reached the wall. Despite this successful defense, the platoon leader now decided to withdraw. There was no protection against grenades in the courtyard and the burning house was throwing out a suffocating heat and smoke. By moving down a ditch single file

(53) Personal knowledge. (54) A-4, p.237.

the platoon regained the battalion line, 400 yards to the rear. The wounded man was left for dead, but managed to crawl back later. (55)

In the battalion area, the situation had not improved. F Company had fallen back again to the high ground 100 yards in their rear. This was done without authority from the battalion commander. It was a serious move, exposing, as it did, the entire left flank of the battalion. D Company was now filling in the gap between E and F.

Our main difficulty at this point was getting the men out of the ditches and up into position on the hedgerow where they could fire at the enemy. Most of the men were frightened, but not panic-stricken. They just did not realize that in order to stop the enemy a continual wall of rifle and machine gun fire must be built up and maintained. There was plenty of ammunition in the line and no danger of running out. The Battalion S4, Lt Peacock, was running jeeploads of ammunition right up to the hedgerows by using the sunken roads. (56) The 81 mm mortar platoon continued to pour heavy concentrations on the hedgerows to the front of the battalion. German 88 mm guns were firing directly on the position at long ranges, but very accurately. (57) Several enemy tanks had been knocked out by the 57 mm antitank gunners and the rocket launchers of the battalion.

The regimental commander, Colonel R. F. Sink, was aware of the precarious situation of the battalion, and had asked Division for aid. The 2d Battalion of the 502 Parachute Infantry was rushed up to the area and was in position to the right of the 2d Battalion, 506 Parachute Infantry, by 1000 hours. (58)

(55) Personal knowledge; (56) A-13, and personal knowledge.
(57) A-13, p 17; (58) A-4, p 237.

25

PARACHUTE RIFLE COMPANY

RELIEF BY 2D ARMORED DIVISION

Unknown to the battalion, help was on the way. Combat Command A, of the 2d Armored Division, had been rushed to the area east of Carentan to meet an expected enemy thrust which did not materialize. They had driven from the Omaha Beach area where they were under the control of V Corps. General Taylor, Commanding General of 101st Airborne Division, hearing that they were close by, requested their help from Corps. This was granted and the armored units began to arrive at 1030 hours. (59)

The situation had eased in the battalion area and no more infantry small arms fire was heard. German tanks, however, continued to fire and small amounts of artillery still fell in the fields to the front and rear.

At 1400 hours the Sherman tanks of the 2d Armored Division rumbled through the battalion lines, accompanied by armored infantrymen. This was a beautiful sight to the battered 2d Battalion. The tanks were firing as they advanced and doing a wonderful job. The tank-infantry team was able to move forward all the way to Baupte, the original objective of the 506 Parachute Infantry. (60) The 2d Battalion, along with the rest of the regiment, was relieved and moved into division reserve in Carentan.

During the day's action, the 81 mm mortar platoon had fired 1000 rounds of ammunition. Lt Heyliger reported that all the paint was burned off the barrels of his mortars. His platoon was down to 50% strength, about ten of his mortarmen being rushed into the line as riflemen to fill the gaps. The average range at which he had fired was from 300 to 500 yards. Most of his casualties were caused by rifle fire, but some from the direct fire of 88's.

(59) A-4, p 237. (60) A-2, p. 93.

He commented that if four of these 88 rounds had not been duds, he would have lost at least a section of men. (61)

D Company was down to a strength of 50 men, while E Company was reduced to 69 soldiers. (62) The men and officers who remained were physically and mentally exhausted. The amazing thing was that there were not more cases of combat exhaustion. Only a few of these were reported. The majority of the men fought bravely, even though the companies were forced to yield ground. The battalion had done its part in defending Carentan, and the men and officers were proud of their job.

The strategic importance of the action of the 101st Airborne Division in holding Carentan can best be summed up by quoting from the report of the Supreme Commander to the Combined Chiefs of Staff.

"On the 12th Carentan fell. The Germans made desperate but fruitless efforts to recover the town and reestablish the wedge between our forces. Our initial lodgement area was now consolidated, and we held an unbroken stretch of the French coast from Quineville to the east bank of the Orne." (63)

ANALYSIS AND CRITICISM

Airborne troops are a strategic weapon. The present doctrine of their use visualizes employment in mass, and for short violent combat operations, using surprise as a vital factor. The 101st Airborne Division was in Normandy for one month, during which time many trained and expert parachutists were killed or evacuated because of sustained ground combat. The point in issue is not that the lives of parachutists are more valuable than

(61) A-14, p.1; (62) A-16, p.3; A-13, p.19; (63) A-19, p.26.

the lives of infantry soldiers. That is not true. The point is that the mere presence of airborne troops in a theater of operations forces the enemy to constantly fear a sudden onslaught from the sky where and when he least desires it. The enemy commander must deploy more troops to guard his lines of communication and vital areas in the rear. The "vertical envelopment" which airborne forces have brought to the art of war has compelled caution by even the most aggressive enemy. But when the airborne forces are employed for long periods as infantry, the enemy can make his plans without fear of the airborne threat.

Sufficient artillery and armor support was lacking throughout the operation. This lack of sufficient organic supporting arms was a factor in the initial success of the German counterattack on 13 June.

On 11 June, when the Carentan battle began, the 2d Platoon had eleven men less than each of the other two platoons of D Company. The company commander should have reassigned men from the other platoons to bring up the strength of the 2d Platoon. This problem does not arise in the infantry because of the arrival of replacements, but airborne units do not receive replacements in combat. When platoons are assigned identical missions in combat, the members of an understrength platoon are forced to fight more fiercely and are in greater danger of sudden death.

There were no decorations awarded to any member of the platoon for bravery in this action. The platoon leader is to be criticized for not submitting recommendations for awards for his men. However, seven of the men of the platoon were promoted to the rank of noncommissioned officer upon the arrival of replacements in base camp.

28

The T/O&E of airborne units during World War II was totally lacking in motor transport from the company level on down. The rifle platoon was weak in having only two rifle squads. The light machine gun was equipped with a tripod but no bipod. The separate tripod was almost useless when units were attacking in hedgerow country. The above inadequacies in the airborne T/O&E have since been corrected. They are mentioned to illustrate the difficulties under which the platoon fought.

During the night march to Hill 30 the platoon moved in single file and had no flank security out. The reasons for such a formation were the tired condition of the men and the blackness of the night. The (fatal results of) such carelessness are obvious. One enemy rifleman could have cut the entire battalion column.

All companies of the battalion at one time or another on the night march lost contact with the unit ahead or to the rear. A double file formation within the companies would have cut the length of the column in half and tightened control of it. Dispersion should have been maintained by connecting files between units down to platoons. These connecting files would be briefed in detail as to their duties, thus minimizing the possibility of loss of contact.

The security elements of D Company on the night of 12 June were far too weak. The night defensive positions of the 2d Platoon consisted of the men digging in along one hedgerow. A normal perimeter defense should have been set up around the four sides of the field. If a German night attack had been launched in strength, the battalion would undoubtedly have been overrun. The failure to set up a night defense was due to the fact that the platoon leader and his men were exhausted and did not realize the gravity of their situation.

29

The dawn attack of the platoon, coinciding as it did with the German tank-infantry assault, was doomed to failure. It seems certain that if the regiment had not moved from its positions, but had been in defense at dawn, that our casualties would have been much lighter and greater damage inflicted on the attackers. The battalion 81 mm mortar platoon had left their positions and were standing in the road ready to follow closely behind the assault companies when the Germans struck. Thus they could not immediately support with mortar fire. (64) Division G2 either was not aware of the coming German attack, or his knowledge was not acted upon.

not previously completed (handwritten)

The platoon leader is to be severely criticized for failing to carry the wounded man back as the platoon withdrew from the house on the 13th. His assumption that the man was dead does not excuse him. His expectation of another enemy assault and his fear that this would find the platoon with no ammunition were the factors causing this grave mistake.

The platoon did not make use of their hand grenades to full advantage. During the fight at the house, grenades should have been thrown into the wooded area to the left front. The casualties that would have resulted in the enemy grenade throwers would have aided the defense. The American hand grenade is a powerful weapon, but the writer feels that a light round grenade would be more valuable. It could be thrown for great distances. More grenades could be carried by the individual. This was the principle of the German egg grenade, which was a successful type.

The crucial point of the German attack on 13 June was just after the entire 2d Battalion had been thrown back to the battalion

(64) Personal knowledge; A-14, p.2.

reserve line. The men of the battalion did not realize that to prevent the Germans from assaulting a second time, a large volume of fire had to be built up on the enemy positions, even though no point targets appeared. The average soldier dislikes exposing himself to fire his weapon without a definite target in sight; however, area fire, and the self confidence gained by firing his own rifle are vital to the defense and the attack. This is the principle behind "marching fire".

The F Company commander was relieved of his command because of his unauthorized withdrawal to positions behind the battalion reserve line. The writer is not personally aware of the enemy situation in the F Company area, but the dangerous situation which this withdrawal created could easily have smashed the entire battalion position. The failure of F Company commander to inform battalion of the situation in his area and request permission to withdraw was a serious violation of tactical doctrine.

LESSONS

The following lessons were brought out by the operation:

1. Strategic use of airborne troops is essential. The attrition of trained parachutists in extended ground combat operations as infantry is wasteful and should be avoided.

2. When assigning missions to lower units, the commander must consider the comparative strength of his units as reduced by previous casualties.

3. Bravery in combat must be recognized by decorations and awards. Morale is raised and incentive provided to perform well in future combat.

4. Tables of Organization and Equipment must be constantly revised to increase the fighting strength and capabilities of the unit.

31

5. Flank security during night movement is essential, regardless of the effect on speed and the physical condition of the men.

6. In night movement all men must be alert to keep contact both to the front and to the rear.

7. When in contact with the enemy at night, one-half of the unit must be alert and in position to repel attacks.

8. Intelligence agencies must keep commanders informed of the enemy indications. Commanders can then adjust their plans in accordance, avoiding the possibility of surprise by the enemy.

9. Wounded men must be carried along when a unit is forced to withdraw, if the situation permits.

10. The hand grenade should be used to full advantage in close combat. The present hand grenade is too heavy for long throws, and, too, it cannot easily be carried in sufficient number for a sustained fight.

11. Soldiers must learn that an enemy assault is repelled by fire power alone. When individual targets cannot be located, continuous area fire must be used.

12. Units are forbidden to withdraw without orders however desperate the situation. Unit commanders must keep higher headquarters informed of the amount of enemy pressure, and request authority to withdraw prior to movement.

32

CHART A

**Unit Strength
2nd Platoon, D Company, 506th Parachute Infantry Regiment
Night of 11 June 1944**

Platoon Headquarters

Platoon Commander
Assistant Platoon Commander
Platoon Sergeant
Messenger
Messenger
Radio Operator

Rifle Squad

Squad Leader
Assistant Squad Leader
Machine Gunner
Assistant Machine Gunner
Ammunition Bearer
Scout
Scout
Rifleman
Rifleman
Rifleman
Rifleman
Rifleman

Rifle Squad

Squad Leader
Assistant Squad Leader
Machine Gunner
Assistant Machine Gunner
Ammunition Bearer
Scout
Scout
Rifleman
Rifleman
Rifleman
Rifleman
Rifleman

60mm Mortar Squad

Squad Leader
Mortar Gunner
Assistant Mortar Gunner
Ammunition Bearer
Ammunition Bearer
Ammunition Bearer

LEGEND
KIA, missing on parachute jump, or WIA during previous fighting

BULLET POINT: GI JIVE

In his 1942 book, *See Here, Private Hargrove*, Private Marion Hargrove offers examples of useful wartime Army jargon:

- *Goldbricking* Loafing. To Avoid one's share of work.
- *Batting the breeze* Shooting the bull; gabbing.
- *Police* Clean up, "to police the area."
- *Fatigue duty* Not part of strictly military training, but the "dirty work."
- *G.I.* Literally "Government Issue," but also to be "G.I." meaning to adhere rigidly to regulations.
- The *PX* The post exchange, or canteen.
- The *old man* The company's COcommanding officer.
- *Top Kick* A first sergeant, he's the company's top non-commissioned officer.
- A *guardhouse lawyer* A self-proclaimed expert on the Articles of War, particularly where Article 96 is concerned, regarding punishment for "conduct unbecoming a soldier."
- *Over the hill* To go AWOL, absent without leave.
- *Chow or mess* Literally, food.
- To *fall out* To get out of the barracks quickly.
- To *fall in* To get into ranks/formation.
- A *yardbird* Typically a low ranking soldier put to menial labor.
- *On the Double* At double time, quickly.
- *Chicken shit* To act in such a way as to incur contempt.
- *Army Bible* The Articles of War; regulations.
- *Blanket drill, horizontal drill* Sleep.
- *Butchershop* A dispensary or hospital.
- *By the numbers* Like clockwork; with precision and efficiency.
- *Chili bowl* Regulation haircut.
- *Chest hardware* Medals
- *Dog robber* An orderly.
- *Holy Joe* Chaplain.
- *Handshaking* Playing up to superiors.
- *Higher brass* the higher ranks of officers.
- *Housewife* a soldier's sewing kit.
- *Mother Machree* a sob story alibi.
- *Ride the sickbook* to goldbrick the easy way by pretending to be ill.
- *Shoulder hardware* the shoulder insignia of a commissioned officer.
- *Sugar report* a letter from the romantic interest back home.

A few more choice expressions are the following.
- *Go to work* Assault or attack.
- *SNAFU* An acronym for "situation normal – all fucked up."
- *Ninety-Day Wonder* A newly minted Second Lieutenant, usually the product of the Officer Candidate School.
- *Meat wagon* Ambulance.
- *The G.I.s* From "gastrointestinal," diarrhea.

And the list goes on and on, and on …

There are some words and phrases that have found their way into reenacting that are historically out of place. One such phrase is "rally point." "Assembly point" is the proper wartime alternative.

BULLET POINT: DOG TAGS FOR DOGFACES

Though only one small part of the overall impression, a pair of issue identification tags can tell a lot about a dogface and go a long way to creating a sense of realism. After nearly two years of trials, the Army, in 1940, adopted the Tag, Identification, M1940 (Stock No.74-T-60). Each soldier was issued two of these tags on the basis as described in The Officer's Guide:

"Identification tags will be worn by each member of the Army at all times, with either uniform or civilian clothing, and may be removed temporarily only as the necessities of personal hygiene require; one tag to be suspended from neck underneath the clothing by a cord or tape 40 inches in length passed through a small hole in the tag, the second tag to be fastened about 2 1/2 inches above the first one on the same cord or tape, both securely held in place by knots. These tags are prescribed as part of the uniform and will be habitually worn by the owner. The tags, embossed as provided in AR 600-35, will be issued to each member of the Army as soon as practicable after entry into service."

"Be certain that this tag contains the data concerning inoculations against disease, and blood type, which are required to be indicated thereon."

Initially, the necklace and extensions were of cotton, plastic, nylon, or rayon. In 1943, the Army adopted a standardized necklace and extension (Stock No 74-N-300) made of metal chain with hinged hooks. Later the well-known beaded stainless-steel necklace supplanted the earlier styles. Issue dog tag silencers became available late in the war, but industrious doggies often made field expedient dog tag silencers by cutting and fitting a section of flexible gas mask hose around each tag.

The tag itself measures 2" by 1-1/8" with a narrow rim on the reverse, and a 1/8" hole for the chain to pass through. World War II era tags are notched (so as to be positioned correctly in any of the several types of embossing machines). Tags were made of brass, monel or steel, but the overwhelming majority were made from stainless steel. Each tag contained five lines of information, each of up to eighteen characters.

The four basic styles of World War II dog tags are as follows:

Style I: ca. December 1940-November 1941

First Line	First name, middle initial, last name
Second Line	Army service number, blood type* (space 17)
Third Line	Name of next of kin
Fourth Line	Street address of next of kin
Fifth Line	City and state of next of kin

Style II: ca. November 1941-July 1943

First Line	First name, middle initial, last name
Second Line	Army service number (spaces 1-8)
	Tetanus immunization (spaces 10-12)
	Tetanus toxoid (spaces 14-15)
	Blood type (space 17)
Third Line	Name of next of kin
Fourth Line	Street address of next of kin
Fifth Line	City and state of next of kin, religious preference (space 18)

Style III: ca. July 1943-March 1944

First Line	First name, middle initial, last name
Second Line	Army service number (spaces 1-8)
	Tetanus immunization (spaces 10-12)
	Tetanus toxoid (spaces 14-15)
	Blood type (space 17)
Fifth Line	Religious preference** (space 18)

Style IV: ca. March 1944-War's End

First Line	Last name, first name, middle initial
Second Line	Army service number (spaces 1-8)
	Tetanus immunization (spaces 10-12)
	Tetanus toxoid (spaces 14-15)
	Blood type (space 17)
Fifth Line	Religious preference (space 18)

Notes: *No Rhesus factor for the blood type (+ or -) is indicated as this information was technologically not yet available wartime. **Religious preference was as follows, 'C' (Catholic), 'P' (Protestant), 'H' (Hebrew) or left blanc.*

Army Service Numbers. During World War II, (c. 1940 onward) a soldier's Army service number consisted of eight characters determined by his military status and the location of his enlistment. Prior to September 1940, Regular Army service numbers consisted of only seven digits.(Rush, 2, pp. 16)

Regular Army service numbers begin with '1', followed by a second digit denoting the Corps Area (a.k.a Service Command) of enlistment (there were nine corps area and four departments in all). Example: **13234634**.

National Guard service numbers begin with '20', followed by a third digit denoting the Corps Area of enlistment. Example: **20337345**.

The service numbers of draftees inducted into federal service by the Selective Training and Service Act, start with '3', followed by a second digit denoting the Corps Area of enlistment. Example: **33757877**.

The service numbers of commissioned officers start with the character 'O', followed by – but not in every case by – a hyphen, then by 2-7 digits. Examples: **O-23587, O2357965, O-125124**. Note: Officers commissioned after the start of 1940 were assigned number 23000 and higher. There were also specific series of service numbers for officers of the Officer Reserve Corps, the National Guard, officers who received direct commissions from civilian status, and graduates of officer candidate school.

Living Historians might wish to use a portion of their own Social Security number to further personalize their identifications tag's Army Service Number.

Regular Army War Department Service Number Range Allocation:
Hawaiian Department (1) **0** then 100,000-199,999
Panama Canal Department (1) **0** then 200,000-299,999
Philippine Department (1) **0** then 300,000-399,999
Puerto Rican Department (1) **0** then 400,000-499,999
First Corps Area (1) **1** then 000,000-999,999
Second Corps Area (1) **2** then 000,000-999,999
Third Corps Area (1) **3** then 000,000-999,999
Fourth Corps Area (1) **4** then 000,000-999,999
Fifth Corps Area (1) **5** then 000,000-999,999

Sixth Corps Area (1) **6** then 000,000-999,999
Seventh Corps Area (1) **7** then 000,000-999,999
Eighth Corps Area (1) **8** then 000,000-999,999
Ninth Corps Area (1) **9** then 000,000-999,999

National Guard War Department Service Number Range Allocation:
Hawaiian Department (20) **0** 10,000-19,999
Puerto Rican Department (20) **0** 20,000-29,999
First Corps Area (20) **1** then 00,000-99,999
Second Corps Area (20) **2** then 00,000-99,999
Third Corps Area (20) **3** then 00,000-99,999
Fourth Corps Area (20) **4** then 00,000-99,999
Fifth Corps Area (20) **5** then 00,000-99,999
Sixth Corps Area (20) **6** then 00,000-99,999
Seventh Corps Area (20) **7** then 00,000-99,999
Eighth Corps Area (20) **8** then 00,000-99,999
Ninth Corps Area (20) **9** then 00,000-99,999

Draftee War Department Service Number Range Allocation:
Hawaiian Department (3) **0** then 100,000-199,999
Panama Canal Department (3) **0** then 200,000-299,999
Philippine Department (3) **0** then 300,000-399,999
Puerto Rican Department (3) **0** then 400,000-499,999
First Corps Area (3) **1** then 000,000-999,999
Second Corps Area (3/4*) **2** then 000,000-999,999
Third Corps Area (3/4*) **3** then 000,000-999,999
Fourth Corps Area (3/4*) **4** then 000,000-999,999
Fifth Corps Area (3) **5** then 000,000-999,999
Sixth Corps Area (3) **6** then 000,000-999,999
Seventh Corps Area (3) **7** then 000,000-999,999
Eighth Corps Area (3) **8** then 000,000-999,999
Ninth Corps Area (3) **9** then 000,000-999,999

*Each of these Corps Area inducted over one million men. After the first 999,999 men were inducted, the digit '4' was introduced as the prefix used for subsequent draftees.

FIRST ARMY AREA
First Corps Area: Connecticut-Maine-Massachusetts-New Hampshire-Rhode Island-Vermont
Second Corps Area: Delaware-New Jersey-New York
Third Corps Area: Maryland-Pennsylvania-Virginia-Washington, DC

SECOND ARMY AREA
Fifth Corps Area: Indiana-Kentucky-Ohio-West Virginia
Sixth Corps Area: Illinois-Michigan-Wisconsin

THIRD ARMY AREA
Fourth Corps Area: Alabama-Florida-Georgia-Louisiana-Mississippi-North Carolina-South Carolina-Tennessee
Eighth Corps Area: Arizona-Colorado-Oklahoma-New Mexico-Texas

FOURTH ARMY AREA
Seventh Corps Area: Arkansas-Indiana-Kansas-Minnesota-Missouri-Nebraska-North Dakota-South Dakota-Wyoming
Ninth Corps Area: Arizona-California-Idaho-Montana-Nevada-Oregon-Utah-Washington

BULLET POINT: CHRONOLOGY OF THE WAR

1939
January 26 – Franco's troops take Barcelona.
May 9 – German-Italian alliance formed.
September 1 – Germany invades Poland, marking the beginning of World War II.
September 3 – Great Britain and France declare war on Germany.
September 8 – President Roosevelt endorses measure enlarging the Regular Army from 210,000 men to 237,000 men, and to enlarge the National Guard to 235,000.

1940
May 10 – Germany invades Belgium, Holland, and Luxembourg.
June – British and French forces narrowly escape destruction, and are evacuated from Dunkirk, France.
June 22 – France formally surrenders to Germany, Collaborationist French government installed in Vichy.
August 27 – National Guard is Federalized for one year's service.
September 16 – Selective Service Act passed into law.

1941
March 11 – U.S. Lend-Lease Act passed.
June 22 – Germany declares war on Russia.
August 9-12 – Roosevelt and Churchill meet; declare Atlantic Charter.
December 7 – Japan opens war with United States by attacking the U.S. naval station at Pearl Harbor, Hawaii.
December 8 – United States declares war on Japan; Niponnese invade Philippines, attack Guam and Wake Islands.
December 10 – Battle for Manila begins.
December 11 – Germany and Italy declare war on U.S. Congress declares war exists between Untied States and Germany and Italy.
December 15 – Russians begin winter drive against German invaders.
December 20 – Japanese submarines raid California waters, attack two ships.
December 22 – Churchill flies to Washington, meets President Roosevelt.
December 23 – Submarine attacks continue; tanker sinks off coast; ship torpedoed off San Pedro.
December 25 – Hong Kong falls, Wake Island captured.
December 26 – Manila declared open city, but Japanese bomb city.
December-January 1942 – ARCADIA (Washington, DC) Conference between Roosevelt and Churchill.

1942
January – Allied leaders confer in Washington, DC.
January 1 – Russians recapture Kaluga, British battle Axis near Bardia.
January 2 – Manila surrenders; Cavite naval base abandoned; MacArthur's forces flee to Bataan; 25 United Nations pledge war to end.
January 4 – Daylight air raids on German begin.
January 11 – Japan invades Dutch East Indies.
January 23 – Japanese land at Rabaul and the Solomons.
January 26 – First American Expeditionary Forces land in Northern Ireland.
January 29 – Axis troops retake Bengazi.
January 31 – U.S. warships shell Marshalls and Gilberts.
February 15 – Singapore falls.
February 23 – Enemy submarine shells California coast at Goleta.

February 27-March 1 – Allies suffer heavy losses in sea battle in Java Sea.

March 14 – Americans land in Australia.

March 17 – General MacArthur reaches Australia to lead Allied forces.

April – Combined chiefs of staff meet in London to discuss a possible invasion of Northwest Europe tentatively scheduled for 1943.

April 9 – U.S. troops on Bataan surrender.

April 18 – Tokyo bombed by U.S. carrier based planes.

May 4 – British troops invade Madagascar.

May 6 – Corregidor surrenders; Japanese complete Burma occupation.

May 9 – U.S. naval forces sink eight Japanese ships in Coral Sea battle.

May 15 – Germans launch drive on Caucasian oil fields.

May 23 – Russians abandon Kerch Peninsula.

June 3 – Japanese planes raid Dutch Harbor, Aleutian Islands.

June 4-6 – U.S. Navy smashes Japanese invasion fleet near Midway Island.

June 7 – Japanese land on Attu and Kiska Islands.

June 20-21 – Japanese submarine shells British Columbia coast; fires shells at Oregon points near seaside; Axis troops capture Tobruk.

June 25 – Axis troops invade Egypt.

July 1 – Sevastopol falls to Germans.

August 7 – U.S. Marines establish bridgehead on Guadalcanal.

August 19 – Operation JUBILEE, Allied raid on Dieppe, France, in which detachment of U.S. Rangers participate.

September 12 – Eisenhower named Commander-in-Chief of Allied Expeditionary Force for intended operations in French Northwest Africa.

September 13 – Germans enter Stalingrad.

October 17 – American troops arrive in Liberia.

October 24 – British begin drive to oust Rommel from Tunisia.

November 3 – British defeat Rommel at El Alamein.

November 8 – Operation TORCH, Allied landings on the west and northwest coasts of Africa.

November 11 – Hitler invades unoccupied France; Admiral Darlan surrenders French Africa to the Allies.

November 21 – Russians begin Stalingrad offensive.

November 27 – French scuttle fleet at Toulon.

December 8 – Dakar port, French fleet given Allies.

December 10 – U.S. troops capture Gona in New Guinea.

December 24 – Darlan assassinated at Algiers.

1943

January 1 – Red Army on the march in the Ukraine.

January 14 – COSSAC (Chief of Staff to the Supreme Allied Commander) planning staff formed by Western Allies at conference in Casablanca; pledge "unconditional surrender."

January 18 – Russians lift siege of Leningrad.

January 23 – British forces take Tripoli.

January 27 – Roosevelt visits Brazil on war plans.

February 7 – General Eisenhower takes command of Allied forces in Africa; Red Army reaches Azov, traps 25,000 Nazis.

February 9 – American troops complete occupation o9f Guadalcanal.

February 20 – U.S. ships shell Japanese in Aleutians.

February 27 – Nazis open drive in Donets area.

March 1 – Lake Ilmen offensive drives Germans south of Leningrad.

March 17 – U.S. planes bomb Kiska six times in day.

April 4 – Northwest African Strategic Air Force under Major General Doolittle strikes Europe for first time, raiding Naples.

May 7 – British take Tunis; American seize Bizerte; U.S. troops occupy Adak and Amchitka in Aleutians.

May 11 – U.S. troops land on Attu.

May 12 – Organized Axis resistance ends in North Africa.

May 12-25 – TRIDENT (Washington, DC) Conference between Roosevelt and Churchill. New date for invasion of Northwest Europe (Operation OVERLORD) set.

May 30 – Yanks recapture Attu, first American soil to be retaken from Japanese.

June 1 – Mexico declares war on Axis.

June 7 – French Committee on National Liberation formed.

June 11 – Pantelleria, island off Sicily, surrenders with 10,000 prisoners.

July 1 – U.S. forces occupy Rendova Island in Solomons.

July 5 – Japanese fleet loses nine warships in battle of Kula Gulf; U.S. cruiser Helena sinks; Allied forces land on New Georgia Island; British land on Crete.

July 10 – U.S., British and Canadian troops invade Sicily; U.S. warships shell Kiska.

July 18 – Nazis on defensive in Orel sector.

July 19 – Rome bombed, for first time, by 521 U.S. planes; Yank bombers raid Japanese base at Parmushiro.

July 23 – U.S. forces take Palermo.

July 25 – Mussolini forced out as dictator, Badoglio forms cabinet.

August 1 – U.S. bombers raid Ploesti oil fields in Romania.

August 6 – U.S. troops occupy Munda in Solomons.

August 15 – U.S., Canadian troops land on Kiska, find island unoccupied.

August 17 – Roosevelt and Churchill meet in Quebec, approve plans for Operation OVERLORD; Allies capture Sicily.

August 23 – Russians recapture Kharkov.

August 28 – King Boris of Bulgaria dies.

September 1 – U.S. task force attacks Marcus Islands, near Tokyo.

September 3 – British-Canadian armies invade Italy.

September 5 – MacArthur's forces land on New Guinea near Lae.

September 8 – Red Army captures Stalino.

September 8 – Italy signs armistice.

September 9 – Operation AVALANCHE, U.S. Fifth Army lands on the Italian mainland south of Naples, in the Gulf of Salerno.

September 11 – Allies in Italy take Salerno.

September 12 – Nazi paratroopers kidnap Mussolini from Allies; Isle of Capri is taken by Allies.

September 14 – Eighty Italian warships surrender to Allies; MacArthur captures Salamaua in New Guinea.

September 16 – Red Army takes Novorossisk.

September 22 – MacArthur's troops land at Finschafen, New Guinea.

September 25 – Red Army retakes Smolensk.

October 1 – U.S. Fifth Army enters Naples.

October 5 – Corsica freed by Allies.

October 13 – Italy declares war on Germany.

November 3 – U.S. Marines invade Bougainville.

November 5 – U.S. Fifth Army enters the German Winter Line.

November 6 – Russians take Kiev.

November 20 – U.S. Army and Marines land on Tarawa and Makin.

November 22 – SEXTANT (Cairo) Conference between Roosevelt, Churchill, and Chaing Kai-shek.

November 26 – EUREKA (Teheran) Conference between Roosevelt, Churchill, and Stalin.

December 10 – General Dwight D. Eisenhower appointed Supreme Commander of the Allied Expeditionary Forces for intended operation in France.

1944

January 2 – U.S. forces land at Saidor, New Guinea.

January 4 – Red Army crosses old Polish border.

January 11 – Allied troops move on Burma; Count Ciano executed.

January 15 – Winter Line Battle ends in Italy.

January 18 – Red Army launches Leningrad offensive.

January 22 – Operation SHINGLE, U.S. and British Forces land behind the German lines on the west coast of Italy, at Anzio.

January 29 – Marines, Army land in Marshalls.

February 2 – U.S. troops enter Gustav line in Italy; Reds enter Estonia.

February 15 – U.S. planes and artillery destroy Monte Cassino Abbey.

February 20 – U.S. fleet raids Truk.

March 4 – New six-ton bombs blast Reich.

March 6 – U.S. troops in action in Asia for first time, capture Walawbum, Burma.

March 13 – Russian troops cross Dneiper.

March 22 – Japanese army penetrates into India.

March 30 – Red Army takes Cernauti, Romania.

April 10 – Soviet troops recapture Odessa.

April 22 – MacArthur's troops land at Hollandia, Dutch New Guinea.

May 9 – Ukrainian troops occupy Sevastopol.

May 11 – Operation DIADEM, U.S. Fifth Army commences attack against the Cassino front.

May 23 – Operation BUFFALO, U.S. 6th Corps breaks out of the Anzio Beachhead.

June 4 – British and American troops march into Rome.

June 6 – Operation OVERLORD, the Anglo-American invasion of France, at Normandy, commences.

June 7 – Allies take Bayeaux.

June 10 – Marines and Army invade Saipan.

June 26 – Allies take Cherbourg.

July 3 – U.S. forces in Normandy enter fighting in the bocage.

July 11 – Moscow reports prewar Russia cleared of Nazis.

July 17 – Soviet army crosses into Latvia.

July 19 – U.S. forces land on Guam.

July 25 – Operation COBRA, the Allied breakout of the Normandy Beachhead commences.

August 1 – U.S. troops enter Brittany through Avranches; Marines take Tinian.

August 15 – Operation DRAGOON (formerly called ANVIL), Allied forces land on the Mediterranean coast of France, between Marseilles and Nice.

August 19 – U.S. tanks enter Paris.

August 23 – Romania surrenders.

August 25 – Germans give up in Paris.

August 28 – Red Army invades Transylvania.

August 31 – U.S. forces reach old Maginot Line.

September 1 – Yanks enter Belgium at Sedan; Canadians take Dieppe.

September 4 – British tanks roll through Brussels and Antwerp to Holland border; Americans reach German border in Belgium; Finland makes peace.

September 10 – American First Army fires first American shells into German near Aachen; Churchill and Roosevelt meet at Quebec.

September 11 – Luxembourg liberated; OVERLORD and DRAGOON forces meet near Dijon, consolidating front line.

September 12 – U.S. forces take Rotgen, inside German; Nazis surrender Le Havre.

September 15 – Yanks occupy Maastricht, Holland.

September 17 – Operation MARKET-GARDEN, Allied land and airborne operation into Holland, to capture bridges at Grave, Nijmegen, and Arnhem; Japanese offensive in China forces U.S. 14th Air Force to abandon its bases; U.S. troops land in Palaus.

September 20 – Brest garrison surrenders.

September 30 – Russians drive into Yugoslavia.

October 2 – Polish resistance forces in Warsaw surrender; U.S. forces commence attack on German West Wall.

October 10 – Reds reach Baltic Sea near Memel.

October 13 – Germans evacuate Athens.

October 17 – MacArthur returns to Philippines as U.S. Army invades Leyte.

October 24 – U.S. battle fleets sink or damage 58 Japanese ships when Imperial navy attempts surprise attack in Leyte Gulf; MacArthur's troops land on Samar Island.

October 28 – Bulgaria signs armistice.

November 20 – Patton's troops enter Metz.

November 24 – Allies take Strasbourg.

December 5 – British fight ELAS forces in Athens.

December 16 – Battle of the Bulge begins, Germans start counterattack through Ardennes that carries 50 miles into Belgium.

December 22 – British strike to halt German offensive; Reds open Baltic offensive.

December 23 – Patton's army strikes at Nazi bulge; planes bomb Germans.

December 25 – Nazi Ardennes drive halted.

December 29 – Germans beaten back in Belgium.

1945

January-February – ARGONAUT (Malta and Yalta) Conferences between Roosevelt and Churchill (the former), and Roosevelt, Churchill, and Stalin (the latter).

January 1 – German Operation NORDWIND counteroffensive strikes U.S. Seventh Army.

January 10 – Yanks land on Lingayen Gulf, Luzon; Nazis flee Ardennes.

January 13 – Navy hits 46 Japanese ships off Luzon.

January 15 – Russians open offensive on Germany with 215 divisions.

January 16 – Allied forces reduce "bulge" in Ardennes.

January 17 – Reds take Warsaw, Krakov.

January 24 – Red Army reaches Oder River.

January 30 – MacArthur lands north of Bataan.

February 4 – Two Yank divisions enter Manila, rescue 3,700 internees.

February 7 – Stalin, Roosevelt and Churchill confer in Yalta.

February 13 – Budapest falls.

February 14 – Nazis blasted in 6,000-plane raid.

February 16 – Tokyo blasted by 1,500 Navy planes.

February 17 – Marines invade Iwo Jima; U.S. Army lands on Corregidor.

February 23 – Operation GRENADE, U.S. Ninth Army operation northeast toward the Rhine; Turkey declares war on Axis; Russians take Poznan; Iwo volcano captured.

February 25 – Tokyo aflame after raids by giant fleet of B-29s and 1,600 carrier planes.

February 26 – MacArthur returns Philippine Commonwealth to Filipino people.

March 7 – Cologne falls to Yanks; U.S. First Army crosses Rhine at Remagen.

March 15 – Operation UNDERTONE launched by Sixth Army Group south of Moselle to close on the Rhone from Koblenz southward.

March 17 – Iwo Jima captured; U.S. Marine casualties 19,938, including 4,198 dead.

March 23 – Operation VARSITY-PLUNDER, the Allied airborne and surface operation of crossing the Rhine River north of the Ruhr in the vicinity of Wesel, Germany.

March 26 – Whole Nazi East Rhine front crumbles; Russians race toward Vienna.

April 1 – U.S. Marine and Army troops invade Okinawa; Yanks close trap in Ruhr.

April 6 – Kioso Cabinet falls as Russians drop pact with Japanese; General MacArthur to head Pacific Army forces; Admiral Nimitz the Pacific naval forces.

April 11 – U.S. Ninth Army at Elbe River.

April 12 – President Roosevelt dies suddenly at Warm Springs; Vice President Truman takes oath as President.

April 14 – U.S. Fifth Army begins attack on German Gothic Line in Italy.

April 20 – Red Army bursts into Berlin.

April 25 – United Nations open conference at San Francisco.

April 29 – Mussolini executed by Italian patriots; Munich and Venice captured.

May 1 – Nazi radio declares Hitler dead, names Admiral Doenitz to succeed him.

May 2 – Russians say Hitler and Goebbels have died in Berlin ruins. German and Italian Fascist armies, number more than one million men in Italy and west Austria surrender; Australian troops invade Tarakan, island off Borneo; German forces in Italy surrender.

May 4 – Nazis in northwestern German, Denmark and Holland surrender; Allies announce Japanese armies in Burma have been "decisively defeated," leaving 97,000 dead.

May 7 – German army commanders surrender to Allies; sign papers at Reims.

May 8 – Churchill, Truman proclaim V-E Day.

May 9 – Stalin hails end of European war as German army chiefs sign surrender to Allies in Ruins of Berlin; Reichmarshal Hermann Goering and Vidkin Quisling, Norse Nazi leader, give up.

May 12 – U.S. forces launch offensive against Japanese Naha line on Okinawa; new amphibious landing on Mindanao.

May 14 – Gigantic air fleet of 900 Navy planes and 500 B-29s blast Nagoya.

May 18 – Navy reveals Japanese air attack on U.S. carrier Benjamin Franklin; 832 men killed and 270 wounded.

May 19 – Chinese troops complete reoccupation of port city of Foochow.

May 24 – 550 Superforts firebomb Tokyo.

May 27 – Chinese troops capture Nanking.

May 28 – MacArthur sets Japanese losses in Philippines at 378,427 dead and captured; American losses 48,044; Yanks take Santa Fe, key city on Luzon.

May 29 – Yokohama firebombed with 3,200 tons of incendiaries.

June 1 – 450 Superforts firebomb Osaka.

June 5 – Koe bombed with 3,000 tons of incendiaries.

June 7 – Osaka again firebombed; Japanese balloons reported in Southern California.

June 11 – Chinese troops take Futing port; seize Lungchow and move on Kwelein.

June 12 – Australians invade Borneo under MacArthur; Okinawa Japanese spurn surrender offer.

June 18 – Lt. General Simon Bolivar Buckner, Jr. killed on Okinawa.

June 21 – Organized resistance ends on Okinawa.

June 24 – Australians complete recapture of Miri oil fields in West Borneo.

June 26 – Yanks seize Kume Island just west of Okinawa.

June 30 – Chinese retake Liuchow, airbase city.

July 1 – Australians land at Balikpapan, Borneo.

July 5 – Entire Philippine Islands liberated, MacArthur says.

July 10 – U.S. Third fleet sends 1,000 carrier bombers against Tokyo.

July 11 – Balikpapan Bay won.

July 14-15 – U.S. Fleet begins first heavy bombardment of Japan's home islands, shelling northern Honshu and Hokkaido.

July 17 – TERMINAL (Potsdam) Conference between Truman, Churchill, and Stalin; British fleet joins in carrier plane raids on Japan.

July 19 – U.S. and British fliers last hiding Japanese fleet at Yokosuka base, Tokyo Bay, sinking 32,700-ton battleship *Nagato*.

July 22 – First Yanks from German front reach Philippines.

July 26 – U.S., Britain and China demand Japan surrender unconditionally.

July 29 – Japan will ignore surrender ultimatum.

August 3 – Japan completely blockaded by B-29s.

August 5 – First atomic bomb dropped on Hiroshima.

August 8 – Russia declares war on Japan.

August 9 – Second atomic bomb hits Nagasaki.

August 10 – Japan offers to surrender if Hirohito is permitted to retain throne.

August 11 – Allies tell Tokyo that Hirohito may remain, subject to Allied commander.

August 13 – The world still awaits word from Japan on Peace.

August 14 – President Truman announces Japan's acceptance of surrender terms.

U.S. Airborne Unit Combat Chronicles

17th Airborne Division
Activated: 15 April 1943. *Overseas:* 17 August 1944. *Campaigns:* Ardennes-Alsace, Rhineland, Central Europe. *Days of combat:* 45. *Distinguished Unit Citations:* 4. *Awards:* MH-3; DSC-4; DSM-1; SS-179; LM-15; SM-6; BSM-727; AM-21. *Nickname:* Thunder from Heaven. *Shoulder patch:* Circular patch in black with stretching claw in gold and arc with word "Airborne" above. *Publications: History of the 17th Airborne Division;* by unit members; and *Pictorial Review;* by unit members; Albert Love Enterprises, Atlanta 2, Ga.; 1944.

Campaign Chronicle
The 17th Airborne Division was stationed in the United Kingdom from 25 August to 23 December 1944. From 23 to 25 December, elements of the Division were flown to the Reims area in France in spectacular night flights. These elements closed in at Mourmelon. After taking over the defense of the Meuse River sector from Givet to Verdun, 25 December, the 17th moved to Neufchateau, Belgium, then marched through the snow to Morhet, relieving the 28th Infantry Division, 3 January 1945. The Division entered the Ardennes campaign, 4 to 9 January, at the Battle of Dead Man's Ridge. It captured several small Belgian towns and entered Flamierge, 7 January, but enemy counterattacks necessitated a withdrawal. However, constant pressure and aggressive patrolling caused the enemy to retreat to the Ourthe River. On 18 January, the Division relieved the 11th Armored Division at Houffalize, pushed enemy remnants from the Bulge, and seized Wattermal and Espeler, 26 January. Coming under the III Corps, the 17th turned toward Luxembourg, taking Eschweiler and Clervaux and clearing the enemy from the west bank of the Our River. Aggressive patrols crossed the river to probe the Siegfried Line defenses and established a limited bridgehead near Dasburg before being relieved by the 6th Armored Division, 10 February. A period of re-equipment and preparation began. Taking off from marshalling areas in France, the 17th dropped into Westphalia in the vicinity of Wesel, 24 March. Operation Varsity was the first airborne invasion over the Rhine into Germany itself. On the 25th, the Division had secured bridges over the Issel River and had entrenched itself firmly along the Issel Canal. Moving eastward, it captured Haltern, 29 March, and Munster, 2 April. The 17th entered the battle of the Ruhr Pocket, relieving the 79th Infantry Division. It crossed the Rhine-Herne Canal, 6 April, and set up a secure bridgehead for the attack on Essen. The "Pittsburgh of the Ruhr" fell, 10 April, and the industrial cities of Mulheim and Duisburg were cleared in the continuing attack. Military government duties began, 12 April, and active contact with the enemy ceased, 18 April. The Division came under the XXII Corps 24 April. It continued its occupation duties until 15 June 1945 when it returned to France for redeployment.

82nd Airborne Division
Activated: 25 March 1942. Designated an airborne division on 15 August 1942. *Overseas:* 28 April 1943. *Campaigns:* Sicily, Naples-Foggia, Rome-Arno, Normandy, Ardennes-Alsace, Rhineland, Central Europe. *Days of combat:* 422. *Distinguished Unit Citations:* 15. *Awards:* MH-2; DSC-37; DSM-2; SS-898; LM-29; SM-49; BSM-1,894; AM-15. *Nickname:* All American. *Shoulder patch:* A blue circle, containing white letters "AA" superimposed on a red square. A blue arc is above containing word "Airborne." *Publications: All American,* by unit members; TI&E, ETOUSA; distributor, secretary, 82d Airborne Division Association, 1945. *Here Is Your Book, Saga of the All-American;* by unit members; Albert Love Enterprises, Atlanta 2, Ga.; 1947. *Paraglide;* Publication of the Airborne Division Association; *All-American Soldier;* a record album by the 82d Airborne Division Association.

Combat Chronicle
The 82d Airborne Division landed at Casablanca, 10 May 1943, and trained. Elements first saw combat in Sicily, when the 505th RCT and part of the 504th dropped behind enemy

lines, 9-10 July 1943, at Gela. The remainder of the 504th RCT dropped, 11-12 July 1943, also near Gela, after running friendly naval and ground force fire. Scattered elements formed and fought as ground troops. The elements were flown back to Tunisia for re-equipment and returned to Sicily to take off for drop landings on the Salerno beachhead. The 504th Parachute Infantry dropped, 13 September 1943, and the 505th the following night; the 325th landed by boat. These elements bolstered Salerno defenses and fought their way into Naples, 1 October 1943. After a period of occupation duty (and combat for some elements in the Volturno Valley and Anzio beachhead), the Division moved to Ireland, November 1943, and later to England, February 1944, for additional training. Moving in by glider and parachute, troops of the 82d dropped behind enemy lines in Normandy on D-day, 6 June 1944, before ground troops hit the beaches. Cutting off enemy reinforcements, the Division fought its way from Carentan to St. Sauveur-le-Vicomte, fighting 33 days without relief. Relieved on 8 July, it returned to England for refitting. On 17 September, it was dropped at Nijmegen, 50 miles behind enemy lines, and captured the Nijmegen bridge, 20 September, permitting relief of British paratroops by the British 2d Army. After heavy fighting in Holland, the Division was relieved 11 November and rested in France. It was returned to combat, 18 December 1944, to stem the von Rundstedt offensive, blunting the northern salient of the Bulge. It punched through the Siegfried Line in early February 1945, and crossed the Roer, 17 February. Training with new equipment in March, the Division returned to combat, 4 April, patrolling along the Rhine, securing the Koln area, later moving across the Elbe, 30 April, into the Mecklenburg Plain, where, 2 May 1945, the German 21st Army surrendered.

101st Airborne Division

Activated: 15 August 1942. *Overseas:* 5 September 1943. *Campaigns:* Rhineland, Central Europe, Normandy, Ardennes-Alsace. *Days of combat:* 214. *Distinguished Unit Citations:* 13. *Awards:* MH-2; DSC-56; DSM-2; SS-456; LM-20; SM-4; BSM-9,488; AM-48. *Nickname:* Screaming Eagle. *Shoulder patch:* Black badge with black arc streaming above; on the badge is white screaming eagle; appearing on arc, in white, is "Airborne." *Publications: Epic of the 101st Airborne Division;* by unit members; 101st Airborne Division Association; *Rendezvous with Destiny;* by First Lt. Leonard Rapport and Lt. Arthur Northwood; The Infantry Journal, Washington 6, D. C., 1947.

Combat Chronicle

The 101st Airborne arrived in England, 15 September 1943, and received additional training in Berkshire and Wiltshire. On 6 June 1944, the Division was dropped into Normandy behind Utah Beach. Against fierce resistance it took Pouppeville, Vierville, and St. Come du Mont. On the 12th, the stronghold of Carentan fell, and after mopping up and maintaining its positions, the Division returned to England, 13 July, for rest and training. On 17 September 1944, taking part in one of the largest of airborne invasions, the 101st landed in Holland, took Vechel and held the Zon bridge. St. Oedenrode and Eindhoven fell after sharp fighting on the 17th and 18th. Opheusden changed hands in a shifting struggle, but the enemy was finally forced to withdraw, 9 October. After extensive patrols, the Division returned to France, 28 November, for further training. On 18 December, it moved to Belgium to stop the German breakthrough. Moving into Bastogne under the acting command of Brig. Gen. Anthony C. McAuliffe, it set up a circular defense and although completely surrounded, refused to surrender on 22 December. Its perimeter held against violent attacks. The 4th Armored Division finally reached the 101st on the 26th and the enemy offensive was blunted. Very heavy fighting continued near Bastogne for the rest of December and January. On 17 January 1945, the Division moved to Drulingen and Pfaffenhoffen in Alsace and engaged in defensive harassing patrols along the Moder River. On 31 January, it crossed the Moder in a three-company raid. After assembling at Mourmelon, France, 26 February 1945, for training, it moved to the Ruhr pocket, 31 March, patrolling and raiding in April and engaging in military government at Rheydt and Munchen-Gladbach. The 101st reached Berchtesgaden by the end of the war and performed occupational duties until inactivation in Germany.

Key:
MH = Medal of Honor
DSC = Distinguished Service Cross
DSM = Distinguished Service Medal
SS = Silver Star
LM = Legion of Merit
SM = Soldier's Medal
BSM = Bronze Star Medal
AM = Air Medal

Regimental and Battalion Organization Chronicles

501st Parachute Infantry Regiment (Separate), *Normandy, Rhineland, Ardennes-Alsace, Central Europe.* 24 February 1942, 1st Battalion redesignated from the 501st parachute Battalion and remainder of regiment activated at Camp Toccoa, Georgia, on 15 November 1942; 1st Battalion inactivated on 2 November 1942, in Australia and assets used to form the 2nd Battalion, 503rd Parachute Infantry there, and new 1st Battalion activated at Camp Toccoa, Georgia on 15 November 1942; assigned to the Airborne Command 15 December 1942 and moved to Fort Benning, Georgia on 23 March 1943; staged at Camp Myles Standish, Massachusetts 2 January 1944, until departed Boston Port of Embarkation on 18 January 1944; arrived in England 31 January 1944, and attached to the 101st Airborne Division in May 1944 past the end of hostilities in Europe; assaulted Normandy, France to capture the Douve River locks at La Barquette, 6 June 1944 and captured Beghel; moved to Rheims, France 28 November 1944 for rehabilitation and sent to Bastogne, Belgium 18 December 1944 where fought until January 1945; entered Germany 4 April 1945 where inactivated on 20 August 1945.

502nd Parachute Infantry Regiment (101st Airborne Division), *Normandy, Rhineland, Ardennes-Alsace, Central Europe.* 24 February 1942 1st Battalion redesignated from 502nd Parachute Battalion and remainder of regiment activated at Fort Benning, Georgia on 2 March 1942. Assigned to the 101st Airborne Division 15 August 1942 and moved to Fort Bragg, North Carolina 24 September 1942; staged at Camp Shanks, New York 25 August 1943 until departed New York Port of Embarkation 5 September 1943; arrived in England 18 September 1943 and assaulted Normandy, France 6 June 1944; returned to England 13 July 1944 and assaulted Nijmegen-Arnhem, Holland 17 September 1944 (attached to the 82nd Airborne Division 4-5 October 1944) and entered Germany 4 April 1945 where inactivated on 30 November 1945.

504th Parachute Infantry Regiment (82nd Airborne Division), *Sicily, Naples-Foggia (inc. Anzio), Rhineland, Ardennes-Alsace, Central Europe.* 1 May 1942 activated at Fort Benning, Georgia and assigned to the Airborne Command; assigned to the 82nd Airborne Division on 15 August 1942 and moved to Fort Bragg, North Carolina 30 September 1942; staged at Camp Edwards, Massachusetts 18 April 1943 until departed New York Port of Embarkation 28 April 1943; landed in North Africa 10 May 1943 and assaulted Gela, Sicily on 9 July 1943; assaulted Anzio, Italy 22 January 1944 and departed Italy 10 April 1944; arrived England 23 April 1944 where remained until assaulted Nijmegen-Arnhem Holland on 17 September 1944; relocated to France 15 November 1944 (attached to the 75th Infantry Division 1-3 January 1945) and crossed into Belgium 26 January 1945 and returned to France 22 February 1945 and entered Germany 8 April 1945; returned to New York Port of Embarkation 3 January 1946 and moved to Fort Bragg, North Carolina 16 January 1946 where remained active through 1946.

505th Parachute Infantry Regiment (82nd Airborne Division), *Sicily, Naples-Foggia, Normandy, Rhineland, Ardennes-Alsace, Central Europe.* 6 July 1942 activated at Fort Benning, Georgia and assigned to the Airborne Command; assigned to the 82nd Airborne Division on 10 February 1943 and moved to Fort Bragg, North Carolina 12 February

1943; staged at Camp Edwards, Massachusetts 21 April 1943 until departed New York Port of Embarkation 28 April 1943; landed in North Africa 10 May 1943 and assaulted Gela, Sicily on 9 July 1943; returned to North Africa 19 August 1943 and England 14 February 1944; assaulted Normandy, France 6 June 1944 and returned to England 13 July 1944; assaulted Nijmegen-Arnhem, Holland 17 September 1944; returned to France 14 November 1944 and crossed into Belgium 18 December 1944 and entered Germany 30 January 1945; returned to France 19 February 1945 and reentered Germany 2 April 1945; returned to New York Port of Embarkation 3 January 1946 and moved to Fort Bragg, North Carolina 16 January 1946 where remained active through 1946.

506th Parachute Infantry Regiment (101st Airborne Division), *Normandy, Rhineland, Ardennes-Alsace, Central Europe.* 20 July 1942 activated at Camp Toombs (renamed Camp Toccoa), and moved to Fort Benning, Georgia 9 December 1942 where attached to the Airborne Command 15 December 1942; transferred to Camp Mackall, North Carolina 26 February 1943 (attached to the 101st Airborne Division 1 June 1943-1 March 1945); relocated to Sturgis Army Airfield, Kentucky 6 June 1943 and to Fort Bragg, North Carolina 23 July 1943; staged at Camp Shanks, New York 29 August 1943 until departed New York Port of Embarkation 5 September 1943; arrived England 15 September 1943 and assaulted Normandy, France 6 June 1944; returned to England 13 July 1944 and assaulted Nijmegen-Arnhem, Holland 17 September 1944; moved to Rheims, France 28 November 1944 for rehabilitation and sent to Bastogne, Belgium 18 December 1944 where fought until January 1945; entered Germany 4 April 1945 (attached to 4th Infantry Division 2-3 may 1945); was assigned 101st Airborne Division 1 March 1945; inactivated there on 30 May 1945.

507th Parachute Infantry Regiment (17th Airborne Division), *Normandy, Rhineland, Ardennes-Alsace, Central Europe.* 20 July 1942 Activated at Fort Benning, Georgia and assigned to the Airborne Command; moved to Barksdale Field, Louisiana 7 March 1943 and to Alliance Army Airfield, Nebraska 23 March 1943 where assigned to the 1st Airborne Infantry Brigade on 14 April 1943; staged at Camp Shanks, New York 23 November 1943 until departed New York Port of Embarkation 5 December 1943; arrived England 16 December 1943 (attached to the 82nd Airborne Division 14 January-27 August 1944) and assaulted Normandy, France on 6 June 1944; returned to England 13 July 1944 (attached to the 17th Airborne Division 27 August 1944-1 March 1945) and landed in France 24 December 1944; crossed into Belgium 25 December 1944 and returned to France 11 February 1945 where assigned to the 17th Airborne Division on 1 March 1945; assaulted Wesel, Germany 24 March 1945 (attached to the XIX Corps 31 March-2 April 1945); arrived Boston Port of Embarkation 15 September 1945 and inactivated at Camp Myles Standish, Massachusetts On 16 September 1945.

508th Parachute Infantry Regiment (Separate), *Normandy, Rhineland, Ardennes-Alsace, Central Europe.* 20 October 1942 activated at Camp Blanding, Florida and assigned to the Airborne Command; moved to Fort Benning, Georgia 5 February 1943 and to Camp Mackall, North Carolina 25 March 1943; staged at Camp Shanks, New York 20 December 1943 until departed New York Port of Embarkation 29 December 1943; arrived northern Ireland 8 January 1944 (attached to the 82nd Airborne Division 14 January 1944-20 January 1945) and England 13 March 1944; assaulted Normandy, France on 6 June 1944 and returned to England 13 July 1944; assaulted Nijmegen-Arnhem, Holland 17 September 1944 and returned to France 20 November 1944; crossed into Belgium 26 January 1945 (attached to 7th Armored Division 21-23 January 1945) (attached to 82nd Airborne Division 24 January 1945-past end of hostilities); returned to New York Port of Embarkation 24 November 1946 and inactivated at Camp Kilmer, New Jersey on 25 November 1946.

513th Parachute Infantry Regiment (17th Airborne Division), *Rhineland, Ardennes-Alsace, Central Europe.* 11 January 1943 activated at Fort Benning, Georgia and assigned

to the 13th Airborne Division and moved to Fort Bragg, North Carolina 1 November 1943, and moved to Camp Mackall, North Carolina 15 January 1944; transferred to the Tennessee Maneuver area 4 March 1944 where relieved from assignment to the 13th and assigned to the 17th Airborne Division on 10 March 1944; relocated to Camp Forrest, Tennessee 24 March 1944 and staged at Camp Myles Standish, Massachusetts 13 August 1944 until departed Boston Port of Embarkation 20 August 1944; arrived in England 28 August 1944 and landed in France 24 December 1944; crossed into Belgium 25 December 1944 and returned to France 11 February 1945; returned to Belgium 21 March 1945 and assaulted Wesel, Germany 24 March 1945; arrived at Boston Port of Embarkation 14 September 1945 and inactivated at Camp Myles Standish, Massachusetts the same date.

517th Parachute Infantry Regiment (Separate), *Southern France, Rhineland, Ardennes-Alsace, Central Europe*. 15 March 1943 activated at Camp Toccoa, Georgia and assigned to the Airborne Command and to the 17th Airborne Division 15 April 1943; moved to Camp Mackall, North Carolina 8 August 1943 and to the Tennessee Maneuver area 8 February 1944; returned to Camp Mackall, North Carolina 5 March 1944 where relieved from the 17th Airborne Division on 10 March 1944 and attached to the Second Army; staged at Camp Patrick Henry, Virginia 7 May 1944 until departed Hampton Road Port of Embarkation 17 May 1944; arrived Italy 28 May 1944 and committed into combat under IV Corps along Highway 1 north of Rome on 17 June 1944; assaulted southern France 15 August 1944 and took St. Vallier on 24 August 1944 (attached to XVIII Airborne Corps 22 November-16 December 1944), (attached to 30th Infantry Division 17-27 December 1944), (attached to 7th Armored Division 28-29 December 1944), (attached to 82nd Airborne Division 1-11 January 1945); attacked 13 January 1945 to take Henumont (attached to 106th Infantry Division 11-17 January 1945), (attached to 82nd Airborne Division 23-26 January 1945, and 3-4 February 1945) and moved to Bergstein area 4 February 1945; attacked through heavily mined area toward Schmidt-Nideggen road on 6-7 February 1945 (attached to 78th Infantry Division 4-7 February 1945) and assembled near Huertgen on 9 February 1945 (attached to 82nd Airborne Division 9-10 January 1945), (attached to 13th Airborne Division 11 February-1 March 1945); assigned to the 13th Airborne Division on 1 March 1945 and arrived at New York Port of Embarkation 20 August 1945; moved to Fort Bragg, North Carolina 23 August 1945 where inactivated on 25 February 1946.

2nd Battalion, 509th Parachute Infantry Regiment (Separate)/509th Parachute Infantry Battalion, *Algeria-French Morocco, Tunisia, Sicily, Naples-Foggia (inc. Anzio), Rome-Arno, Southern France, Rhineland, Ardennes-Alsace*. 2 November 1942 the 2nd Battalion redesignated from 2nd Battalion, 503rd Parachute Infantry Regiment in England and assaulted Oran and Youks-les-Bains, North Africa 8-15 November 1942; attached to 82nd Airborne Division for assault of Sicily on 9 July 1943; assaulted Salerno, Italy 9 September 1943, and parachuted onto Avellino 14 September 1943; badly decimated in ensuing battle and withdrawn from front to guard Fifth Army Headquarters in Italy, redesignated as the 509th Parachute Infantry Battalion on 10 December 1943; assaulted Anzio 21 January 1944; assaulted Le Muy, southern France 15 August 1944; (assigned to the 101st Airborne Division 18 November 1944-18 December 1944); 22-30 December 1944 defended Sadzot, Belgium; January 1944 attacked vic. St. Vith, Belgium; inactivated 1 March 1945.

1st Battalion, 551st Parachute Infantry Regiment (Separate), *Rome-Arno, Southern France, Rhineland, Ardennes-Alsace*. 26 November 1942 1st Battalion activated at Fort Kobbe, Panama Canal Zone and arrived in Italy about June 1944; assaulted southern France 15 August 1944 under the 1st Airborne Task Force and moved into Belgium where attached to the 82nd Airborne Division 26 December 1944-13 January 1945 and 21-27 January 1945; inactivated in Europe on 10 February 1945.

D-Day morning. Paratrooper turns to face his comrades and begins to signal them to take cover.

Once you hit the ground, that was the end of uniformity, but it's one of the few ways we have to build some kind of esprit in the unit. It is a necessity to do it right. – A 101st Airborne Division Living History Unit CO

Introduction. In order to properly portray the U.S. Army parachute infantryman on the Western Front, 1944-1945, every reenactor must make an effort to interpret the variety of uniforms, insignia and equipment relevant to the setting, and endeavor to outfit himself accordingly. The wear of authentic-looking uniforms and equipment is of paramount importance, not only for one's own satisfaction, but as a courtesy to others whose enjoyment of this hobby is heightened by (and in many cases dependent on) interaction with those who share similar goals and who put forth similar efforts to achieve them. Furthermore, a sense of duty to history and to the memory those whom reenactors portray must not be taken lightly.

In World War II reenacting, 'authenticity' is the word that describes the yardstick by which all aspects of this hobby are measured … by which reenactors most often measure themselves and others. But this standard is often misinterpreted, and often it is not uniformly applied to all aspects of this hobby. *Webster's New World Dictionary* says that 'authenticity' has two meanings: 1, *reliable, credible*; and 2, *genuine, real.* This guide covers many facets of World War II reenacting. Its goal is to reveal credible ways in which to bring the past alive.

The discussion of uniform authenticity brings a number of issues to rise. Most reenactors feel that original uniforms, or at least "authentic-looking" uniforms, are a basic necessity. This is undoubtedly true, for the reasons already stated. However, there is a time and a place for both. With the quality reproduction uniforms available today, reenactors need not risk the destruction of rare, original pieces of uniform and equipment by wearing them during tactical battle recreations. However, with regard to displays for the public, original items of uniform and equipment should be offered whenever possible.

Care should be taken to see that, whatever the situation, uniforms and equipment are carefully researched with respect to the historical setting and with respect to the unit being portrayed. This may be accomplished in a number of ways, depending on one's level of interest. Reference guides are plentiful. Official books and documents (such as tables of basic allowance, TBAs, and tables of organization and equipment, T/O&Es) may be obtained from government or military archives. Photographic materials illustrating the units covered in this guide are available at the National Archives, the Army War College, and through a wide variety of published works.

Through conducting research for two previous books, and *Parachute Rifle Company,* the author is well-familiarized with the historical record concerning uniforms and equipment used by U.S. Army combat infantry units during World War II. What follows is a composite of that information, that which is most relevant to the subject at hand.

PART I: UNIFORMS

The Purpose and Importance of Uniforms. Simply stated, the purpose for the wearing of an approved military uniform by personnel of a particular nation or army is both to secure homogeneity within that force, and to promote *esprit de corps*. Furthermore, such a military uniform confers upon its wearer, should he become a prisoner of war, rights to approbatory treatment under the Geneva Conventions. In the context of this book, this section is meant to help living historians differentiate between the typical types of uniforms worn by the disparate U.S. Army units, particularly in the identification of figures in period photographs, and in creating one's "shopping list."

Kinds of Uniforms. Historically, commanding officers – typically theater commanders, division commanders, or the commanders of separate units – prescribe the components of uniforms and equipment to be used by officers and men under their command. Such a directive is based on the climatic conditions and weather encountered in each particular theater of operations, and on the duty that is to be performed. During the first few years

of America's active involvement in World War II, these factors, especially the latter, are the basis for the U.S. Army's decision to develop separate uniforms and equipment for its parachute jumpers, its dismounted infantry, and its mountain/alpine troops. By the end of 1942, the Army's way of thinking changes, and it takes steps to develop uniforms that will be worn by members of all of the arms and services. However, the degree to which individual units are able to meet, or maintain, the Army's uniform and equipment standards is, in some cases, influenced by the actual availability of certain items at a given point in time.

It is standard practice within the Army of the United States, to exhaust supplies of earlier-pattern issue before allotments of more up-to-date patterns are made available. As a hypothetical example: A quartermaster who has on hand both *shovels, entrenching, M1910*, and *shovels, entrenching, M1943*, will, as a matter of course, fill any requisitions for shovels by first exhausting his supply of the M1910 pattern shovels. This, in many ways, accounts for the inevitable degree of variance, indeed the lack of strict homogeneity, in the clothing and equipment of a given military organization, especially one which finds itself in the midst of combat operations. In the field, the unit will be challenged, with not only battling the enemy, but with managing a bewildering turnover in personnel, and with adequately equipping and, when the need arises, re-equipping its personnel so that it may carry out its duty.

But, there is a chaotic element at work that, whether unintentionally, or out of life or death necessity, sometimes finds itself in direct conflict with the Army's attempts at order.

Gunner and assistant gunner turn away from the muzzle blast of their 60mm M2 mortar as the weapon coughs out its 3-pound bomb and sends it on its high-trajectory flight to a target up to 2,000 yards distant. The mortar squad's leader, a buck sergeant, gazes through his binoculars to check the accuracy of their fire, while his platoon leader relays information to other company elements over the field telephone. There seems to be only one small detail amiss in this historical recreation: the back sight on the M1A1 carbine carried by the man second from right. It's of the post-war variant. In Living History, the Devil is in the details.

This agent of disorderliness is the individual soldier. The individual soldier, especially when in the field, is prone to satisfying his own uniform and equipment needs by whatever solution is at hand, regardless of what the Army might have to say. He trades his coat for one that is warmer. He discards equipment that he does not want. He obtains additional weapons that he thinks he may need. He re-arranges his pack and web gear. He sews extra pockets on his trousers. He tapes, he cuts, he makes holes where none are designed to be. In terms of reenacting, these subtleties must be considered acceptable variations, based on valid history.

However, all stories must have a starting place. The story of the U.S. Army parachute infantryman's uniforms, worn behind the lines, and on the front lines of the Western Front during 1944, and 1945, begins with the applicable standards outlined by Army regulations. Of those prescribed by the U.S. Army during the years in question, there are three basic uniform combinations that will, under most circumstances, and with acceptable variation,

Boots, Parachute Jumper. These boots were made for walking ... and more specifically for parachute jumping. Influenced heavily by both German parachutist's boots and the boots utilized by U.S. Forest Service firemen, and after a period of testing and modification, the standard pattern, pictured here, was approved by the U.S. Army in August 1942. Note the M3 fighting knife in its M8 sheath strapped to this paratroopers leg; a nearly-universal practice among airborne soldiers, so as to have the knife handy should one need to cut himself free of his suspension lines on landing by parachute.

fully meet the needs of most reenactors. These are as follows: *The Work Uniform, Olive-drab, Herringbone*; *The Service Uniform, Wool, with Coat* (*a*, officers' and *b*, enlisted men's); and *The Field Uniform* (for *a*, dismounted troops, *b*, parachute jumpers, and *c*, First Special Service Force).[1]

I. The Work Uniform, Olive-drab, Herringbone. Army regulations as of 1944, prescribe that officers and enlisted men, when engaged in training out of doors or under such conditions as may cause one to soil their clothing, will wear a work uniform consisting of the herringbone twill cap, and the herringbone twill jacket and trousers. And, although the one-piece olive-drab herringbone twill suit is specified for use by members of the armored force, mechanics , and parachute jumpers only, in practice it is widely used by infantry soldiers, too. The work uniform will be worn in combination with appropriate foot wear – field service shoes and leggings, or parachute jumper's boots. The worksuit is, during colder times, worn over olive-drab wool serge trousers (worn with an M1937 web waist belt) and an olive-drab wool flannel shirt, itself sometimes worn over a white cotton T-shirt or other undergarment(s).

Depending upon a particular unit's standard, a soldier may also wear a field jacket when weather dictates. There are any number of jacket styles that might be appropriate. In the case of some airborne units, soldiers may don a leather A2 flight jacket. Perhaps an M1941 or M1943 field jacket is worn. Perhaps a winter combat jacket. Historical research will yield insight. Topping off the ensemble will often be an M1941 wool knit cap, or an M1941 herringbone twill cap. But, if the training area is in a combat zone, or if the training is being taken under combat conditions, a steel helmet will normally be worn. In cases where the weather is cold, the high-neck olive-drab wool sweater, or an appropriate substitute, and gloves, may be worn. Insignia will be as appropriate to one's rank and unit.[2]

In practice, such as was the case, for instance, with many members of the 1st Airborne Task Force in Operation Dragoon, the HBT uniform was worn as an outer garment in the field. *But that is another story …*

II-a. The Winter Service Uniform, Wool, with Coat, Officers'. The standard service uniform for U.S. Army infantry officers whose units serve on the Western Front circa 1944-1945, is the Winter Service Uniform with Coat. *For the sake of this discussion, the officers' service uniform will be discussed only as it applies to non-combat dress. Combat or field uniforms will be discussed separately, later in this chapter.* The officers' service uniform consists of the following components: Winter Service Coat with Officers' Belt; Service Trousers; Service Shirt; Necktie; Garrison Cap; Service Cap; Waist Belt; Shoes or Boots; Overcoats; Wool Muffler; and Gloves.

The officers' winter wool service coat is a four-pocket blouse in the dark color, olive-drab shade No.51, typically cut from wool elastique, but which may be of whipcord or barathea, too. It is equipped with epaulettes, brass buttons throughout, and an integral cloth belt in matching color and fabric, with a brass buckle. Mohair braid, in the color olive-drab shade No.53 adorns the cuffs. Regulations offer that officers' service trousers may be either in the color matching the service coat, or in a light gray known as drab shade No.54. The service shirt is allowed in a number of different fabric and color combinations. Approved colors for woolen versions include dark olive-drab shade No.51, drab shade No.54, and khaki shade No.1. Cotton service shirts are permitted only in khaki shade No.1. The woolen officers' necktie is in olive-drab shade No.3. The officers' web waist belt with brass 'roller-bar' buckle is khaki or light olive drab in color, although finer belts, in drab shade No.54, are also permissible. At certain times it may be prescribed that the officers' service uniform be worn without the service coat. In such cases, the necktie will be tucked into the shirt between the first and second visible buttons.

There are, under most circumstances, two types of headgear that an officer may wear with the wool service uniform. The primary item of headgear is the garrison cap constructed of the same fabric as the service coat. The secondary item of headgear is the service cap. This latter item, according to *The Officer's Guide*, may be worn by officers "when not in formation with troops."

There are two primary types of footgear that are authorized for wear with the service uniform: Shoes (low or high) and 'semi-dress' boots (parachute jumper's boots). Shoes are the standard footgear for officers of infantry, armored infantry, glider infantry, and Ranger formations. These must be of Army russet leather and of a commercial pattern, and are to be worn with tan or brown socks. It seems reasonable, however, to assume that regulations allow for the wearing of ankle-high Army russet leather service shoes, too. For officers of parachute infantry formations and the First Special Service Force, parachute jumper's boots are to be worn, with one's trousers neatly bloused.

By 1944, there are two basic overcoats in use by officers. The first is the short overcoat. The second is the trench coat. Officers' short overcoats may be constructed of melton, kersey, beaver or doeskin fabrics, and the regulation color is olive-drab shade No.52. The officers' trench coat (also known as the overcoat, field, long) is made up of a number of components: A reversible wool lining, a detachable hood, and a water repellent poplin/twill outer shell with integral waist belt. The prescribed color for this garment is either olive drab shade No.2 or No.7. Regulations allow that the outer shell of the officers' overcoat may serve dual purpose as a raincoat when needed. With the overcoat, an officer may wear an olive-drab wool muffler at his discretion. Wool gloves are authorized for wear with the service uniform when prescribed, and at the choice of officers when not on duty. For all items of the officers' service uniform, insignia will be as appropriate, and will be discussed later in the section, *Insignia*.

II-b. The Service Uniform, Wool, with Coat, Enlisted Men's.
The standard service uniform for U.S. Army infantry enlisted men whose units serve on the Western Front circa 1944-1945, is the Winter Service Uniform with Coat. *As with the officers' service uniform above, the components of the enlisted men's service uniform will be discussed here only as they pertain to non-combat dress. Enlisted men's combat or field uniforms will be discussed separately, below.* The enlisted men's service uniform consists of the following components: M1939 Service Coat; Trousers; Shirt; Necktie; Garrison Cap; Waist Belt; Shoes or Boots; Overcoat; Wool Muffler; and Gloves.

The enlisted men's M1939 service coat is a four-pocket garment cut from olive-drab wool serge, and much more simply rendered than the officers' style coat. Enlisted men's trousers are also of olive-drab wool serge. The shirt worn with this uniform is the olive-drab wool-flannel coat-style shirt. It comes standard with gas flaps at the cuffs and collar. Enlisted men's neckties are of cotton mohair in olive drab shade No.5. Headgear consists of a garrison cap cut from olive-drab wool serge. The standard waist belt used by enlisted men is the M1937 model of cotton web with an open-faced brass buckle, usually with a dulled finish. Footgear for enlisted men is as is prescribed for use with officers of corresponding units. At certain times it may be prescribed that the enlisted men's service uniform be worn without the service coat. In such cases, the necktie will be tucked into the shirt between the first and second visible buttons.

The enlisted men's overcoat is a full-length garment constructed of wool melton, has epaulettes, a notched roll collar, and is double-breasted. The buttons are brass or olive-drab colored plastic. The use of the olive-drab wool muffler and olive-drab wool gloves is as with officers. For all items of the enlisted men's service uniform, insignia will be as appropriate, and will be discussed later in the chapter, *Insignia*.

III-a. The Field Uniform, Dismounted Troops.
Infantry, armored infantry, and Ranger infantry, all fall under the heading of dismounted troops. For the most part, personnel of these three types of infantry troops all share the same basic field uniform evolution. On June 6, 1944, when U.S. troops stormed the beaches of Normandy, France, American infantrymen, armored infantrymen, and Rangers, with few exceptions, were clothed and equipped as had been their counterparts who had taken part in operations in the Mediterranean for nearly two years previous.

The basic field uniform of the 'foot slogging' infantryman, armored infantryman, and Ranger of the Normandy and Northern France Campaigns consists of olive-drab wool serge trousers, olive-drab coat style wool flannel shirt, Army russet leather field service shoes worn with M1938 dismounted leggings, an M1941 field jacket (or, in some cases,

Toting his M3A1 submachine gun, Platoon Sergeant Allen emerges from a Norman thicket. He is clad in the M1942 parachutist jacket and trousers, with elbows and waist coat pockets, and knees and trouser-side pockets all reinforced with heavy olive drab canvas cloth by unit parachute riggers. The Airborne establishment learned from its experience early in the Italian campaign that pockets crammed with ammunition and grenades would, from the opening shock of the T5 parachute, tear and spill their contents into the void below. Reinforcement of the knees and elbows would give the uniform longer wear with hard use.

Clad in M1942 parachute jumper jackets and trousers, a pair of airborne infantrymen patrol along a Norman country lane. This photo makes clear the difference between a uniform that has been reinforced, r, and the unadorned version.

winter combat jackets), and an M1 helmet. In the 2nd and 5th Ranger Infantry Battalions, the wearing of parachute jumpers' boots is commonplace in the field. Often, two-piece olive-drab herringbone twill work suits are worn over the wool field uniform. As the weather warms in France, infantry soldiers take to wearing the herringbone twill uniform components ever increasingly *as* the field uniform. Gloves, wool sweaters, wool mufflers, overcoats, and raincoats, are worn as weather dictates. Throughout all, the only substantial difference between officers' and enlisted men's field service dress is that officers' wool flannel shirt is equipped with epaulettes. Officers, too, usually wear enlisted men's style olive-drab wool serge trousers in the field. Photo evidence also indicates that officers have a knack for acquiring the winter combat jacket which normally is prescribed for wear by members of the armored force.

During the Normandy Campaign, components of the M1943 field uniform begin to make an appearance among the Army's dismounted troops. This new uniform, field tested in Italy beginning in September 1943, incorporates the best features of earlier combat clothing used by the Army's various arms and services, and is to be the new standard throughout the Army. The M1943 field uniform is a clothing system made up of numerous pieces meant to be layered to suit climatic conditions as they are encountered by U.S. Army troops. M1943 uniform consists of the M1943 field jacket with adjustable waist cord and detachable hood, the M1943 pile jacket meant as a liner for the field jacket, the M1943 trousers and suspenders which can be worn atop wool serge trousers if need be, the M1943 field cap, and M1943 'double buckle' combat boots. All clothing items are in olive-drab shade No.7. In addition to the clothing items, the Army also develops numerous items of field equipment during the same time period, which will be discussed in the chapter, *Equipment*.

The best intentions of the U.S. Army manage only to see that the updating of field uniforms for the Army's dismounted troops is accomplished slowly. In fact, in spite of the severe weather encountered during the Ardennes-Alsace Campaign, many combat troops enter battle without suitable winter clothing of any kind. Rubber goloshes with felt uppers – called arctic overshoes by the Army – and shoe pacs, one of the most desperately needed items of winter gear, only arrive in sufficient numbers after the Battle of the Bulge has neared its conclusion. Still, by the outset of the campaign for Central Europe, most units have been issued with M1943 combat boots, and M1943 field jackets.

III-b. The Field Uniform, Airborne Troops. In order to cover this category properly, it must first be broken down into two separate parts: parachute jumpers, and gliderborne troops. At the commencement of the Normandy Campaign, U.S. Army parachute jumpers are clad in the same uniform as was worn when U.S. paratroopers first saw action in World War II, in French North Africa, the M1942 parachute jumpers' jacket with integral belt and trousers, and M1942 parachute jumpers' boots. However, for Operation OVERLORD, most paratroopers have modified their jackets by adding reinforcing at the elbows and lower pockets, and even adding extra pockets at the sleeves and tails. Similarly, the trousers are modified to include reinforcing at the knees and cargo pockets, as well as tie-down straps at both thighs. The trousers are usually supported by Air Corps suspenders. This uniform is designed to be worn over the olive-drab wool shirt and trousers if necessary. Lined and unlined horsehide riding gloves are also an item favored by paratroopers. Paratroops are also issued a specially modified steel helmet and liner. The earliest model of this helmet is the M2 with a fixed 'D' bale. The later model, the M1C, is equipped with a standard swivel bale. The liner for each of these helmets is equipped with an added leather chin cup and harness, and provision is made to affix the liner to the helmet by means of snaps added to the helmet's web chin straps.

By the commencement of the Rhineland Campaign on September 15, 1944, the uniform of all U.S. airborne troops had been standardized as the M1943 field jacket and trousers, and M1943 combat boots. The trousers, in most instances, are modified to include cargo pockets and tie down straps at the thighs, mimicking the setup of the earlier M1942 parachute jumpers' trousers. And while the M1943 combat boot was prescribed as the item of issue with respect to footgear, in practice, many paratroopers continued to wear their earlier 'jump' boots.

During cold or inclement weather, airborne troops must rely on the same garments for comfort as do any other of the Army's soldiers: arctic overshoes or shoe pacs; the enlisted men's raincoat or officers' trench coat; the enlisted men's wool overcoat, or the officers' short wool overcoat; the M1943 pile jacket as a liner for the M1943 field jacket; and any other garment that resourceful 'troopers may be able to scrounge.

III-c. The Field Uniform, Alpine Troops (First Special Service Force). The garments most widely worn by the First Special Service Force during combat operations are mountain trousers and the M1943 field jacket. Mountain trousers, baggy, are designed to be worn over the olive-drab wool serge trousers when weather dictates. Mountain trousers are usually worn in conjunction with either a pair of issue mountain trouser suspenders or a variety of Air Corps types, and an M1937 web waist belt, too. Though the M1943 field jacket was the most widely used, the M1941 field jacket, the winter combat jacket (a.k.a. 'tanker' jacket), and the reversible parka, are all highly suitable for an individual's combat uniform impression.

Reversible parkas are produced in two basic types: type I and type II. Neither of these are to be confused with the reversible ski parka that, while appearing infrequently at the front, was used by the Force predominantly during its early training in the United States. The type I reversible parka is cut to hang down to the knees, and is ruffed with wolf fur at the cuffs and around the hood. It is produced in two variants, the first having slash front pockets at the chest, the second having buttoned flaps to cover said pockets. The type II reversible parka is shorter, has buttons rather than fur at its cuffs, has button closures for its chest pockets, and has buttons at the neck. In the field, Forcemen utilized the M1943 pile jacket (designed as the liner for the M1943 field jacket) as an insulating liner for the reversible parka. Often the long tails of the parkas are rolled up to allow the Forceman easier access to his trouser pockets.

The standard foot gear for the field is the parachute jumper's boot. However, during the invasion of south France, M1943 combat boots began to supplant the parachute boot. In wet or colder weather, either rubber or cloth arctic overshoes were worn over an individual's boots. Other items commonly used in the field were the olive-drab wool high-neck sweater; the olive-drab wool knit toque; the olive-drab wool M1941 knit cap; the olive-drab wool muffler; leather-palm olive-drab wool gloves, trigger finger mittens with olive-drab wool knit inserts, or, olive-drab wool knit wristlets. In cases where an individual does not have or wish to use mountain trousers as part of his combat impression, olive-drab wool serge trousers are the best alternative.

Care of and Manner of Wearing the Uniform. The manner in which an officer or enlisted man should wear his uniform – especially his service uniform – is set forth in Army regulations. The uniform must be kept in good repair, clean and neatly pressed, with no missing buttons. Buttons and insignia on the service uniform are to be of bright finish. "Overcoats, coats, and shirts will be worn buttoned throughout." And service hats (overseas caps) will have the appropriate hat cord (piping) sewed on.

It is recommended that uniforms – wool uniforms most especially – be dry cleaned as a measure to ensure they do not shrink, fade, or loose their shape. In most cases, the brass buttons for both officers' and enlisted men's service uniforms will be given a lacquer coating that will keep them bright. However, if they should dull through wear, they should be cleaned with a small amount of ammonia applied to a damp rag. Harsh abrasives should be avoided. Other suitable commercial products may also be used.[3]

A dirty business. *No clean shaves, no clean uniforms at the front.* In light of the realities of combat, the Army's proscribed manner in which to wear one's uniform was completely absurd. One common complaint from veteran soldiers is that living historians look *too* clean. Or, rather, not dirty enough! When in combat, troops could go for weeks – if not months – on end without a bath, and without any change of clothes. They seldom shaved, and personal hygiene was difficult to manage at best. Would it not be interesting to one day see an event where all the reenactors, on both sides of the field, appeared in this authentic state?

Standing knee-deep in his shallow foxhole, this PFC wears the M1943 field jacket and trousers, the latter modified by unit riggers to include the large side pockets similar to the setup of the M1942 parachute jumper's trousers, and tie down tapes at the thighs. Note that he is equipped with the OD #7 colored M1944 field suspenders.

PAGE 90
The only feature of this paratrooper's uniform that differentiates him from a private is the small yellow bar painted on the front of his helmet. It became common practice that officers shed bright metal insignia in the field, less they become a target of enemy snipers. He is clad in an M1943 field jacket and trousers; the trousers modified in the normal airborne manner with the addition of large side pockets of heavy, impregnated OD canvas, and tie-down tapes at the thighs.

QUARTERMASTER CLOTHING FOR FIELD USE
As Proscribed for Parachute Jumpers

WAR DEPARTMENT
Based on Table of Basic Allowance 21
Washington, January 7, 1943 (modified)

Item		Quantity	Remarks and basis of issue
Belt, cloth, O's	ea	1	Per O.
Belt, web, waist, M-1937	ea	1	Per O, EM.
Boots, parachute jumper's	pr	1(1)	Per parachutist.
[Boots, combat, M-1943	pr	1	Per parachutist, ca. September 1944.]
Brassard, arm, U.S. National Ensign	ea	1	[Per individual in parachute units when authorized by CO.]
Cap, herringbone twill	ea	1	Per EM.
Cap, wool, knit, M-1941	ea	1	Per individual.
Coat, parachute jumper's, M-1942	ea	1(1)	Per parachutist.
Drawers	pr	3	Per O.
Drawers, cotton, shorts, or drawers, wool	ea	5(2)	Per EM (not to exceed 2 may be wool as directed by CO).
Gloves, horsehide, riding, unlined	pr	1	Per individual in parachute units when authorized by CO.
Gloves, wool, OD	pr	1	Per O, WO (for field service as directed by CO).
Gloves, wool, OD, leather palm	pr	1	Per EM.
Handkerchief, cotton, white	ea	4(2)	Per O, EM.
Helmet, steel, [M-2, or] M-1[C], complete, consisting of:			
Body, helmet			
Liner, helmet			
Band, head			
Band, neck			
[Chin cup]	ea	1	Per individual.
Hood, cloth	ea	1	Per EM (see note 2*a*).
Insignia, collar, O's	pr	2	Per O (state arm).
Insignia, grade	ea	2	Per O, according to grade.
Insignia, shoulder sleeve:			
Divisions	ea	(1)	Per coat, parachute jumper's; field jacket; shirt when worn as an outer garment; as authorized b AR 600-40.
Insignia, sleeve, chevron: Service, cotton,			
(khaki device on dark blue back)	pr	1	Per cotton shirt, combat jacket, field jacket, herringbone twill jacket, and herringbone twill one-piece suit for NCO and PFC authorized by AR 600-35 and AR 600-40.
Insignia, sleeve, chevron: Service, wool,			
(OD device on dark blue back)	pr	1	Per flannel shirt, overcoat for NCO and PFC authorized by AR 600-35 and AR 600-40.
Jacket, field[, M-1943]	ea	1	[Per parachutist, ca. September 1944.]
[Jacket, pile, M-1943	ea	1	Per jacket, field, M-1943.]
Mittens, asbestos, M-1942	pr	1(2)	Per gun, machine, cal. .30; per mortar.
Mittens, insert, trigger finger	pr	2	Per EM (see note 2*a*).
Mitten-shells, trigger finger	pr	1	Per EM (see note 2*a*).
Muffler, wool, OD	ea	1	Per EM (see note 2*a*).
Necktie, cotton, mohair, OD	ea	1	Per O.
Overcoat, OD, O's [trench coat]	ea	1	Per O.
Overcoat, short, O's	ea	(1)	Per O.
Overcoat, wool, roll-collar	ea	1	Per EM.
Overshoes, arctic	pr	2	Per male individual when authorized by CO.
Raincoat	ea	1	Per EM
Shirt, flannel, OD	ea	2(1)	Per EM.
Shirt, wool, OD	ea	2(1)	Per O.
Socks	pr	6	Per O (at least one pair to be plain tan or brown).

Study of the officer's overcoat, left, and the enlisted men's raincoat. Both were knee-length, but by comparison, the officer's water repellent trench-style overcoat, with its removable wool lining, was a luxurious garment. Operating as they so often did at the extreme front of the Army's advance, paratroopers, most often without the use of their bedrolls, would simply wrap themselves in their raincoats to keep out the dampness and get what sleep they could in the bottom of their slit trenches.

Socks, light wool or heavy wool	pr	3	Per EM.
Suit, one-piece, herringbone twill	ea	2(1)	Per parachutist.
Supporter, athletic	ea	1	Per parachutist.
Suspenders, trousers	ea	(1)	Per parachutist.
Sweater, high-neck	ea	1	Per individual.
Trousers, wool, OD	pr	2(1)	Per O, EM.
Trousers, parachute jumper's	ea	1(1)	Per parachutist.
[Trousers, field, M-1943]	ea	1(1)	[Per parachutist, ca. September 1944.]
Undershirts	ea	3	Per O.
Undershirt, summer, sleeveless, or undershirt, wool	ea	5(2)	Per EM.
Wristlets, knit	pr	1	Per EM issued gloves, horsehide, unlined.

Note 2a: For theater outside the United States as approved by War Department.

PART II: INSIGNIA & DECORATIONS

INSIGNIA

Definition of Insignia. The term *insignia* includes all metallic or embroidered articles which are worn on the uniform that serve to identify the wearer as a member of the Army of the United States – his grade and arm of service, his organization in some instances, and other incidents of his service such as overseas and service stripes.

Except as otherwise prescribed, insignia for wear upon uniform clothing will be made of gold or gold color material. Insignia of grade for shoulder loops may be embroidered. Metal insignia of grade may be knurled or smooth.

Officers who find the use of metallic insignia objectionable, especially under field conditions, should make use of embroidered cloth insignia which may be sewed permanently on all garments.[4]

Headgear Insignia and Ornamentation. Helmet. Insignia of grade will be worn by officers on the front of the steel helmet, and/or helmet liner, centered on the front of the helmet or liner, with center of the insignia 2 1/2 inches from the lower edge of the helmet or liner. Insignia will be painted on the helmet or liner, and of standard size. Bars will be worn perpendicular to the bottom edge of the helmet or liner. Leaves will be worn with stem down. The eagle will be worn, beak to the wearer's right. The star will be worn point upward. The star(s) will be centered on the front of the helmet or liner. The line of centers will be parallel to the base of the helmet or liner and spaced 5/8 inch apart.

Cap, garrison. General officers: cord edge braid (piping) of gold bullion, rayon, or metallized cellophane of gold color. Other officers: cord edge braid of gold bullion, rayon or metallized cellophane of gold color and black silk intermixed. Warrant offices: cord edge braid of silver bullion, rayon, or metallized cellophane and black silk intermixed.[5] Enlisted men: cord edge braid of light blue denoting Infantry arm of service.

Officers' and NCO's "aiming stake" tactical markings on the back of the steel helmet. In an attempt by the Army to make it easier on the battlefield for troops to divine those in a position of leadership, the vertical bar denotes officers, while the horizontal bar denotes non-commissioned officers. Note that the field expedient camouflaged helmet has its aiming stake rendered in the reverse.

LEFT
Field expedient camouflage paint pattern applied to the MI helmet. Photographic evidence reveals a multitude of styles and patterns throughout the war.

CENTER
Unit tactical markings (in this case 2/508 PIR's double lightning bolts, "Conquest from the Clouds") were devised as a means of instant recognition between troops, and as a way to promote unit esprit.

RIGHT
Normandy, June 1944. Corporal Dautrich uses a scrap of camouflaged parachute panel as a helmet cover to good effect. Photo evidence show this practice was not uncommon.

Insignia of grade will be worn by officers on the garrison cap, on the left side, centered on the curtain, with center of the insignia 1 1/2 inches from the front. The bars of lieutenants and captains will be worn perpendicular to the bottom edge of the cap. The leaves of majors and lieutenant colonels will be worn with stem down. The eagle of colonels will be worn beak to the front. The star of a brigadier general will be worn point upward. Additional stars will extend to the rear of the first star and be placed 5/8 inch apart. Miniature insignia of grade is authorized for general officers, and when worn, additional stars will be placed at a relatively smaller interval.[6]

Cap, service. Officers wear the coat of arms of the United States. Warrant officers wear the warrant officers' insignia.[7]

Tactical Markings On the Steel Helmet *(see color plates)*. Note: Historical photographs show that the tactical markings painted on helmets were most often done by hand and often in a more crude manner than is depicted by the graphic.

Tactical Markings On the Steel Helmet

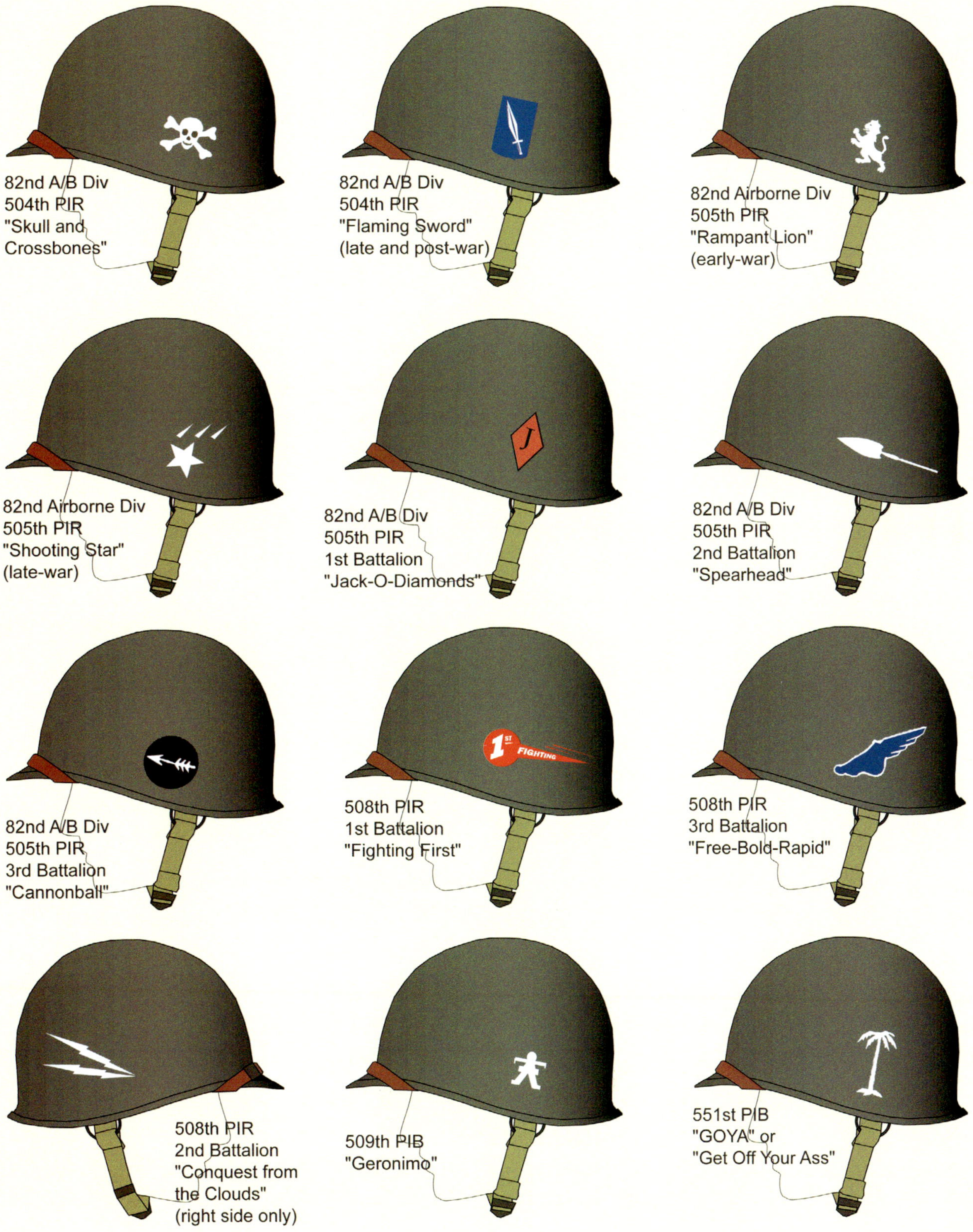

82nd A/B Div
504th PIR
"Skull and
Crossbones"

82nd A/B Div
504th PIR
"Flaming Sword"
(late and post-war)

82nd Airborne Div
505th PIR
"Rampant Lion"
(early-war)

82nd Airborne Div
505th PIR
"Shooting Star"
(late-war)

82nd A/B Div
505th PIR
1st Battalion
"Jack-O-Diamonds"

82nd A/B Div
505th PIR
2nd Battalion
"Spearhead"

82nd A/B Div
505th PIR
3rd Battalion
"Cannonball"

508th PIR
1st Battalion
"Fighting First"

508th PIR
3rd Battalion
"Free-Bold-Rapid"

508th PIR
2nd Battalion
"Conquest from
the Clouds"
(right side only)

509th PIB
"Geronimo"

551st PIB
"GOYA" or
"Get Off Your Ass"

Tactical Markings On the Steel Helmet

101st A/B Div
501st PIR
1st Battalion

101st A/B Div
502nd PIR
2nd Battalion

101st A/B Div
506th PIR
3rd Battalion

101st A/B Div
326th Airborne
Medical Company

Combat
Medic

Field
Expediant
Camouflage

Bottom, l-r: Second lieutenant, first lieutenant, captain.
Below, l-r: Officers' 'aiming stake', and non-commissioned officers' bar.

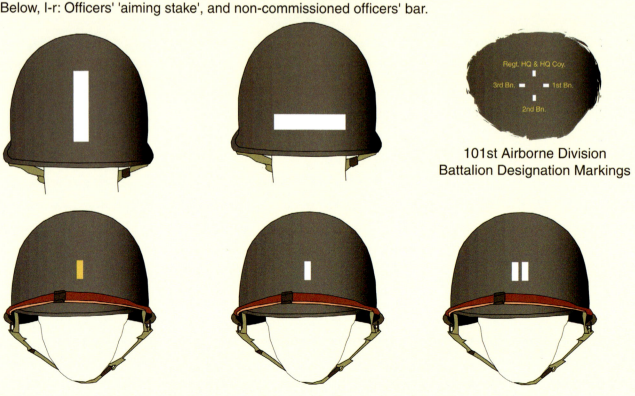

Regt. HQ & HQ Coy.

3rd Bn.   1st Bn.

2nd Bn.

101st Airborne Division
Battalion Designation Markings

Insignia on Collar or Lapel of Service Coat. The insignia worn on the collar or lapel of the service coat is of metal, consisting, on each lapel, of the letters "U.S." and insignia indicating the arm to which the individual is assigned. Officers wear the letters "U.S." on the collar (lapel) horizontally, lower edge one-half inch above the horizontal line of the lapel, the center of the "U.S." at the center of the collar. The insignia of arm is worn horizontally on the lapel, upper edge one-half inch below the horizontal line of the lapel, and *centered* below the "U.S.". Warrant officers wear the insignia of warrant officers in lieu of the insignia of arm.[8]

Insignia On Shirt. When the olive drab or khaki shirt is worn without the service coat, insignia will be worn as follows: *On the collar.*

All officers, except general officers. On the right side, 1 inch from the end, the insignia of grade; on the left side, 1 inch from the end, metal insignia indicating arm. Bars will be worn parallel with the front edge of the collar. Leaves will be worn with stem down. The eagle will be worn beak to the front.

General officers of the line. On both sides, 1 inch from the end, the insignia of grade. Additional stars will extend to the rear of the first star and be placed 5/8 inch apart. General officers are authorized to wear miniature insignia of grade. Additional miniature stars will be placed at a relatively small interval.

Warrant officers. On the right side, 1 inch from the end, the insignia of grade, on the left side, 1 inch from the end, insignia of arm, service or bureau. If not on duty with arm or service, the coat of arms of the United States 9/16 inch in height within a ring 3/4 inch in diameter. Bars will be worn parallel with the front edge of the collar.[9]

Paratroop platoon leader. Insignia worn by officers in the field was extremely limited, this by virtue of Army regulations, and for the simple reason that obvious insignia made them a lucrative target for enemy snipers. This first lieutenant's metal rank insignia is worn on his right shirt collar point, and the metal crossed rifles of his infantry arm are pinned to the left. His Parachutist's Badge is the only badge proscribed for wear in the field and is pinned on his left breast. Note the souvenir parachute cloth scarf, cut from the canopy after his landing in Normandy.

Colors and Insignia of the Arms. Each of the combat arms has a distinctive insignia and a distinctive color. The insignia is worn on the uniform as heretofore described. The hat cord worn by enlisted men is the color prescribed by their branch. Distinctive branch color is used on the shoulder straps of the blue dress uniform and on other gold braid decorations. It is also used in the blue dress uniforms as cape linings and other purposes. The colors and insignia of the arm pertinent to this work is as follows:

Branch	Color	Insignia
Infantry	Light blue	Crossed rifles[10]

Shoulder Loop Insignia for Officers. On each shoulder loop of the service coat, the long overcoat, the short overcoat, the raincoat, the field jacket, and on each shoulder of work clothing, metal or embroidered insignia of grade will be worn as follows: Second and first lieutenants, and warrant officers wear the bar in the middle of the loop parallel to and 5/8 inch from the sleeve end of loop. Captains place the bars in a similar manner with the lower bar parallel to and 5/8 inch from sleeve end of loop. Majors and lieutenant colonels place the leaves, point up, in the middle of loop, stem of leaf 5/8 inch from sleeve end of loop. The eagle worn by a colonel is placed in the middle of the loop, head up, beak to the front, talons 5/8 inch from the sleeve end of loop. Brigadier generals place the star, point up, in the center of loop. Major generals place the center of the two stars, points up, 2 1/2 inches apart, the stars equidistant from the sleeve end of the loop and the outer edge of the bottom. Lieutenant generals place the three stars, points up, equidistant each from the other. Generals place the four stars, points up, equidistant one from the other.[11]

When an officer wears the work uniform, insignia is worn as prescribed for the olive drab shirt.[12]

Shoulder Loop Insignia for Warrant Officers. *Chief warrant officer.* One gold bar 3/8 inch width and 1 inch in length, with rounded ends, having a brown enameled top and a longitudinal center of gold 1/8 inch in width. *Warrant officer (junior grade).* One gold bar 3/8 inch in width and 1 inch in length, with rounded ends, having a brown enameled top and a latitudinal center of gold 1/8 inch in width. Warrant officers wear insignia as prescribed for lieutenants.[13]

Overcoat Sleeve Insignia for General Officers. On the overcoat of general officers two bands of black mohair braid are worn on both sleeves. The 1 1/2-inch band is placed with its lower edge 2 1/2 inches above and parallel to the end of the sleeve; the 1/2-band is placed with its lower edge 1 1/2 inches above the upper edge of and parallel to the other band.[14]

Service Stripe. Each enlisted man who has served honorably in the military service for 3 years wears the service stripe. This stripe is worn 4 inches from the end of the left sleeve of the service coat. For each additional period of 3 years, another service stripe is worn.[15]

Wound and War Service Chevrons. Wound and war service chevrons are not authorized for wear by Army personnel for World War II. However, personnel authorized to wear such insignia for service during the First World War are authorized to wear both wound chevrons and war service chevrons as part of their service uniforms. They are worn only on the woolen service coat, with the wound chevrons on the right sleeve and the service chevrons on the left sleeve. They are worn point down. When service stripes are worn the war service chevron is worn above the uppermost stripe. In terms of reenacting, one must note that due to their age – at least 43 years old – few such individuals would have been rank and file combat infantrymen in 1943.

Overseas Stripes. Gold-colored 1/2-inch by 1-3/8-inch stripe embroidered onto olive drab woolen material. Each stripe represents six-month's overseas service. This stripe is worn 4 inches from the end of the left sleeve of the service coat. For each additional period of 6 months, another overseas stripe is worn.

Rank Insignia
How To Identify Your Officers

GENERAL
OF THE
ARMY

GENERAL

LIEUTENANT
GENERAL

MAJOR
GENERAL

BRIGADIER
GENERAL

COLONEL

LIEUTENANT
COLONEL

MAJOR

CAPTAIN

FIRST
LIEUTENANT

SECOND
LIEUTENANT

WARRANT OFFICERS
(CHIEF)   (JUNIOR GRADE)

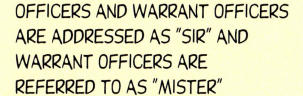

OFFICERS AND WARRANT OFFICERS
ARE ADDRESSED AS "SIR" AND
WARRANT OFFICERS ARE
REFERRED TO AS "MISTER"

NON-COMMISSIONED GRADES

RIGHT:
INSIGNIA, SLEEVE, CHEVRON:
SERVICE, COTTON
(KHAKI DEVICE ON DARK BLUE BACK)

MASTER
SERGEANT
(1ST GRADE)

FIRST
SERGEANT
(1ST GRADE)

TECHNICAL
SERGEANT
(2ND GRADE)

STAFF
SERGEANT
(3RD GRADE)

TECHNICIAN
(3RD GRADE)

RIGHT:
INSIGNIA, SLEEVE, CHEVRON:
SERVICE, WOOL
(OD DEVICE ON DARK BLUE BACK)

SERGEANT
(4TH GRADE)

TECHNICIAN
(4TH GRADE)

CORPORAL
(5TH GRADE)

TECHNICIAN
(5TH GRADE)

PRIVATE
FIRST CLASS

Graphic Design by Robert Todd Ross

Combat Leader Insignia. During the last few months of the war in Europe, the Combat Leader insignia begins to make an appearance with both officers and non-commissioned officers who command units "whose mission is to combat the enemy by direct means or methods."[16] For NCOs the Combat Leader insignia takes the shape of a 1/2-inch by 2-inch horizontal dark green wool felt bar stitched to the sleeve of the service coat centered and one inch below the rank chevrons. Officers wear a loop of similar material around both epaulettes of the service coat.

Shoulder Sleeve Insignia. Shoulder sleeve insignia are authorized for wear by individuals assigned to units such as divisions, separate units (regiments and battalions), and others specifically authorized. It will be worn on the upper part of the outer half of the left sleeves of the service coat, overcoat, field jacket, and the shirt when worn as an outer garment, the top of the insignia to be one-half inch below top of the shoulder-seam.[17]

Distinctive Insignia and Trimmings. Organizations classified in general as regiments, separate battalions, or separate companies are authorized to adopt distinctive insignia or trimmings for wear by members thereof as a part of the uniform as a means of promoting *esprit de corps*. Distinctive insignia bear the organization badge or coat of arms, or similar device, having historical significance connected with the organization, such as the ornament of the organization when originally organized, or that worn in some prior war. Colored trimmings will not be worn with the cotton service uniform. Distinctive insignia will be worn by officers as follows: On the service coat centered on the shoulder loops. Distinctive insignia is not worn by officers on the service shirt or garrison cap.[18]

BADGES

Parachutists' Badge. "… Parachutists' badge may be worn when equipped for the field and while on field duty, and may be worn on the olive-drab shirt when worn without the coat."[19]

Bronze Star Appurtenances. One bronze star appurtenance 3/16 inch in diameter will be worn on the pertinent service ribbon for participation in each operation (campaign) announced by the War Department in General Orders as authorizing participants to wear such recognition. Where more than five bronze star appurtenances have been earned, silver star appurtenances 3/16 in diameter may be substituted for the bronze in the ratio of one to five. The bronze star appurtenance which may be worn on a theater ribbon is not to be confused with the Bronze Star Medal, a decoration in its own right.

Bronze Spearhead Appurtenances. One bronze spearhead appurtenance, of a scale similar to the bronze star appurtenance, will be worn on the pertinent service ribbon for participation in each invasion announced by the War Department in General Orders as authorizing participants to wear such recognition.

Note: While officially unauthorized, it was common practice among parachute troops to attach bronze star and spearhead appurtenances to their parachutists' badge on the same basis as was proscribed for the wearing of such appurtenances on the theater ribbon.

Combat Infantryman and Expert Infantryman Badges. The present war has demonstrated the importance of highly proficient, tough, hard, and aggressive infantry, which can be obtained only by developing a high degree of all-round proficiency on the part of every infantryman. As a means of attaining the high standards desired and to foster *esprit de corps* in infantry units, the Expert Infantryman and Combat Infantryman badges are established for infantry personnel. The Combat Infantryman badge is the higher award.

Infantrymen, including officers, establish eligibility to wear the Expert Infantryman badge by attaining the standards of proficiency established by the War Department or by satisfactory performance of duty in action against the enemy. The Combat Infantryman badge may be won by Infantrymen, including officers, by exemplary conduct in action against an enemy, or by satisfactory performance of duty against an enemy in a major operation as determined and announced by the theater commander.[20]

Badges, When Worn. Badges (except as prescribed for the parachutists' badge) will not be worn on the olive drab service shirt, overcoat, or when equipped for the field; neither will they be prescribed for troops in the field. They may be worn on the khaki shirt. Officers suspended from rank and command, or from either, and enlisted men serving sentence of confinement, are prohibited from wearing decorations, medals, or substitutes therefor.[21]

PART III: EQUIPMENT

Introduction. In addition to the uniforms required by reenactors, most living history events – bivouacs, tactical battle recreations and displays – will require that participants provide other items in order to fully take part. Provided below is the table, EQUIPMENT FOR FIELD USE (EFU). This table is based on *Table of Basic Allowances No.21, War Department, Washington, January 7, 1943*, as well as other U.S. Army World War II tables of organization specific to the period airborne rifle company. While not all encompassing, it has been thoughtfully prepared to be comprehensive enough to 'cover the waterfront' with regard to the parachute infantry impression for nearly all reenactment field events.

Table EFU encompasses items commonly used by parachute infantry units that have been developed by several of the U.S. Army's arms and services, including the Quartermaster Corps, the Signal Corps, the Chemical Warfare Service, the Ordnance Department, and the Corps of Engineers. In order to streamline this information, certain items listed in TBA 21 not pertinent to this book have been deleted, while other items, gleaned from such sources as period tables of organization and equipment (T/O&E), and operations reports, have been included. As well, both enlisted men's and officers' items are carried on the same lists, rather than separately.

The phrases, "Per parachutist," and "Per individual" appear throughout the *Basis of Distribution and Remarks* column of Table EFU. These phrases could be interchanged with "As appropriate" – Appropriate to one's impression as per his unit's wartime T/O&E; appropriate to the setting of the tactical battle in which one is participating; appropriate to the weather conditions in which one finds himself; *and appropriate to one's budget for this hobby.* World War II reenacting is, after all, a hobby, and one hasn't the luxury of being issued a complete set of the necessary clothing and equipment as were actual U.S. Army soldiers. Each reenactor's goals and expectations for this hobby are different, and each individual budgets himself accordingly.

When using Table EFU, other rules of thumb will apply. The number listed in the *Allowances* column represents the basic unit of issue of each particular item. Numbers appearing in parentheses denote an increase in issue of a particular item either as suggested by wartime doctrine, or for practical reasons with an eye toward the modern reenacting environment. The abbreviation 'O' stands for officer; 'EM' stands for enlisted men; and 'OD' stands for olive-drab.

If a criticism on an individual point could be leveled against a large number of reenactors, it is that they wear their field equipment far to low on their person, almost in 'gun-slinger' fashion. Study of period photographs is recommended, and the *Soldier's Handbook* offers the following advice. "Put on equipment, slipping the arms through [field] suspenders as through sleeves of a coat. By means of adjusting buckles on [field] suspenders, raise or lower the belt until it rests well down over hip bones and below pit of abdomen. Raise or lower it in rear until adjusting strap lies smoothly across small of the back. By means of adjusting straps on [field bag], raise or lower the load on the back until the top of [field bag] is on a level with top of shoulders, so that [straps] from their point of attachment on the [field bag] to the shoulders will be horizontal. The latter is essential to proper adjustment of the load."

Strewn about this rocky redoubt is much of the typical impedimenta of war. Cartridge belts, wire cutters, canteens, bandage cases, bandoleers, assorted ordnance, a field bag and a shoulder holster. The parachute infantryman was trained and equipped to carry out his job, that being to engage and destroy the enemy with an array of small arms. All of the soldier's equipment was devised to help him to accomplish this mission.

The M2 pocket knife, a switchblade, was carried by paratroops in the coat knife pocket of the M1942 jump jacket attached to a lanyard that was looped around one of the jacket's epaulets. This knife was widely issued to other infantry and Ranger personnel but is synonymous with The Airborne. It was as handy in a street fight as it was for cutting one's self free from tangled parachute suspension lines.

EQUIPMENT FOR FIELD USE
As Proscribed for Parachute Jumpers

WAR DEPARTMENT
Based on: Table of Basic Allowance 21, 7 January 1943;
T/O & E 7-37 Infantry Rifle Company, Parachute, 17 February 1942 (and 1 August 1944);
T/O 7-35T, Infantry Parachute Battalion, 24 February 1944.

Section I - *Individual Equipment, Quartermaster*

Item		*Allowances*	*Basis of distribution and remarks*
Bag, Barrack	ea	1(1)	Per EM.
Bag, canvas, field, OD, M1936	ea	1	Per O, EM of parachute units.
Belt, cartridge, cal. .30, dismounted M-1923	ea	1	Per individual armed with rifle, M1.
Belt, magazine, M-1937, BAR	ea	1	Per automatic rifleman; assistant automatic rifleman; am carrier auto rifle squad.
Belt, pistol or revolver, M-1936	ea	1	Per individual not otherwise issued cartridge or magazine belt.
Blanket, wool, OD, M1934	ea	1(1)	Per individual.
Book, memorandum, pocket, with pencil	ea	1	Per O.
Book, message, Signal Corps, M210A	ea	1	Per individual.*
Box, match, waterproof, with compass	ea	1	Per individual.*
Can, meat, M-1932	ea	1	Per individual.
Canteen, M-1910	ea	1	Per individual.
Cover, canteen, dismounted, M-1910	ea	1	Per individual.
Cup, M-1910	ea	1	Per individual.
Disc, luminous	ea	1	Per parachutist.*
Fork, M-1926	ea	1	Per individual.
Goggles, M-(1943; 1944), Polaroid, all-purpose, 1021	pr	1	Per parachutist*
Holster, pistol, M-1916 (or holster, shoulder)	ea	1	Per pistol, automatic, cal. .45, M-1911A1.*
Kit, cleaning, cal. .30	ea	1	Per carbine; rifle; BAR; LMG.*
Knife, M-1926	ea	1	Per individual.
Knife, pocket	ea	1	Per O.
Knife, pocket, M-2	ea	1	Per parachutist.
Lanyard, pistol	ea	1	Per pistol, automatic, cal. .45, M-1911A1.*
Mirror, trench	ea	1	Per O.
Necklace, identification tag, w/extension	ea	1	Per individual.
Packet, first aid, parachute jumper's	ea	1	Per parachutist.*
Pen, fountain	ea	1	Per O.
Pin, tent, shelter, wood	ea	5(5)	Per tent, shelter half.

Pocket, magazine, double web, M-1923	ea	1	Per individual armed w/ pistol.
Pocket, magazine, for carbine, cal. .30 M1	ea	5	Per individual armed w/ carbine, M1.
Pocket, magazine, for gun, SNG, cal. .45, M-1A1	ea	1	Per gun, submachine, cal. .45, M-1A1.*
Pole, tent, shelter	ea	1(1)	Per tent, shelter half.
Pouch, first aid packet, M-1924	ea	1	Per individual.
Pouch, magazine or clip, Air Corps type	ea	4	Per rifle; carbine.*
Roll, bedding, waterproofed, M-1935	ea	1	Per O.
Rope, parachutist, 5/8" x 30'	ea	1	Per parachutist.
Rope, tent	ea	1(1)	Per individual
Sling, web, OD, carbine	ea	1	Per carbine, cal. .30, M-1A1.*
Sling, leather, rifle, M1907	ea	1	Per rifle, U.S., cal. .30, M-1.*
Spoon, M-1926	ea	1	Per individual.
Strap, carrying, OD, bag, canvas, field	ea	1	Per bag, canvas, OD, field, M-1936.
Suspenders, belt, M1936	ea	1	Per individual.
Tag, identification	pr	2	Per individual.
Tape, ankle, 2"	roll	1	Per parachutist.
Tent, shelter, half	ea	1(1)	Per individual.
Toilet articles: brush, shaving; brush, tooth; comb, rubber; razor, safety, with 5 blades	set	1	Per individual.
Towel, bath	ea	1	Per individual.
Towel, huck/face	ea	1	Per individual.
Watch, 7-jewel or better	ea	1	Per O.

Section II - *Organizational Equipment, Army Air Forces*

Item		*Allowances*	*Basis of distribution and remarks*
Bag, flyer's, kit, type A-3	ea	1	Per parachute.
Holder, rifle clip (Limited Standard, 442575)	ea	4(2)	Per rifle, (per carbine).*
Holder, SMG clip (Limited Standard, 442590)	ea	4	Per SMG M-1A1.*
Holster, assembly, parachute:			
Rifle	ea	1	Per individual armed w/rifle.
Submachine gun	ea	1	Per SMG.
Parachute, complete, training, type, T-5	ea	1	Per individual plus 20 percent.
Vest, life preserver, type B-4	ea	1	Per individual.

Section III - *Organizational Equipment, Chemical*

Item		*Allowances*	*Basis of distribution and remarks*
Mask, gas, combat M5-11-7	ea	1	Per individual.
Anti-dim			
Cover, protective, individual			
Eye protector, M-1			
Kit, gas mask, waterproofing, M-1			
Sleeve, gas, detection	ea	1	[Per individual in parachute units when authorized by CO.]*

Section IV - *Organizational Equipment, Engineer*

Item		*Allowances*	*Basis of distribution and remarks*
Compass, lensatic, luminous dial type, with case	ea	1	Per O; 1st sgt; t sgt; s sgt; plat guide; s sgt; sqd ldr; sgt.
Compass, wrist, liquid filled	ea	1	Per parachutist not issued compass, lensatic.
Demolition equipment; set No. 5, individual	set	1	Per rifle sqd.

Net, camo, cotton, twine, fabric garnished, 15x15ft.. ea 1.................. Per LMG; mort.
Templet, map, plastic, transparent, M-2.................... ea 1.................. Per O.

Section V - *Organizational Equipment, Ordnance*

Item		Allowances	Basis of distribution and remarks
Bayonet, M-1 with scabbard	ea	1	Per rifle, U.S. cal. .30, M-1.
Binocular, M-3 w/ case M-17	pr	1	Per O; t sgt, plat; s sgt, plat guide.
Carbine, cal. .30, M-1A1	ea	2	Per T/O 7-37
Knife, fighting, M-3, w/sheath, M-6 (or scabbard, M-8)	ea	1	Per individual.
Gun, machine, Browning, cal. .30, M-1919A4(A6)	ea	1	Per T/O 7-37.
Gun, submachine, cal. .45 M-1A1(3, 3A1)	ea	1	Per T/O 7-37.
Launcher, grenade, M-7	ea	1	Per T/O 7-37.
Launcher, rocket, 2.36-in. M-1A1(9A1)	ea	1	Per T/O 7-37.
Mortar, 60-mm, M-2, with mount, M-3	ea	1	Per T/O 7-37.
Mount, tripod, machine gun, cal. .30, M-2	ea	1	Per MG, cal. .30.
Pistol, automatic, cal. .45, M-1911A1	ea	1	Per T/O 7-37.
Projector, pyrotechnic, hand, M-9	ea	1	Per T/O 7-37.
Rifle, Browning, automatic, cal. .30, M-1918A2	ea	1	Per T/O 7-37.
Rifle, U.S. cal. .30, M-1	ea	1	Per individual armed with carbine per T/O 7-37.
Rifle, U.S. cal. .30, M-1C	ea	1	Per T/O 7-37.
Rifle, U.S. cal. .30, M-1903A4	ea	1	Per T/O 7-37.
Watch, wrist:			
7-jewel	ea	1	Per 1st sgt; t sgt, plat; s sgt, sup; sgt, comp; opr, rad tp; watch, wrist may be issued in lieu thereof.

Section VI - *Organizational Equipment, Quartermaster*

Item		Allowances	Basis of distribution and remarks
Axe, entrenching, M-1910	ea	1	Per 10 EM.
Bag, carrying, ammunition, general purpose, w/ strap	ea	1(2)	Per launcher, grenade; SMG; 2 per am bearer.
Bag, carrying, rocket, M-6, parachutist	ea	2	Per launcher, rocket.
Carrier, axe, entrenching, M-1910	ea	1	Per Axe, entrenching, M-1910.
Carrier, pick-mattock, entrenching, M-1910	ea	1	Per pick-mattock, entrenching, M-1910.
Carrier, shovel, entrenching, M-1910 (or M-1943)	ea	1	Per shovel, entrenching, M-1910 (or M-1943).
Carrier, wire-cutter, M-1938	ea	1	Per cutter, wire, M-1938.
Case, canvas, dispatch, M-1938	ea	1	Per O.
Case, magazine, 30-round, with shoulder strap	ea	1	Per gun, submachine, cal. .45, M-1A1.*
Cover, muzzle, canvas, rifle or carbine	ea	1	Per rifle; carbine.
Cutter, wire, M-1938	ea	2	Per 10 EM.
Machete, 18-inch-blade, M-1942	ea	1	Per squad.
Mask, face, launcher, rocket	ea	2	Per launcher, rocket.
Outfit, cooking, 1-burner	ea	1	Per 12 individuals, or major fraction thereof.
Pick-mattock, entrenching, M-1910, with handle	ea	2	Per 10 EM.
Scabbard, canvas, carbine, cal. .30, M-1A1	ea	1	Per carbine, cal. .30, M-1A1.
Sheath, machete, 18-inch-blade, M-1942	ea	1	Per machete.
Shovel, entrenching, M-1910 (or M-1943)	ea	7	Per 10 EM.
Sling, carrying, machine gun and ammunition	ea	2	Per LMG.
Stone, sharpening, pocket	ea	1	Per machete.
Whistle, thundered	ea	1	Per O, 1st sgt; t sgt; s sgt; sgt.

Standing alongside a quiet country lane in Normandy, two paratroopers of the 508th Parachute Infantry Regiment stand over the body of a dead enemy soldier. Fighting in Normandy was fierce. One paratrooper commented that, after landing, in the most terrible sense it was "dog eat dog." The soldier on the right carries a U.S. .30 caliber M1 rifle with attached M1 bayonet. On his right shoulder, he wears a gas detection sleeve meant to change colors when exposed to poisonous gas.

Section VII - *Organizational Equipment, Signal Corps*

Item	Allowances		Basis of distribution and remarks
Flag set M-133	ea	2	Per company.
Flashlight, TL122 (A/B/C)	ea	1	Per O, 1st sgt; t sgt, plat; s sgt, sup; s sgt, sqd ldr; opr, rad tp.
Lantern, electric, portable, hand	ea	4	Per company.
Panel set AP-50-( )	ea	4	Per company.
Radio, set, complete, SCR-536 w/case	ea	6(2)	Per company (plus 2 spare).
Radio set, complete, SCR-300			*
Reel equipment, CE-11	ea	2	Per company
Signal lamp equipment, SE11 (M277)	ea	1	Per company
Signal, very, light, (Red, Green, White)			*
Switchboard, field			*
Telephone, field, battery powered, EE8B w/ case			*
Telephone, sound power			*
Wire, W-130-A on spool DR-8. (Authorized substitutes in order of preference are Wire WD-3/TT or W-130	mi.½		Per company

*Additional items <u>not</u> mentioned on wartime airborne rifle company-level T/O&Es or TBAs but included by author, as they nevertheless found their way into use.

BULLET POINT: THE BEDROLL

The pitching of tents has no real place in a combat recreation. More often than not, soldiers simple dug slit trenches and curled themselves up in their raincoats and fell asleep. If they were lucky, they may have had use of their bedrolls. At reenactment events set in the field, whenever possible, the use of a bedroll is an historically accurate way to provide a modicum of shelter and comfort.

In the book, *G Company's War*, Lee Otts, a lieutenant in the 26th Infantry Division, describes frequently the ubiquitous blanket roll. "Whenever possible our blanket rolls were carried on trucks and brought up to us at night. Blanket rolls contained from two to four blankets, and to keep them dry we rolled them inside a shelter half. At first we also placed our personal articles inside the blanket rolls, but after fumbling in the dark trying to find our bedroll out of a stack of two hundred we gave up the idea and settled for the first roll we came to ... Two men with eight blankets could sleep very comfortably; the only difficulty was getting the eight blankets. We would put one shelter half and our raincoat with about three blankets below us and the other five blankets and another shelter half (if we had one) over us. It was much warmer in the holes than on the outside, so we hated to get out of them."

Ingredients: 1, shelter half; 1(2-4), OD wool blanket(s); 5, tent pegs; 1, tent pole; and 1, tent rope.

FM 21-100, Basic Field Manual, Soldier's Handbook, on page 63, states the following: "To make the roll – Spread shelter half on the ground and fold in triangular end [or ends for late war models] so that the shelter half forms a rectangle. Make a second fold by carrying folded edge to opposite edge. Fold the blanket twice parallel to its longer axis so that blanket is now one-fourth its previous width, and then fold once at the middle so as to bring the ends together. Place blanket symmetrically in center of folded shelter half; place underwear, socks, and handkerchief between folds of blanket. Place tent pole on that end of the blanket from which the rolling is to begin. Place pins ... next to and parallel with pole ... Fold sides and then the near end of shelter half snugly over the blanket; fold 10 inches to far end of shelter half toward the blanket and, beginning at near end, roll tightly into folded end of shelter half, thus making an envelope roll." Tie up the roll with the tent rope.

With the front settling down to something of a stalemate, First Sergeant Weaver gets some much needed rest at the bottom of his foxhole with the relative comfort provided by a little hay gathered from a local barn, a shelter half as a ground cloth, and a wool blanket.

Silhouetted against the skyline, is this heavily-laden paratrooper, every pocket crammed with needed equipment, food and ammunition.

Where to Carry Articles of Equipment
BASED ON FM 31-30, TACTICS AND TECHNIQUE OF AIRBORNE TROOPS, ET. AL.

RIGHT CHEST POCKET, COAT
KIT, PARACHUTE, ESCAPE
SULFADIAZINE TABLETS, 1 PACKET
MORPHINE, 1 SYRETTE
SULFANILAMIDE, 2 PACKETS

WATCH POCKET OR BELT
COMPASS, WATCH OR LENSATIC

RIGHT WAIST POCKET, COAT
GRENADES, FRAGMENTATION, 2

RIGHT HIP POCKET
HANDKERCHIEF
SOCKS, PAIR, 2

RIGHT LEG POCKET
"K" RATION, 1 MEAL
"D" RATION, 2 BARS
SPOON, M-1926

COAT KNIFE POCKET
KNIFE, POCKET, M2

LEFT CHEST POCKET, COAT
NOTEBOOK AND PENCIL
WATCHES
TOILET PAPER, 48 SHEETS
HALAZONE, TABLETS, 1 BOTTLE
TOOTH BRUSH
MAP
WHISTLE, THUNDERER

LEFT WAIST POCKET, COAT
GRENADE, COLORED SMOKE, 1
GRENADE, WHITE PHOSPHOROUS, 1

LEFT HIP POCKET, TROUSERS
POCKET BOOK

LEFT LEG POCKET
ROPE, PARACHUTIST, 30'
PACKET, FIRST AID, PARACHUTE JUMPER'S

ITEMS TO BE PACKED IN BARRACK BAG
(TO BE LEFT WITH REAR ECHELON)
DRAWERS, 2 PAIRS
UNDERSHIRTS, 2
SOCKS, WOOL, 3 PAIRS
COMBAT UNIFORM, SPARE
CAP, GARRISON, OD
HANDKERCHIEFS, 2
BLANKETS, WOOL, OD, 2
TOWEL, BATH, 1
BOOTS, SPARE, 1 PAIR
TENT, SHELTER, HALF, 1
POLE, TENT, 1
PEGS, TENT, 5
ROPE, TENT, 1
CAN, MEAT, WITH KNIFE AND FORK

ADDITIONAL ITEMS CARRIED
IN BAG, FIELD, M-1936
KIT, CLEANING, CAL. .30
RAINCOAT
"K" RATION, 2 MEALS
"D" RATION, 4 BARS
PATCHES, CLEANING
SOAP AND RAZOR WITH 4 BLADES
TOWEL, HUCK
TAPE, ANKLE
BOX, MATCH, WATERPROOF
LACES, 1 PAIR, SPARE
DRAWERS, 1 PAIR
UNDERSHIRT, 1

"Contrary to film staging, where we see men point guns at and shoot individual enemies, in real modern war long-range weapons have abstracted the enemy to the far horizon: he is rarely seen; only the incoming rounds give notice of his presence. Men dying at the hands of unseen antagonists added to the terror of combat."[1]

PRINCIPAL WEAPONS OF U.S. ARMY PARACHUTE INFANTRYMEN IN WORLD WAR II

PART I: INDIVIDUAL WEAPONS

Rifle, Caliber .30, MI. Designed by John C. Garand, the M1 rifle is accepted for U.S. service in 1936, replacing the M1903 Springfield. Mass production commences in 1939, and soon after the M1 achieves the status of becoming the world's first general issue self-loading (semi-automatic) rifle. The M1 is gas-operated. Chambered in .30 caliber M1906, with a muzzle velocity of 2,800 feet per second, the effective range of the M1 is approximately 500 yards, although the maximum range is up to 3,000 yards. Ammunition, loaded into the rifle's internal magazine, comes in the form of eight-round *en bloc* clips. When the last round is fired, both the empty shell casing and the en bloc clip are ejected at once. The bolt remains open as a signal to reload. The length of this weapon is 43 1/2-inches and, at 9 1/2-pounds, the M1 is heavy. Yet, the M1's high rate of fire, coupled with its rugged reliability, wins it high regard.

The M1 accepts the standard M1 bayonet with its 10-inch blade and issue M7 scabbard. Some riflemen may be detailed as grenadiers. Using an M7 rifle grenade launcher, and an M15 grenade launcher sight, fitted to the muzzle of their M1s, these men may project a number of pieces of ordnance including M9A1 antitank rifle grenades, T2 impact fragmentation rifle grenades, as well as standard MkIIA1 fragmentation grenades that are married to M1A2 grenade projection adapters.

Rifle (Sniper), Caliber .30, M1903A4. The M1903A4 sniper rifle fires the standard .30 caliber M1906 ball cartridge from a five-round internal box magazine. Due to the configuration of the sight vis-à-vis the receiver bridge, rounds must be loaded into the magazine one at a time. The 2.5 power Weaver 330C telescopic sight (M73B1) is adjustable up to 1,200 meters. No bayonet lug is provided.

Automatic Pistol, Caliber .45, M1911A1. Called the *Colt* after its designer, and also the '45', the M1911A1 is a self-loading, semi-automatic weapon that utilizes a reliable recoil operation to cycle ammunition from its seven-shot magazine housed in the grip. An eighth round may be loaded in the breach. Though its .45 caliber projectile leaves the muzzle at relatively low velocity, its mass is enough to bring down almost any opponent no matter where he may be struck. The weapon is approximately 8 1/2-inches in length, and, fully loaded, weighs nearly 2 1/2-pounds. This sidearm is typically carried in an issue M1916 russet brown leather holster.

Carbine, Caliber .30, M1 (M1A1, M1A3, M2). During World War II, the M1 carbine fills a practical need for a lightweight weapon that may be easily wielded by troops such as vehicle drivers, engineers, and artillery and mortar crewmen, as well as being an adequate weapon for officers in the field. It is a gas operated, semi-automatic weapon that, like the M1 rifle, is chambered in .30 caliber, but which fires a pistol-shaped cartridge. The M1 carbine is magazine fed, accepting 15-round detachable box magazines. As oftentimes happens, military arms undergo a certain evolution. In the case of the M1 carbine, it has been modified from its original form to include a folding wire stock and a wooden pistol grip. This variant is classified as the M1A1 carbine. With the stock folded it is very compact, making it an ideal weapon to be carried by airborne troops. Both M1 and M1A1 carbines are fitted with a flip site graduated to 300 yards, although this weapon is at its best

at distances well inside of 100 yards. Late war T/O & Es list the M1A3 and M2 carbines (the former equipped with a pantograph stock more rigid than that of the M1A1; the latter being selective fire, between semi- and fully-automatic). There is no evidence that either of these weapons saw use by airborne troops in combat before the end of hostilities in Europe.

Thompson Submachine Gun, Caliber .45, M1A1. The M1A1 variant of the Thompson submachine gun is a modified version of the earlier M1928A1, simplified for mass production. Eliminated are the lock, actuator, breech oiler, buttstock catch, compensator and barrel fins. A straight forehand replaces the forward pistol grip, and a simple flip sight takes the place of the predecessor's complex backsight. A further simplification is the M1A1's fixed firing pin positioned on the face of the bolt. Adopted by the U.S. Army as its standard submachine gun in April 1942, the M1A1 has a cyclic rate of 600-800 rounds per minute and chambers the same man-stopping .45 caliber ammunition as does the M1911A1 automatic pistol. The Thompson accepts both 20- and 30-round detachable box magazines, and when fully loaded weighs in at about 11-pounds. A selector switch allows the operator to fire either single shots or fully automatic. In the latter mode, this weapon's recoil is such that its muzzle tends to climb. Nevertheless, it is a tremendously popular weapon.

No matter what, a soldier's weapon had to operate properly when it was called to due so. So it had to be kept clean. Here, two paratroopers field strip their M1 rifles.

OPPOSITE
Study of the U.S. Army's main battle rifle, the semi-automatic .30 M1. The paratrooper at right wears the ten-pocket cartridge belt that carries the 8-round en bloc clips for the M1, as well as a bandoleer of spare ammunition.

BELOW
Prior to 24 February 1944, Table of Organization 7-37 proscribed that every member of the parachute rifle company be issued the M1911A1 automatic pistol as sidearm. With revisions occurring after this date, the issue of the M1911A1 was stopped. Photographic evidence shows that the "Colt" remained a popular sidearm and was widely used, suggesting that those who had received the pistol prior to February 1944 retained them rather than turning them in.

Submachine Gun, Caliber .45, M3 (M3A1). By the close of 1944, the U.S. Army begins to phase out the Thompson replacing it with the less-costly .45 caliber M3 and M3A1 submachine guns; the M3 model having been introduced two years earlier. Nicknamed 'Grease Gun', the weapon bears a strong resemblance to that automobile repair shop tool, as it is manufactured chiefly from stamped parts, save for the barrel and the bolt. It weighs 10 1/2-pounds and, instead of a wooden buttstock, the Grease Gun employs a retractable wire stock. Utilizing 30-round detachable box magazines, the M3 is full-automatic only, but with a relatively low cyclic rate of 450 rounds per minute, allowing an experienced man to squeeze off single shots if necessary. Fitted with fixed sights, this compact weapon has very little recoil, virtually eliminating the tendency to 'climb' during long bursts of fire.

Browning Automatic Rifle, Caliber .30, M1918A2. Designed by John M. Browning, the gas-operated Browning automatic rifle first sees action in the closing stages of World War I, where it wins popularity, if not widespread use. In 1940, the basic design is updated to include a lightweight bipod, a flash hider, and a buttstrap. Like most U.S. infantry weapons of its day, the BAR is chambered in .30 caliber M1906. Rounds are fed into the weapon by 20-round detachable box magazines. While this weapon may be fired on full-automatic only, one may select from two cyclic rates – 350 or 600 rounds per minute.

The Browning automatic rifle is the standard squad-level automatic weapon used throughout the U.S. Army during World War II. Though heavy – weighing in at 19 1/2-pounds – this weapon is reliable. Typically, a BAR gunner is accompanied by a rifleman who acts as assistant gunner, carrying additional magazines for the BAR.

LEFT
Detail of the standard shoulder holster and double-web magazine pouch for the M1911A1 automatic pistol.

OPPOSITE
Lieutenant Soltis presents the M1A1 .30 carbine. Within the parachute rifle companies, M1A1 carbines served as officers' weapons and as 'backup' weapons for mortarmen and machine gunners. It was a handy, lightweight weapon, but lacked the range, accuracy, and stopping power of the standard .30 caliber M2 ball ammunition fired by the M1 rifle.

BELOW
With its wire stock folded, the M1A1 carbine was only about two feet in length.

OPPOSITE

TOP
His face blackened with singed cork, Private Allen holds the M1A1 Thompson submachine gun with 30 box magazine. Chambered in .45 ACP, the TSMG, nicknamed among other things the "Trench Broom" was a devastating weapon at close range and was, regardless of its reputation, issued quite sparingly within the parachute rifle companies. Tables of Organization listed but six TSMGs, these being in the company weapons pool.

BOTTOM
Detail of the M3A1 submachine gun. Chambered in the same .45 caliber ammunition as the Thompson SMG, the M3 submachine gun (or "grease gun") was made mostly of stamped parts and cost the government only a fraction of the former's price. Even by the time of the Normandy operation the M3 and M3A1 SMGs were making their appearance in the field and would continue to do so in ever-increasing numbers through the end of the war.

RIGHT
Trooper Domitrovich shows the details of a modified M1928A1 Thompson submachine gun, with simplified wartime economy barrel and foregrip.

Grenadier Corporal Benfer places a MkIIA1 fragmentation grenade with adapter onto the grenade launcher affixed to the muzzle of his M1 rifle. Typically the assistant platoon leader filled the role of grenadier within the platoon, but this practice does not seem to have been strictly followed.

Corporal Benfer prepares to fire a standard antitank rifle grenade from his M1 rifle.

PART II: CREW-SERVED WEAPONS

Browning Light Machine Gun, Caliber .30, HB, M1919A4/A6. The advent of the light machine gun was the realization of the need for a portable support weapon which could be employed *by* the attacking infantry, rather than by support troops away from the point of contact. The Browning light machine gun is an air-cooled weapon, with a perforated barrel jacket. It is recoil-operated and fires from an open bolt which further helps to ventilate this weapon while in operation. The gun weighs 31-pounds. In the ground mode it is used with a collapsible M2 tripod. The tripod weighs 14-pounds. Between the rear two legs of the tripod is fixed a traversing bar. To that is attached a mounting gear incorporating a wheel that manages the elevation and depression of the gun. The gun's integral pintle mount mates it to the tripod and is latched in place.

The M1919A4 is crew-served, manned by a machine gunner, an assistant machine gunner and, in most cases, two additional men assigned as ammunition carriers. Ammunition for this weapon comes in 150-round canvas belts with a brass tab at either end to assist loading, and are transported in olive drab metal tins with hinged lids. The cyclic rate of the Browning LMG is roughly 500 rounds per minute, while its sustained rate of fire is 150 rounds per minute. Late-war modifications to this weapon – the addition of a rifle-like buttstock, a carrying handle, a bipod, and a flash suppresser – have rendered it an even more suitable close support weapon for soldiers afoot.

Antitank Rocket Launcher, 2.36", M1 (M9). The M1 'Bazooka', so named because of its resemblance to "a comic wind instrument played by a well-known American entertainer," is the very first truly portable antitank weapon introduced into the U.S. Army. It is the first modern rocket launcher, and the first launcher to employ shaped charge antitank rockets. This weapon's primary component is its 61-inch smooth bore tube into the rear of which is inserted the rockets. Typically the Bazooka is operated by a two-man team – one man to load, the other to fire. The rocket is ignited by means of an electrical discharge produced by a pair of flashlight batteries. The sudden ignition of the rocket's propellant produces a devastating back blast, so the front end of the tube is fitted with a lightweight mesh screen to shield the gunner. The Bazooka weighs approximately 13-pounds. Its M6A1 rockets weigh approximately 3 1/2-pounds each, and can penetrate armor up to 4 1/2-inches thick at a maximum range of 300 yards, though it is measurably more effective at shorter ranges. Though this rocket launcher is designed first and foremost to be used against enemy armor, it is also highly effective against blockhouses and other hardened enemy positions. The M9 Bazooka is a wartime improvement on the M1 design, allowing most notably for the M9 to be broken-down into two sections of equal length for easier portage.

Mortar, 60mm, M2, w/ Mount, M2. The M2 60mm mortar is the standard American light infantry mortar. It consists of four basic parts, the barrel or 'tube', the bipod, the base plate, and the sight. This mortar is a crew-served weapon typically operated by a four-man team comprised of a mortar gunner, an assistant mortar gunner, and two ammunition carriers. This weapon is aimed using its M4 sight, that while being transported is detached and carried in its square leather case. The tube is smooth bore and measures just over 28 inches. The total weight of this mortar is 42-pounds. This mortar's shells are called bombs, and most often it is M49A2 high explosive shells that are fired; although M83 illumination shells may also be fired from this weapon. Mortar bombs weigh approximately 3-pounds. Their range is from 100 yards to the maximum being just short of 2,000 yards. To fire this weapon the loader simply drops a shell, stabilizing fins first, down the barrel. When the shell reaches the bottom of the tube, the propellant is ignited sending it on its high-trajectory flight to the target.

OPPOSITE
First Lieutenant Soltis loads an armor piercing rocket into the M1 2.36" rocket launcher held by 'Trooper Feige. The "bazooka," as it was more commonly called, was issued to each parachute rifle company on the basis of one for each of three rifle platoons, and one in the company weapons pool. This weapon was a simple affair but could penetrate up to 4-1/2 inches of armor at 300 yards, and was also very effective against bunkers and other fortified positions.

On the combat jump, antitank rockets for the bazooka are issued on the basis of twelve per weapon, carried on individuals, one round per man. Once the company has organized itself on the ground, the rounds are redistributed and are carried by the bazooka team, six rounds in each of two M6 antitank rocket carrying bags.

PART III: HAND GRENADES

Hand Grenades. Augmenting each soldier's individual weapons are a variety of hand grenades. All employ the same basic mechanism and are small enough to be thrown by an individual soldier. Grenades are either filled with an explosive or some form of chemical. Each type incorporates a fuze assembly comprised of a safety pin, a handle or 'spoon', a striker, a cap, the fuze-proper, and the charge. Grasping the grenade in one hand while holding the spoon in place, the soldier will next pull the pin from the fuze assembly by its ring. As long as the spoon is depressed it will prevent the striker from firing the cap and thus igniting the fuze. When either the grenade is thrown, or the spoon is released, the ventilated fuze will begin to burn down and, in a few brief moments (about 4-5 seconds), detonate the charge contained in the body of the grenade.

Most commonly carried is the MkIIA1 fragmentation hand grenade. Weighing about 1 1/2-pounds, this grenade has a deeply scored cast metal shell which causes it to be called the 'pineapple'. Filled with TNT (or in some cases EC blank fire powder) it packs a devastating blast that sends jagged fragments in a 30 yard radius. Other grenades include the smooth cased MkIIIA1 offensive hand grenade, the Thermite-filled incendiary hand grenade, the white phosphorous/smoke hand grenade, as well as a variety of colored smoke grenades.

BULLET POINT: THE COMBAT LOAD

The term, combat load, refers to the ammunition supply allocated to an individual soldier, with respect to the type of weapon, or weapons, with which he is armed.

In the book by Gary Howard, *America's Finest, U.S. Army Airborne Uniforms, Equipment and Insignia of World War Two (ETO)*, there is a chart on page 100 that outlines the "Tentative Plan On Basic Ammunition Loads" as set forth by H. Hanner, S-3 of the 506th Parachute Infantry Regiment for Operation Overlord. While there may have been some variation from regiment to regiment, division to division, and campaign to campaign, any difference was probably very little. The following proscribes for each weapon the amount of ammunition allocated, and the method for carrying this ammunition. The management of the initial combat load was extremely important as it contributed to the maximum allowable gross weight of troops and equipment aboard transport aircraft for airborne operations.

.30 M1 Semi-Automatic Rifle: 136 rounds; carried on individual; 128 rounds in four U.S. Army Air Corps Rifle Clip Holders, U.S.A.A.F. stock number LS 442575 (four *en bloc* clips per pocket), one 8-round *en bloc* clip in rifle, hand or jump suit pocket. (55% ball; 40% AP; 5% tracer). In lieu of the "Holder, Rifle Clip" (commonly, if incorrectly, referred to as "rigger" pouches) an individual would carry his ammunition in a cartridge belt and in a cloth bandoleer or the pockets of his jump suit.

.30 M1(M1A1) Semi-Automatic Carbine: 175 rounds; carried on individual; 160 rounds in two Air Corps pockets (two 15-round magazines and one 50-round box per pocket); one 15-round magazine in hand, or jump suit pocket. (100% ball).

.45 M1(M1A1, M3, or M3A1) Submachine Gun: 300 rounds; carried on individual; fourteen 20-round magazines in general purpose ammunition bag, one 20-round magazine in gun, hand, or jump suit pocket. Note: In cases where 30-round magazines are used, the individual would carry the load as ten 30-round magazines (six being borne in a magazine case) the rest in the gun and pockets of the jump suit. (100% ball). U.S. Army Air Corps Submachine Gun Clip Holders, U.S.A.A.F. stock number LS 442590, holding four 20-round clips each, may also be employed.

.45 M1911A1 Semi-Automatic Pistol: 21 rounds; carried on individual; two 7-round magazines in pouch, one 7-round magazine in the pistol. (100% ball).

.30 M1903(M1903A4) Rifle: 145 rounds; carried on individual; 140 rounds in four Air Corps pockets (seven 5-round clips per pocket), one 5-round clip in rifle, hand, or jump suit pocket.

Rifle Grenades: 10 grenades; carried on two individuals; five in each of two general purpose ammunition bags. (Six fragmentation, and four antitank).

MkIIA1 Fragmentation Hand Grenades: carried on individual; four grenades in jump suit pockets (if a general purpose ammunition bag is employed, six may be carried).

2.36" M1 (M9) Antitank Rocket Launcher: Twelve rockets per weapon, carried on individuals, one round per man; to be collected and carried by crew after jump, six rockets in each of two M6 antitank rocket carrying bags.

60mm M2 Mortar: 80 rounds; dropped in bundle, and carried on seven men (four riflemen jump with one round each, three mortar squad members jump with four rounds each in a general purpose ammunition bag); 54 rounds dropped in bundles and carried in an M3A4 Utility Hand Cart (four carts per company).

Paratroopers line up to receive bandoleers of M2 ball ammunition, each containing six, 8-round en bloc clips, brought forward by regimental service company Peeps to the battalion ammunition point or AP. 1/2 ton trucks, known alternately at Peeps or Jeeps, were the mainstay of organic transportation for the airborne divisions, and were delivered by glider to the combat zone.

During a lull in fighting two paratroopers spend time loading .30 caliber M2 ball, armor piercing and tracer ammunition into 20-round magazines for their squad's Browning automatic rifle.

81mm M1 Mortar: 54 rounds; dropped in bundle; 30 rounds in cart; six rounds on each of four men, *or five rounds on four men and four rounds on one man.* (80% HE, 20% WP).

.30 M1919A4 (M1919A6) Light Machine Gun: 3,250 rounds; with machine gun platoon 2,000 rounds dropped in bundle and carried on 81mm mortar cart, the remaining 1,200 rounds to be carried with riflemen as one belt of ammunition each (this may be used in M1 rifles if warranted by situation). Additionally, 6,250 rounds of ammunition (constituting reserve) will be dropped in bundle.

The ammunition loads as Hanner specifies above are considered to be all that troops could carry away with them from the field, regardless of how much and by what method ammunition and weapons either in bundles or as personal loads might be dropped.

PART IV: KNIVES AND EDGED WEAPONS

Trench Knife, M3. The M3 trench knife is the standard fighting knife issued to U.S. Army troops during World War II. The M3 is approximately 12-inches in length. The blade measures just over 7-inches. The top of the metal cross-guard curves forward, and the heavy steel hilt is flat. All metal parts have a dull, Parkerized finish. The grip is fashioned from leather washers. Early in the war, the M3 trench knife is issued with an M6 leather sheath. Later in the war, the M6 sheath is supplanted by the M8 plastic scabbard.

Trench Knife, M1918 MkI. The M1918 MkI, while being of roughly the same overall length as the M3 trench knife, is markedly different in overall appearance, featuring a double edged blade, and a heavy brass handle which incorporates fearsome brass knuckles tipped with dull spikes, and a pommel spike. The MkI is issued with a metal scabbard employing a crudely fashioned belt hanger.

PART V: ANTITANK MINES AND ANTIPERSONNEL MINES

Mines in General. By and large, mine warfare – the deliberate construction of minefields, and the recovery of and disarming of mines – is the domain of the U.S. Army's Combat Engineers. However, the British-made N°75 Hawkins mine, capable (at least in theory) of damaging the track of an enemy tank, or severing a steel rail, is issued in great numbers to U.S. paratroops for the invasion of France. As well, U.S. infantrymen may, under certain circumstances, employ mines such as the M1A1 antitank mine (1944) by simply laying them on road surfaces in plain view to deny enemy vehicles use of the road. In such cases, these mines should be covered by fire to prevent their removal by enemy troops. Rules for the employment of mines in reenacting are discussed later in this chapter.[2]

Mine fields are, in military terms, a class of 'obstacle'. An obstacle is anything other than fire power used to impede the enemy. It may be either a natural terrain feature or artificial work of destruction or construction and includes antitank and antipersonnel mines and demolitions.[3]

The purpose of an obstacle is to assist in the destruction of enemy troops by delaying them under fire, by restricting their power of maneuver, by forcing them into positions where the defense can most efficiently deal with them, and by disorganizing their plan of attack. The effectiveness of an obstacle is determined by three factors: The type of obstacle, the difficulty of adjacent terrain, and the strength of covering fires. One should note that obstacles covered by fire delay the enemy for the length of time required to drive off the defenders plus the length of time required to remove the obstacle. In order to be effective, *all obstacles must be covered by fire.*[4]

The N°75 Hawkins mine, shown here strapped to a paratroopers calf, is British ordnance, and was a device intended to use in hasty minefields to damage enemy tanks (their tracks or suspension) and other vehicles.

For tactical battle reenactments, artificial obstacles created as a result of destruction include simulated destroyed bridges and simulated road craters. The most germane artificial obstacle created as a result of construction is a simulated mine field.

Tactical Employment of Antitank Mines. The antitank mine is used tactically in almost all types of operations, offensive as well as defensive. It is the best quickly placed antimechanized obstacle available to the Army at the present time. It is designed to immobilize any vehicle passing over it.

The purpose of a mine field is to delay enemy armored forces under fire until they are destroyed by that fire or by counter attack; and to divert them into areas best suited to the defender. Antitank mine fields are used to close gaps in the main natural obstacles on which a defensive position is based; or as a continuous field where a natural obstacle does not exist. Antitank mine fields are also used as protective bands around individual defense areas; as an obstacle in barriers, and (in reenactment terms) especially for road blocks.

As stated above, a mine field must be defended by fire to be effective. Undefended mine fields delay the enemy only for the relatively short time it takes to bypass them or to remove enough mines to permit passage.[5]

Procurement of Antitank Mines. During World War II, the procurement, storage, and issue of antitank mines is a responsibility of the Ordnance Department. Antitank mines are supplied to the using arms and services in the same manner as are other class V supplies (all classes of ammunition, pyrotechnics, and chemicals).

Antitank mines are normally drawn in boxes by the using agency from ammunition distributing points and delivered by trucks to a covered position in rear of the mine field and as close to it as possible, where they are unboxed, fuzed, and assembled. In some cases the unboxed mines are reloaded on trucks and delivered to the mine field site. However, in some cases it may be necessary to hand-carry antitank mines for considerable distances where it is impracticable to bring a truck close to a selected mine field site.[6]

Characteristics of Mine Fields. *Hasty mine fields.* The hasty mine field is laid in expectation of immediate attack. The primary objective is immediate protection. The field is shallow in pattern. Generally no provision is made for burying mines, for activating (booby trapping) selected mines, or for installing antipersonnel mines. A variation of this pattern is the antitank mine road block. No special training is required for the laying of hasty mine fields. They may be laid or removed on order of any unit commander by troops of any arm or service.[7] Therefore the simulation of hasty mine fields are advocated for the purpose of tactical battle reenactments with the caveat that any mine simulator be of a standardized type. And while Army doctrine proscribes a distinct pattern for the laying of a hasty mine field, in actual practice this is perhaps too cumbersome for use during a tactical battle reenactment.

Deliberate mine fields. A deliberate mine field is one laid when time permits detailed preparation. The mines of a deliberate field are buried and carefully camouflaged. The field is deep in pattern and normally includes activated and antipersonnel mines. The laying and removal of deliberate mine fields and the removal of enemy mine fields require special training and, therefore, are the technical specialties of the Corps of Engineers.[8] Given the nature of most tactical reenactment events, the planning and construction of simulated deliberate mine fields should be the responsibility of event planners and organizers; the mine field to be installed prior to the commencement of the event.

Density of Antitank Mine Fields. The density of an antitank mine field is defined as the number of mines per yard of front. The standard hasty and deliberate minefields are laid with a density of 1 1/2 mines per yard of front. A scarcity of antitank mines may require that minefield be laid with lesser density. The antitank mine road block pattern is laid with a density of three mines per yard of front.[9]

TOOLS OF A GRIM TRADE

Antitank Mine Strings. When a road must be kept open for use by friendly vehicles it cannot be mined by ordinary methods. To provide protection of outposts from the sudden incursion of hostile vehicles, or to provide for continuity in a line or band of obstacles, antitank mine strings are used. They consist of antitank mines tied every few feet along a light rope. Mine strings used in pairs are employed in the following manner: Mine string is hidden at side of road. A rope leads from mine string to man hidden across road. The rope must be camouflaged well enough so enemy vehicle crews cannot see it until too late. When enemy vehicles approach, string-puller draws the mine string across road directly in the path of enemy vehicle. This action must be timed so that vehicle cannot stop or evade mines.[10]

U.S. Antitank Mine, M1A1. The M1A1 is a cylindrical, steel encased, 10-2/3 pound antitank mine filled with six pounds of cast TNT. Its dimensions, inclusive of its spider, are 4-inches by 8-inches. Its color is either olive drab, yellow, or olive drab with a yellow band and bottom.[11]

U.S. Antitank Mine, M4. The M4 antitank mine is identical to the M1A1, and additionally has two booby trap wells.[12]

U.S. Light Antitank Mine T7(M7). The T7 is employed in hasty minefields to protect forward troops, in road blocks, and as an antipersonnel mine as it is equipped with a fuze well. This mine is capable of disabling light tanks and vehicles. Its dimensions are 4 1/2-inches, by 2 1/2-inches by 7-inches. The T7's plated steel case is painted olive drab. The mine is filled with 3 1/2-pounds of Tetrytol, and the overall weight of this mine is 4 1/2-pounds.[13]

British No.75 Hawkins Grenade Mine, Mark I. This mine is utilized in an antitank role. Its steel case is painted olive drab in color, and is filled with 1 1/2 pounds of Nobel's Ammonal 704. The overall weight of the Hawkins mine is 3 pounds. This mine is ideal for use in road blocks or in hasty minefields to protect forward troops by disabling light tanks and vehicles. This mine measures 6 1/2 inches by 3-5/8 inches.[14]

Antipersonnel Mines in General. The antipersonnel mine is employed against personnel, and is laid to perform a definite tactical mission. Antipersonnel mines are used in antitank mine field and other obstacles, to give warning of enemy parties as well as for their effect against them. They are also laid independent of other installations as antipersonnel mine fields, to deny the enemy the use of assembly in such areas. Antipersonnel mines are also used as booby traps.

Detached units such as patrols and flank guards may make temporary installations of antipersonnel mines for local protection without special authorization. However, it is the responsibility of these detached units to remove these mines when they leave the immediate vicinity.[15]

U.S. Antipersonnel Mine, M3. The cast iron case of the M3 mine is painted olive drab with black lettering. It is filled with 0.9-pounds of flaked TNT, and its overall weight is 9.6-pounds. The M3 is a fragmentation type mine that when fired on the surface of the ground is capable of causing casualties to all personnel within 10 yards, and is dangerous up to 100 yards. The M3 mine is 3 1/2-inches by 3 1/2-inches by 5-3/8-inches. This mine accepts a variety of fuzes, and is typically activated by a trip-wire connected to the firing devise.[16] The German counterpart to the U.S. M3 mine is the Stock Mine (Concrete). The gray-colored case of the stock mine is cylindrical, constructed of formed concrete imbedded with steel fragments, and measures 6 1/2 inches and weighs 4 1/2 pounds. Each stock mine is issued with a wooden stake 2 feet in length. The stake is pounded 19 inches into the ground, and the stock mine is impaled on the stake. The explosive contained in the stock mine is the standard German borehole charge, which is detonated by means of a pull fuze ignitor and trip wire setup. The stock mine will cause personnel casualties up to 50 feet.

U.S. Antipersonnel Mine, M2. "The M2 mine consists of an explosive shell contained in an upright thin-walled steel tube welded to a base plate. A 1/2-inch pipe nipple threaded to the base plate connects the firing mechanism to the mine.

"The propelling charge, 20 grains of back powder in a small bag, is located in a cavity at the bottom of the tube; the tube is sealed at the top with a cap. The primer and igniter assembly are fitted onto the pipe nipple; a cap screwed over the primer protects it until the mine is assembled and placed.

"The mine is dull olive drab in color except for the base flange, which is yellow. Stenciled on the flange is the type and model of the mine, the lot number, manufacturer's symbol, and date of loading.

"The shell itself weighs approximately 3 pounds, of which 12 percent or about 1/3 pound is high explosive [TNT-filled]; and is cylindrical, 9 1/2 inches in height, and 3 1/2 in diameter. The overall weight of the device is 6 1/2 pounds.

"The [M2] mine is similar to a [60mm mortar shell]. When the fuze is actuated, the primer sets off the igniter. The flash from the igniter sets off the propelling charge in the base plate. The propelling charge projects the shell into the air and at the same time ignites the delay fuze. When the shell is at a height of approximately 6 feet above the base plate, the delay fuze fires a tetryl booster which detonates the high explosive in the shell. Upon explosion, the shell bursts into fragments effective over a radius of 30 feet."[17]

Details of the M1A1 .30 cal. carbine. Also note the strips of British-made burlap scrim woven into his helmet netting.

BULLET POINT: ACHTUNG! MINEN!

Simulated Deliberate Mine Fields for Tactical Battle Recreations

No tip-toe through the tulips! The use of antipersonnel and antitank mines by the Allied and the Axis powers during World War II was extensive. The effect of their use was measured both physically and psychologically. By incorporating mine fields into a tactical scenario, one will expand the dimension of the reenactment environment by adding increased realism and an additional challenge. For the purpose of simulating deliberate mine fields as part of tactical battle scenarios, one will consider all mine fields constructed by German reenactors to be composed of buried antitank mines and antipersonnel mines, the latter of the *S-Mine* variety. Similarly, deliberate mine fields laid by U.S. reenactors will be mixed fields of buried antitank mines laid in the prescribed pattern interspersed with buried antipersonnel mines, the latter of these being the M2 antipersonnel mine type.

The Mine-Simulator consists of a yellow paper flag (shown to scale in the corresponding figure) suspended from a nine-inch wire post. To lay the mine, simply press the post into the earth. Deliberate mine fields will be laid in almost every case by *pioneer* or engineer reenactors, or event organizers, before and during a given tactical battle recreation. Mines must be laid in fields of at least thirty and must be spaced at two-yard intervals in a regular staggered pattern. Mines may be booby-trapped to 'explode' if an attempt is made to remove them. This may be accomplished by affixing an second flag to the end of the post that is inserted in the ground. Keep in mind though, each side may start with only a fixed number of mine flags. Booby-trapping mines will require one to use two flags per simulator, rather than just the single flag required for a normal mine.

Any reenactor who strays into a mine field will become an instant casualty, so be careful! If one does find himself in the kill zone, he is required to take his 'hit', either seriously wounded or 'KIA', as supervised by *Umpires*. Unarmored vehicles that ride into a minefield will be considered destroyed; their crew and passengers seriously wounded or 'KIA'. Armored vehicles that ride over a mine will be considered immobilized (as if, for instance, a track was severed); their crew and passengers shall be considered lightly wounded or unharmed at the discretion of a supervising *Umpire*.

Only *pioneer* or engineer reenactors may remove mines once placed. To recover the mine(s), or to clear a path through the minefield, the Mine-Simulator is simply pulled from the earth. However, if a booby-trapped mine is removed, the engineer will become 'KIA'. Engineers may clear safe lanes through mine fields by removing Mine-Simulators from a swath at least six-yards wide, but each safe lane must be marked with engineer's yellow tape to allow any reenactor other than he who cleared the lane to pass. Once a safe lane is cleared, medical personnel may be called upon to remove the wounded and dead from the mine field and to render necessary medical aid.

Deliberate Minefields (employ minemarkers) vs. **Hasty Minefields** that employ actual simulators.

PART VI: DEMOLITIONS AND EXPLOSIVES

Demolitions and Explosives. Like mines, demolitions and explosives are generally employed by Engineer troops. However, certain individual infantry soldiers, as well as some infantry organizations as a whole, receive demolitions training as standard practice. Commonly used types of explosives are *trinitrotoluene* (TNT), *tetrytol* (M1 and M2 demolition block), composition C-2 (M3 and M4 demolition block), and ammonium nitrate. An additional demolitions device that must herein be acknowledged but which, however, will not be discussed is the wire-breaching charge known as the Bangalore torpedo.

Trinitrotoluene. TNT comes in the form of 1/2-pound and 1-pound packages, crated in 50-pound wooden boxes. TNT is an all purpose explosive that burns at 21,000 feet per second, and which may be used to cut trees and timber beams, and steel members. It is also highly effective in the destruction of concrete walls and obstacles, and may be used to good effect in cratering roads.[18]

Blocks, Demolition, Chain, M1 (Tetrytol). Tetrytol M1 is packaged as eight 2 1/2-pound blocks on detonation cord (also known as primacord) in a haversack – the well-known satchel charge. M1 demolition block burns at a slightly faster rate than does TNT, and its overall effectiveness is roughly 1 1/2 that of a comparable weight charge of TNT, although it is slightly less effective as a cratering charge. Each M1 block measures 2 inches by 2 inches by 11 inches, and is packaged in olive drab-colored asphalt-impregnated paper. There is 8 inches of primacord between each block and 2 feet of primacord at either end of the chain. On the obverse of the package is printed "BLOCK, DEMOLITION, CHAIN, M1" and on the reverse is printed, "1-BLOCK = 5, 1/2 POUND TNT BLOCKS."[19]

Block, Demolition, M2 (Tetrytol). The M2 demolition block is the same as M1 block only that M2 blocks are packaged individually and are fitted with a threaded cap well at each end. On the obverse of the package is printed "BLOCK, DEMOLITION, M2" and on the reverse is printed, "1-BLOCK = 5, 1/2 POUND TNT BLOCKS."[20]

Composition C-2. A more stable improvement over the earlier Composition C, C-2 burns at 26,000 feet per second and, overall, is an even more powerful explosive than tetrytol. C-2 explosive is issued in two distinct packages: Demolition Block, M3 or Demolition Block, M4. M3 demolition block is packaged in olive drab cardboard cartons measuring 2 inches by 2 inches by 11 inches, weighing 2 1/2 pounds apiece. The face of the carton is marked, "DEMOLITION BLOCK, M3, COMPOSITION M-2" and on the reverse is "HIGH EXPLOSIVE, ONE BLOCK EQUIVALENT TO SIX ONE-HALF POUND TNT BLOCKS."

M4 demolition block is packaged in olive drab cardboard cartons measuring 1 inch by 1 1/2 inches by 6 inches. The carton is marked, "DEMOLITION BLOCK, M4 (COMPOSITION C-2), 1/2 POUND NET, HIGH EXPLOSIVE."[21]

Ammonium Nitrate Cratering Explosive. Though combusting at less than half the rate of TNT, and with less than half the explosive force, ammonium nitrate is the explosive of choice when it comes to cratering roads. It comes packaged in 40-pound metal tins.[22]

Components of Demolition Sets.
• **Blasting machine.** – A ten-cap blasting machine (a.k.a. "Hell box") is standard in squad and platoon demolition sets. It weighs about 5 pounds.
• **Galvanometer.** – Used to test the electrical firing wires and firing circuits.
• **Reel, wire, firing.** – Metal reel carrying 500 feet of two-conductor, standard, No.18 gauge (B&S), rubber-covered firing wire.
• **Caps.** – See below.
• **Fuze, blasting, time.** – Also known as safety fuze, a black powder fuze that burns at a rate of 30-45 seconds per foot, issued in rolls of 50 feet.

OPPOSITE

TOP
Members of a rifle squad plant explosive charges on a bridge as a precaution against enemy attack. Each rifle squad was issued a complete demolition set containing a blasting machine, galvanometer, wire and reel, caps, fuze and detonating cord, cap crimper, fuze lighters, M1 explosive priming adapter, blasting cap protectors, cap sealing compound and firing devices.

BOTTOM
At a save distance from the bridge, a trooper affixes the wires to a 10-cap blasting machine.

BELOW
With enemy forces advancing and "Hell box" in hand, this paratrooper prepares to fire the bridge.

Detonating cord (primacord). – Greenish-yellow, waterproof textile covering with a relatively rough, waxy finish. Detonating cord is filled with *pentaerythritetranitrate* (PETN) and burns at a rate of 20,000 feet per second. Packaged as 100-foot lengths on wooden reels.

- **Cap crimper.**
- **Fuze lighters.**
- **Adapter, priming, explosive, M1.**
- **Blasting-cap protector.**
- **Cap sealing compound.**
- **Standard firing devices.**
    – Pull-type firing device, M1 and M2.
    – Pressure-type firing device, M1.
    – Release-type firing device, M1.
    – Combination firing device, M1.
    – Delay-type firing device, M1.[23]

All of these above-named explosives may be fired either by a delay method, or by electrical method using a blasting machine. The delay method requires the use of safety fuze. In this method, one attaches a 'special blasting cap' to the explosive charge. The blasting cap is crimped onto a length of slow-burning safety fuze that is cut to the desired length. To the other end of the safety fuze is connected a pull fuze ignitor – an M1 fuze lighter, or an M2 weatherproof fuze lighter. Pulling the ring of the igniter starts the safety fuze burning. The fuze burns into the blasting cap, setting it off, detonating the explosive. In the case of the electrical method, an electrical blasting cap is fitted to the explosive charge. Firing wire is strung from the blasting cap a safe distance to a 10-cap blasting machine called a 'Hell box'. The Hell box produces an electrical charge that travels down the wire, setting off the blasting cap which in turn detonates the explosive charge. Linked together with detonation cord, explosive charges of two or more components may simultaneously be detonated.

Along a Norman roadway, this paratrooper's kit includes a rigger-made version of the Air Corps clip holder on his right front, a MkIIA1 fragmentation hand grenade, a smoke grenade, and an M1A1 folding stock carbine. M1A1 carbines are proscribed for issue to machine gunners and mortar gunners (as a backup weapon), and to officers. The initial combat load was 175 rounds distributed in two 50-round boxes and five 15-round magazines.

"Send me men who can shoot and salute." – General John Joseph "Black Jack" Pershing

PART I: THE BASICS

Telling time in the Army. The services tell time by a different method than do people in civilian life, so reenactors should familiarize themselves with the 24 hour clock. By looking at the clock diagram one can see that, instead of using PM, the Army goes right on past 12 o'clock noon (1200 hours) to 1300 for one o'clock PM (1300 hours). Anything up to the 1200 hour is in the morning; anything after 1200 hours is the afternoon or night before midnight. Thus, 1100 hours is 11 o'clock AM; 0300 hours is 3 o'clock AM, 1400 hours is 2 o'clock PM; 2200 hours is 10 o'clock PM. Minutes after the hour are added onto the number. For example 0415 hours is 4:15 AM; 1737 hours is 5:37 PM.[1]

Dates – days, months and years – and times are often used in conjunction with one another in military field orders, journals, and reports. Example: 230630 May 44 stands for 6:30 o'clock AM (0630 hours), May 23, 1944. Likewise, 161800 Dec 44 stands for 1800 hours, December 16, 1944.

Discipline. During World War II, an important mark of the trained soldier is discipline – that mental attitude which made obedience and proper conduct instinctive under all circumstances. As with U.S. Army soldiers of World War II, reenactors should quickly begin the practice of immediate and unstinting compliance with all commands and requests by their officers and non-commissioned officers while participating in living history and tactical battle recreation events. Just as it was for those who reenactors portray, discipline is the trademark of a soldier, a privilege, and a duty.[2]

Military courtesy. In your home and school you were taught to be polite and considerate in your speech and attitude to your parents, your teachers and your comrades. That was courtesy. Military courtesy is the same thing except that the military man is so proud of his profession and has such high respect for the men who belong to it that courtesy is more carefully observed than in civil life. Military courtesy is a part of military discipline. The disciplined soldier is always courteous whether on or off duty, whether to members of the military or civilians.[3]

The correct use of titles. Commissioned Officers. As it is stated in *The Officer's Guide*, "lieutenants are addressed officially as "Lieutenant." However, the adjectives "first" and "second" are used in written communications." The same is the case when addressing other officers: brigadier generals, major generals, and lieutenant generals should all be addressed as "General." Lieutenant colonels should be addressed as "Colonel." It is acceptable for senior officers to refer to their subordinates as "Smith" or "Jones," states *The Officer's Guide*, but never are subordinates permitted this privilege.

Warrant Officers. Chief warrant officers and warrant officers junior grade will be addressed as "Mister."

Chaplains. Chaplains, regardless of rank, should be addressed as "Chaplain." Catholic chaplains may also be addressed as "Father."

Non-Commissioned Officers. Master sergeants, technical sergeants, and staff sergeants are all addressed as "Sergeant." Corporals are addressed as "Corporal."

Privates. Officers and NCOs should address privates either by "Smith" or "Jones," or simply as "Private."

Written Communications. In official written communications, the full titles of officers and non-commissioned officers will be used.

Uncovering. As a general rule, officers and enlisted men remove their headdress when indoors, including, offices, hallways, mess halls, kitchens, orderly rooms, amusement rooms, bathrooms, libraries, dwellings, or other places of abode. Such structures as drill halls, riding halls, gymnasiums, and other roofed structures used for drill or exercise of troops are considered "out of doors" in the application of military courtesies.

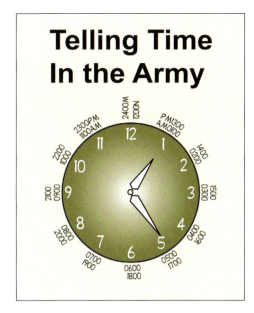

Telling Time In the Army

Uncovering When Under Arms. The expression "under arms" will be understood to mean: With arms in hand or having attached to the person a hand arm or equipment pertaining directly to the arm, such as a cartridge belt, pistol holder, or automatic rifle belt. Exception: Officers wearing the officers' belt, M1921, without arms attached. As a rule, officers and enlisted men who are "under arms" generally do not uncover except when: Seated as a member or in attendance on a court or board (Sentinels over prisoners do not uncover); Entering places of divine worship; Indoors when not on duty and it is desired to remain informally; In attendance at an official reception.[4]

The military salute. The *military salute* is, beyond the exercise of normal soldierly discipline, the way in which a soldier demonstrates his respect for the men and the Army to which he belongs, and is the courteous recognition between members of the armed forces of the United States. The salute is a privilege enjoyed only by members of the military service in good standing; prisoners do not have the right to salute. Although there are different types of salutes, the following paragraphs will be confined primarily to the discussion of the *hand salute*, that which is most pertinent to the reenacting environment. Please note that the procedures described herein apply to uniformed troops in dismounted service, i.e. soldiers on foot.[5]

An enlisted man or officer will render the salute when he meets those who are entitled to it: namely officers or superior officers of the United States Army, Navy, Marine Corps, and Coast Guard. Officers of friendly nations are also to be saluted. However, enlisted men will not render a salute to other enlisted men nor to non-commissioned officers. Furthermore officers of *unfriendly* nations are definitely *not* entitled to a salute. Officers will render a salute to a superior officer, or in reply to a salute from a subordinate officer or enlisted man.[6]

To execute the hand salute correctly, explains *The Officer's Guide*, "stand or walk erectly with your head up, chin in, and pull in on the stomach muscles. Look squarely and frankly at the person to be saluted. Raise the right hand smartly until the tip of the forefinger touches the lower part of the headdress or forehead above and slightly to the right of the right eye, thumb and fingers extended and joined, palm to the left, upper arm horizontal, forearm inclined at 45°, hand and wrist straight; at the same time turn the head toward the person saluted. To complete the salute, drop the arm to its normal position by the side in one motion, at the same time turning the head and the eyes to the front.[7] Execute the two movements of the salute in the cadence of marching, *ONE*, *TWO*. If you are saluting a superior officer, execute the first movement and HOLD the position until the salute is acknowledged, and then complete your salute by dropping the hand smartly to your side."[8]

Company CO Captain Bauman and acting platoon leader Technical Sergeant Allen synchronize their watches preparatory to launching an attack. Technical sergeants normally fill the role of Platoon Sergeant in each platoon, and assist the platoon leader in keeping their the unit organized. So far in this campaign the fighting has felled both Sergeant Allen's platoon leader and assistant platoon leader, rendering Allen next in the chain of command to take over.

Although salutes were not normally exchanged under combat conditions, this officer is far enough behind the main line of resistance as to have drawn a hand salute from this young paratrooper-messenger.

As stated in *The Officer's Guide,* "The smartness with which the officer or soldier gives the salute is held to indicate the degree of pride he has in his profession. A careless or half-hearted salute is discourteous."[9]

When out of doors, a salute should be rendered when one can easily recognize the individual entitled to receive it. Usually this is at a distance of not more than 30 and not less than 6 paces, in order that the officer may have time to recognize and return it. For the sake of reenactment, this procedure should be followed while within the bounds of all military posts, camps, and stations, but only while all parties concerned are *in* uniform. If the officer remains in your immediate vicinity without talking to you, no further salute is necessary when he departs. If a conversation takes place however, you should again salute when either you or he leaves.[10]

When reporting to an officer (or superior officer) in his office, the soldier will first remove his headdress, unless under arms, and enter when told to do so. He will march to within two paces of the officer's desk, halt, salute, and state, "Sir, Private _____ reports to _____ ." (For example, "Sir, Private Smith reports to the Platoon Commander." or "Sir, Lieutenant Jones reports to the Company Commander.") After reporting, carry on the conversation, and when it is ended, salute, make an about face, and withdraw. Unless under arms, always remove your headdress when entering a room where an officer is present.[11]

If you are one of a group of soldiers, not in formation, call the group to attention as soon as you recognize an officer approaching, unless some other member of the group has already done so. If the group is out of doors, all members of the group salute; if indoors or in a tent, all remove their head covering and stand at attention unless otherwise directed by a superior. If the group is in formation out of doors, it is called to attention by the one in charge and he alone gives the salute.[12]

If you are talking to an officer (or your superior officer), do not interrupt your conversation to salute another officer. However if the officer to whom you are talking salutes his senior, you will also salute. If you are in ranks and not at attention and an officer speaks to you, come to attention, but do not salute. The officer or non-commissioned officer in command of your unit will give the salute for the entire organization to the person entitled to it.[13]

If an officer (or superior officer) enters the mess room or mess tent, you remain seated, "at ease," and continue eating unless the officer directs otherwise. If the officer (or superior officer) speaks directly to you, remain seated "at attention" until the conversation is ended, unless he directs otherwise."[14] When an officer enters a squad room or tent, individuals rise, uncover (if unarmed), and stand at attention. If more than one person is present, the first to perceive the officer calls, 'Attention!'"[15]

"A group of enlisted men within the confines of military posts, camps, or stations and not in formation, on the approach of an officer, is called to attention by the first person noticing him; in formation, by the one in charge. If out of doors and not in formation, they all salute; in formation, the salute is rendered by the enlisted man in charge. If indoors, not under arms, they uncover … The salute is rendered but once if the senior remains in the immediate vicinity and no conversation takes place."[16]

Note that when indoors, salutes are generally not exchanged except when reporting to an officer or senior officer. Enlisted men meeting an officer in a hallway or on stairs halt and stand at attention, but do not salute. "An enlisted man in ranks and not at attention comes to attention when addressed by an officer" but does not salute. Individuals engaged in work do not salute; the officer or non-commissioned officer in charge of a work detail will salute for the entire group. Do not salute when carrying articles with both hands or when you are otherwise so occupied as to make saluting impracticable. "In churches, theaters, or places of public assemblage, or in public conveyance, **salutes are not exchanged, [nor are they exchanged] when on the march, in campaign, or under simulated campaign conditions.**" Vehicle drivers do not salute unless the vehicle is halted, though individuals riding in the vehicle salute whether the vehicle is in motion or halted.

If you are driving a motor vehicle, salute only when the vehicle is halted. Any other soldier in the vehicle salutes whether the vehicle is at a halt or in motion, unless there are a number of soldiers in the vehicle with an officer or non-commissioned officer in charge. In this case only the officer or non-commissioned officer gives the salute.[17]

After landing by parachute, paratroops became, in essence, elite light infantry afoot. Dry socks and clean feet served to maintain circulation and avoid "immersion foot," and the more commonly known trench foot. If an infantry soldier was unable to walk he was as useless as if he had been felled by enemy fire.

When not in formation and the National Anthem is played, or "To the Colors" sounded, at the first note face the music, stand at attention and give the salute. At "Escort of the Color" or "Retreat," face toward the color or flag, and render the salute. If you are passing, or being passed, by an uncased national color, render the same honors as when the National Anthem is played.[18]

Physical Training "Thorough technical, psychological, and physical training is one protection and one weapon that every nation can give to its soldiers before committing them to battle, but since war always comes to a democracy as an unexpected emergency, this training must be largely accomplished in peace. Until world order is an accomplished fact and universal disarmament a logical result, it will always be a crime to excuse men from the types and kinds of training that will give them a decent chance for survival in battle."[19] In his book, *The Sky Men*, the author states, "By the end of A Stage, every man could run five miles in fifty minutes, do at least fifty push-ups, sixteen chin-ups, and climb a forty foot rope using only his arms. The constant exercise had not only toughened the

Lathering up for a shave in the field. A steel helmet suspended by its chinstraps from a fighting knife plunged into the tree serves as a water basin. The shaving soap is in a 'liberated' **SS** coffee cup, it's former owner not having use for it any longer.

Shaving was accomplished using a **PX** razor and a polished steel mirror. Water, let alone hot water, was a luxury, and dry shaving was how the job often got done.

men, but had taught them that they were able to go beyond the limits of ordinary physical exertion. It also instilled in the men the confidence that they were serving with men they could trust in combat, men who wouldn't quit when things got rough. More importantly, each man knew that if he dug down deep inside himself he could find the will to keep going, no matter what. This set the paratroopers apart from other soldiers." For wartime Army doctrine concerning physical training of soldiers, please refer to FM 21-20. Under wartime conditions, and in everyday life, physical fitness is extremely important to one's overall wellbeing and quality of life. Please take a page out of the paratrooper's experience and endeavor to get in shape, and stay in shape!

BULLET POINT: SOUND OFF!

Marching songs have been a tool to raise the spirits of, and instill pride and unity in, troops for centuries. Whether during periods of physical training or close order drill, or while on one's march to the battlefront, here is a cadence and a few songs that have a decidedly "airborne" flavor.

The Duckworth Chant. This marching cadence traces its origin to Fort Slocum, New York, in 1944, authored by one Private Willie Lee Duckworth (1924-2004) of Sandersville, Georgia, and fostered by post commanding officer, Colonel Bernard Lentz (already known in the U.S. Military for his book, *The Cadence System of Teaching Close Order Drill*). Duckworth's improvised chant features *Joe the Grinder*, (a.k.a. *Joe De Grinder* and *Joe D. Grinder* subsequently shortened to simply, *Jody*) a mythical ladies' man of the day's blues and jazz songs that seduces the wives and sweethearts of prisoners and soldiers. In the context of Army life, Jody became known as a "civilian back home who has stolen the affections of the soldier's sweetheart."[1] As the troops marched, the cadence was called, and the soldiers would answer in time with the step. And although Duckworth's original words may be lost to time (and in fact may be so obscure as to make little sense to others than who were at Fort Slocum at the time), the spirit of his immortal chant is encapsulated in the lines that follow.

Forward … Harch!

Cadence: Hut, hup, hareep, four!

Call: The heads are up, the chests are out.
Call: The arms are swinging. In cadence, count!

REFRAIN:
Call: Sound off!
Reply: One, two!
Call: Sound off!
Reply: Three, four!
Call: Cadence count.
Reply: One, two, three, four, one, two three, four!

Call: Eeny, meeny, miney, mo.
Call: Let's go back and count some mo'.

[REFRAIN]

Call: It won't get by if it ain't GI.
Reply: It won't get by if it ain't GI.

Call: It won't get by if it ain't GI.
Reply: It won't get by if it ain't GI.

[REFRAIN]

Call: I don't mind to take a hike.
Reply: If I could take along a bike.
Call: I don't mind a bivouac.
Reply: If I could take along a WAC.

[REFRAIN]

Call: I had a good home, but I left.
Reply: You're right!
Call: I had a good home, but I left.
Reply: You're right!
Call: Jody was there, when I left.
Reply: You're right!
Call: Jody was there, when I left.
Reply: You're right!

[REFRAIN]

Call: Am I right or wrong?
Reply: You're right!
Call: Am I right or wrong?
Reply: You're right!
Call: You know I'm right. So tell me . . .
Reply: You're right!
Call: Am I right or wrong?
Reply: You're right!

Call: You left your gal a'way out west.
Reply: I thought this army life was best.
Call: Now she's someone else's wife.
Reply: And I'll be marchin' the rest of my life.

[REFRAIN]

Call: Jody was home when you left.
Reply: You're right!
Call: Your baby was there when you left.
Reply: You're right!
Call: You had a good wife when you left.
Reply: You're right!
Call: But Jody was home when you left.
Reply: You're right!

[REFRAIN]

Call: There ain't no use in goin' back.
Reply: Jody's livin' in your shack!
Call: Jody's got somethin' you ain't got!
Reply: It's been so long, I almost forgot!

[REFRAIN]

Call: They signed you up for the length of the war!
Reply: I never had it so good before!
Call: The best you'll get in a bivouac?
Reply: Is a whiff of cologne from a passing WAC!

[REFRAIN]

Call: The Captain rides in a jeep.
Reply: You're right!
Call: The Sergeant rides in a truck.
Reply: You're right!
Call: The General rides in a limousine, but we're just out of luck.
Reply: You're right!

[REFRAIN]

Call: The Second Platoon is just like Krauts.
Reply: They're all afflicted with the gout!
Call: The Third Platoon can't stand the gaffe.
Reply: They're tryin' to get on the General's staff!

[REFRAIN]

Call: If I get shot in a combat zone?
Reply: Just box me up and send me home.
Call: The WACs and WAVEs will win the war.
Reply: So tell us what we're fighting for?

[REFRAIN]

Cadence: Hut, hup, hareep, four!

Call: **Comp'ny . . . Halt!**

Blood On the Risers
Sung to the melody of John Brown's Body

He was just a cherry trooper and he surely shook with fright
As he checked all his equipment and made sure his pack was tight
He had to sit and listen to the awful engines roar,
And he ain't gonna jump no more.

CHORUS:
Gory, Gory, What a hell of a way to die
Gory, Gory, What a hell of a way to die
Gory, Gory, What a hell of a way to die
He ain't gonna jump no more.

"Is everybody happy?" cried the Sergeant, looking up.
Our hero feebly answered "yes," and then they stood him up.
He leaped right out into the blast, his static line unhooked.
He ain't gonna jump no more.

[CHORUS]

He counted long, he counted loud, he waited for the shock;
He felt the wind, he felt the clouds, he felt the awful drop;
He jerked his cord, the silk spilled out and wrapped around his legs.
He ain't gonna jump no more.

[CHORUS]

The risers wrapped around his neck, connectors cracked his dome;
The lines were snarled and tied in knots, around his skinny bones;
The canopy became his shroud, he hurtled to the ground.
He ain't gonna jump no more.

[CHORUS]

The days he'd lived and loved and laughed kept running through his mind;
He thought about the girl back home, the one he'd left behind;
He thought about the medics and wondered what they'ed find.
He ain't gonna jump no more.

[CHORUS]

The ambulance was on the spot, the jeeps were running wild;
The medics jumped and screamed with glee, they rolled their sleeves and smiled;
For it had been a week or more since last a chute had failed.
He ain't gonna jump no more.

[CHORUS]

He hit the ground, the sound was splat, his blood went spurting high;
His comrades were then heard to say, "A heck of way to die";
He lay there rolling 'round in the welter of his gore.
He ain't gonna jump no more.

[CHORUS]

There was blood upon the risers, there were brains upon the 'chute.
Intestines were a-dangling from his paratrooper suit.
He was a mess, they picked him up and poured him from his boots.
And he ain't gonna jump no more.

A Catchy Li'l Ditty

We pull up on the risers and we fall down on the grass.
We never land upon our feet, we always hit our ass.
Aye aye, Christ Almighty, who the Hell are we?
Zim zam, God damn, we're Airborne Infantry!
Hooray!

The Company Headquarters, and
The Platoon Members and Their Functions

Introduction. As most reenactment units number no more than thirty or forty members – some as few as only ten – information describing the organization of platoon- and squad-sized formations is most appropriate to reenacting, especially for tactical battles. Furthermore, as the infantry is the backbone of United States Army ground forces during World War II, and as the organization of all other types of combat infantry formations follow, chronologically, the development of the former, the standard infantry rifle platoon is discussed herein in more detail. When the occasion arises that the personnel of several reenactment units – two or more platoons – be combined under one command for the purpose of a tactical battle scenario, an infantry company headquarters will be established for this task.

Company Headquarters, Rifle Company, Rifle Regiment. An infantry rifle company headquarters is composed of two distinct elements, the command group and the administrative group. The command group is employed by the company commander in order to prepare the company for combat, and to maintain control of the company during combat. The command group consists of the following personnel: The second-in-command (or executive officer), the first sergeant, the communication sergeant, the bugler, messengers, and the orderly.

In terms specific to the *Company Headquarters, Infantry Rifle Company*, as per T/O 7-37, 24 February 1944, the personnel are as follows:

– Captain, Company Commander
– First Lieutenant, Company Executive Officer
– First Sergeant
– Sergeant, Communication
– Sergeant, Operations (intelligence)
– Privates or PFCs, Messengers (3)
– Privates or PFCs, Radio Telephone Operators (3)
– Privates or PFCs, Riflemen (5)
– Enlisted Cadre (14, various ranks and duties)

Toward the close of 1944, the Army increased the strength of the Parachute Infantry Rifle Companies. T/O & E 7-37T of 16 December 1944, authorized changes and increases in personnel to the parachute rifle company headquarters as follows:
– Captain, Company Commander
– First Lieutenant, Company Executive Officer
– First Sergeant
– Staff Sergeant, Mess
– Staff Sergeant, Supply
– Sergeant, Communication
– Corporal, Company Clerk
– Technician Grade 5, Armorer-articifer
– Private or PFC, Bugler
– Technicians Grade 4, Cooks (2)
– Technician Grade 5, Cook
– Privates or PFCs, Cook's Helpers (2)
– Privates or PFCs, Messengers (2)
– Privates or PFCs, Radio Telephone Operators (1)
– Privates, Basic (12)
– Enlisted Cadre (22, various ranks and duties)

In historical terms, the company commander is responsible for the discipline, administration, supply, training, tactical employment, and control of his company. In reenactment terms, all of these duties apply, with the possible exception of supply and training which, as is the nature of this hobby, is the responsibility of the individual and, to a lesser extent, the reenactment unit to which he belongs.

The company commander must supervise the tactical employment of all elements of the company. He makes his plans after considering available intelligence information, his own reconnaissance and, if possible, that of his subordinates, and after weighing the advice of his subordinates if such is offered. It is also the company commander's responsibility to continuously supervise his subordinates in order to insure they properly carry out their assigned tasks. He is also responsible for the security of his company. However, when applicable, reports as to the location of the company and its progress with regard to its mission, will be rendered by the most rapid means possible to the higher commander (battalion commander) when applicable. Many of these conditions, however, are presented to the company commander, and others concerned, as the rudimentary elements of the setting and scenario for the given tactical battle recreation.

The Company Headquarters Command Group. During a tactical battle scenario, the second-in-command (usually a first lieutenant), is in charge of the command post and keeps himself apprised of the tactical situation as it effects the company. He is ready to replace the company commander should the former become a casualty, or, at the orders of the company commander, to take over one of the platoons. He maintains communication with the elements of the company and the company commander, and, when need be, with the battalion headquarters. The second-in-command also dispatches messengers to notify elements of the company and battalion headquarters as to changes in location of the company command post.[20]

The first sergeant is at the disposal of the company commander. If need arises, the first sergeant may take command of a platoon. He assists the second-in-command at the direction of the company commander, and assumes the second-in-command's responsibilities when the latter leaves the command post. The first sergeant also takes charge of the command post when no officer is present.[21]

The communication sergeant is knowledgeable in the use of wire and radio-telephone communication, as well as visual signals, in the preparation of sketches and overlays, and as an observer. His most important role is to supervise the establishment of observation over the company front, and to supervise the installation of the company's wire and other communications equipment. He furthermore receives and dispatches messengers who are with the company commander.[22]

The bugler – a title somewhat contrary to his role – is a trained observer who is deployed to assist the company commander with observation and in the control of the company. In the context of a tactical battle scenario, the bugler would signal the approach of enemy armored vehicles by sounding a whistle signal.[23]

As many as six messengers may be assigned to the company headquarters group. One messenger accompanies the company commander and carries messages to the command post or to other elements of the company as specified. If circumstances of a tactical battle recreation dictate, one messenger is dispatched to the battalion's command post when the battalion develops for combat.[24]

In some cases, a basic private may be detailed as the company orderly. While perhaps being a trained messenger and observer, he has another more vital role. He accompanies the company commander wherever he goes and acts as his personal bodyguard.[25]

The Company Headquarters Administrative Group. The administrative group in a World War II-era rifle company headquarters consists of the following personnel: the supply sergeant, the mess sergeant, cooks and cook's assistants, the armorer-articifer, and the company clerk. While, from an historical perspective, it is fitting to acknowledge these troops, the duties and functions that these personnel traditionally performed are less applicable to tactical battle scenarios. Rather many of the services provided by such troops are, as is the case with many larger reenactment events, provided by the event organizers, or are the responsibility of the reenactors themselves.[26]

The additional enlisted cadre and the basic privates are at the disposal of the company commander, ostensibly to provide security for the company headquarters when in combat, and to be used to replace casualties throughout the company during combat.

Rifle Platoon, Infantry Division. U.S. Army infantry rifle platoons, during the latter portion of World War II, consist each of a command group and three rifle squads, totaling some forty five men. The traditional duties and functions of these elements of the platoon follow. However, some omissions or additions have been made in order to incorporate the historical evidence into a format more useful to reenacting.

The command group consists of a *platoon leader* (first lieutenant), an *assistant platoon leader* (second lieutenant), a *platoon sergeant* (technical sergeant), a *platoon guide* (staff sergeant), a *radio-telephone operator* (RTO), two *messengers*, and basic privates as replacements. The platoon leader is responsible for discipline, control, and tactical employment of the platoon. The assistant platoon leader will take command when the platoon leader is absent or if he becomes a casualty. The platoon sergeant will assist the platoon leader in keeping the platoon organized. The platoon guide will attempt to prevent straggling, enforce orders concerning concealment, cover and discipline, and check the security of the platoon's rear and flanks. The platoon guide will also check to make sure troopers have enough ammunition. Extra ammunition for the platoon, if such may be the case, will be stored on a weapons carrier, if available, or at a company ammunition point (AP) for distribution. The RTO and messengers are at the disposal of the platoon leader.

It is important to keep one thing in mind: the confusion of real combat caused breakdowns in the ability of individuals to properly carry out their assigned duties. To expect anything less than 'breakdowns' during the course of a reenactment's tactical battle would be expecting too much. Because there will be confusion, it is important that all soldiers follow the directions of the command group.

Organization of the Infantry Rifle Company, Parachute Per T/O 7-37 (with changes No. 1 and No. 2) 24 February 1944

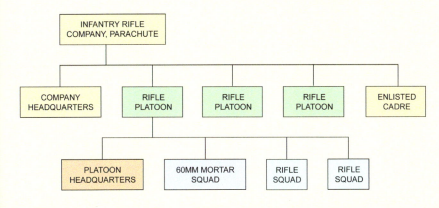

Parachute Rifle Company (8 Os, 119 men)
Plus Enlisted Cadre (14)

Headquarters, Rifle Company (2 Os, 14 men)
3 x .30 M1A1 Carbines
13 x .30 M1 Rifles
6 x .45 M1A1 Submachine Guns (Company Pool)
1 x 2.36" M1A1 Rocket Launcher (Company Pool)

Headquarters, Platoon (2 Os, 5 men)
2 x .30 M1A1 Carbines
5 x .30 M1 Rifles
1 x 2.36" M1A1 Rocket Launcher (Platoon Pool)

Rifle Squad (12 men)
1 x .30 M1919A4 Light Machine Gun
1 x .30 M1A1 Carbine
11 x .30 M1 Rifles

60mm Mortar Squad (6 men)
1 x 60mm M2 Mortar
2 x .30 M1A1 Carbines
4 x .30 M1 Rifles

Organization of the Infantry Rifle Company, Parachute Per T/O & E 7-37T (with changes No. 1 and No. 2), 16 December 1944

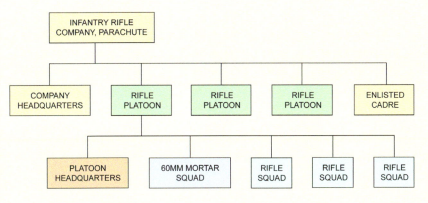

Parachute Rifle Company (8 Os, 168 men)
Plus Enlisted Cadre (22)

Headquarters, Rifle Company (2 Os, 27 men)
2 x .30 M1A1 Carbines
27 x .30 M1 Rifles
6 x .45 M1A1 Submachine Guns (Company Pool)
1 x 2.36" M1A1 Rocket Launcher (Company Pool)

Headquarters, Platoon (2 Os, 5 men)
2 x .30 M1A1 Carbines
5 x .30 M1 Rifles
1 x 2.36" M1A1 Rocket Launcher (Platoon Pool)
1 x .30 M1C Rifle (Platoon Pool)

Rifle Squad (12 men)
1 x .30 M1919A4 Light Machine Gun
2 x .30 M1A1 Carbines
1 x Browning Automatic Rifle
10 x .30 M1 Rifles

60mm Mortar Squad (6 men)
1 x 60mm M2 Mortar
2 x .30 M1A1 Carbines
4 x .30 M1 Rifles

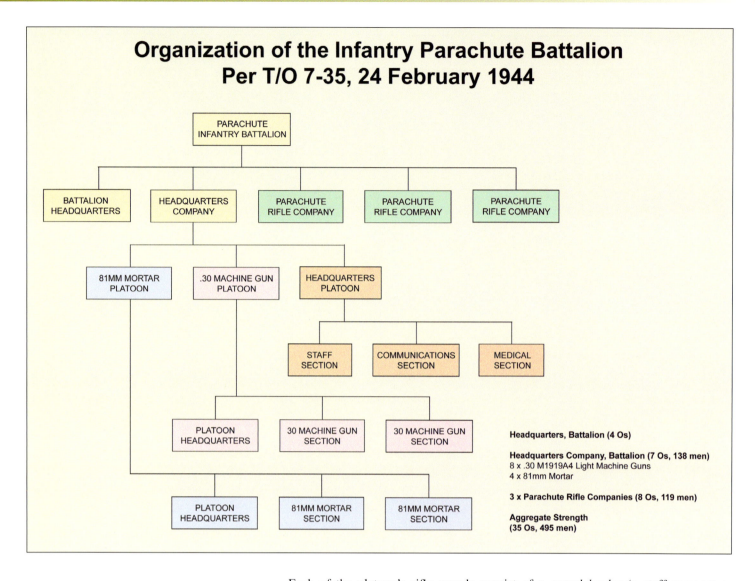

Each of the platoon's rifle squads consist of a *squad leader* (a staff sergeant or sergeant) an *assistant squad leader* (a sergeant or corporal), a Browning automatic rifle team, and seven riflemen. The squad leader is responsible for the discipline, control, and conduct of his squad. He leads the squad in combat and reports on its ammunition supply to the platoon guide. The assistant squad leader, positioned at the rear of the squad to prevent straggling, helps the squad leader maintain control and organization of his men, and is also equipped as the grenadier. The BAR team consists of an automatic rifleman and two other riflemen, both of whom act as ammunition bearers, and one of whom is additionally designated as the assistant automatic rifleman. Two of the remaining riflemen are designated as scouts. Typically, all men in the squad, save for the BAR gunner, are armed with M1 rifles, although the ammunition bearers may instead each carry an M1 carbine.

Before the advance is begun, the platoon leader designates one squad as the *base squad* on which the other two squads will regulate their movement. The pair of scouts from each squad will deploy under the command of the platoon leader, "lock and load, scouts out!," and move boldly to the front and flanks of the advancing platoon; the platoon moving in a formation determined by the platoon leader. In each pair, one scout watches for signals from the platoon leader and covers the lead scout as the latter reconnoiters as much as 500 yards ahead. If scouts are fired on by the enemy – and do not become immediate casualties – they will endeavor to designate the target for the platoon leader. At this time, the squad leaders assemble their squads and watch for the platoon leader's orders.

The parachute infantry rifle platoon is discussed below. Please note that for the sake of historical accuracy, mention is made of platoon-component mortar and grenadier elements. However, for reasons of safety, this guide does not endorse the employment of mortars and grenade projectors for tactical battles, only for display.

The Infantry Platoon, Parachute, ca. 24 February 1944, consists of thirty-five enlisted personnel, commanded by a first lieutenant. This platoon is comprised of a platoon HQ, two rifle squads, and a mortar squad. The platoon HQ consists of two officers and five enlisted men. In the platoon pool of weapons are six cal. .45 submachine guns and a bazooka. Within the platoon are two rifle squads, each consisting of twelve men, and an M2 60mm mortar squad consisting of six men.

The rifle squads are each allocated eleven M1 rifles, an M1A1 carbine, and a .30" light machine gun. Before late February 1944, each man in the parachute rifle company is also armed with a .45" automatic pistol. After February 24, 1944, in correspondence with T/O & E 7-35T, the automatic pistol was withdrawn from issue, although many soldiers seem to have retained this weapon in actual practice.

The Infantry Platoon, Parachute, ca. 16 December 1944, consists of forty-seven enlisted personnel, and two officers: a first lieutenant in command, and a second lieutenant as assistant platoon leader. This late-war platoon is comprised of a platoon HQ, three rifle squads, and a mortar squad. The platoon HQ consists of two officers and five enlisted men. Each of the three rifle squads consists of twelve men lead by a staff sergeant, and an M2 60mm mortar squad consisting of six men, lead by buck sergeant.

Each rifle squad is allocated ten M1 rifles, a .30" light machine gun, and a Browning Automatic Rifle. Additionally, the squad is allocated two cal. .30 M1A1 carbines carried as backup weapons by the BAR gunner and the machine gunner.

A pathfinder operates a Eureka beacon to guide incoming aircraft to a drop zone in Normandy. Pathfinders were volunteers from the airborne organizations that were specially selected and trained. While not the subject of this book, the perilous job of pathfinders was integral to the mission of the rifle companies, and indeed, all the airborne forces.

BULLET POINT: FORM FOR FIELD ORDERS

Field Orders. Prior to the commencement of a military operation, field orders are commonly produced and distributed to all headquarters concerned. Written orders are vital in communicating the exact missions and responsibilities of all parties to any operation. The basic components of a complete written field order are as follows.[1]

Issuing unit
Place of issue
Date and hour of issue
FO_____
Maps: (Those which correspond to the order).

1. **Information:** Include appropriate information covering:

a. *Enemy:* Composition, disposition, location, movements, strength; identifications; capabilities. Refer to intelligence summary of report when issued.

b. *Friendly forces:* Missions or operations, and location of next higher and adjacent units; same for covering forces or elements of the command in contact; support to be provided by other forces.

2. **Decision or Mission:** Decision or mission; details of the plan applicable to the command as a whole and necessary for coordination.

TROOPS
(Composition of tactical components of the command, if appropriate.)

3. **Tactical Missions for Subordinate Units:** Specific tasks assigned to each element of the command charged with the execution of tactical duties, which are not matters of routine or covered by standard operating procedure. A separate lettered subparagraph for each element to which instructions are given.

Instructions applicable to two or more units or elements or to the entire command, which are necessary for coordination but do not properly belong in another subparagraph.

4. **Administration Matters:** Instructions to tactical units concerning supply, evacuation, and traffic details which are required for the operation (unless covered by standard operating procedure or administrative orders; in the latter case, reference will be made to the administrative order).

5. Signal Communication.

a. *Orders for employment* of means of signal communication not covered in standard operating procedure. Refer to signal annex or signal operation instructions, if issued.

b. Command posts and axes of signal communication: Initial location for unit and next subordinate units; time of opening, tentative subsequent locations when appropriate. Other places to which messages may be sent.

Commander

Authentication
Annexes (listed)
Distribution

Author's Note: The U.S. Naval Observatory website, http://aa.usno.navy.mil/data/docs/RS_OneDay.html, is an ideal place to obtain specific information about the phases of the moon, sunrise, and sunset for the purpose of preparing an accurate weather report to be featured as an Annex to a Field Order.

BULLET POINT: THE QUICK AND THE DEAD

The Aid Station and the Battalion Medical Section

Hey, somebody call for a medic! During the course of tactical battle recreations, some reenactors will assuredly become casualties. The following article will briefly explain what steps may be taken to evacuate casualties from the battle area to an *aid station* of the *battalion medical section*, and how to move fresh replacements to the front. This process is easy, systematic, and can be accomplished quickly. The idea of actively reenacting the duties of combat medics will make the reenactment more realistic for everyone.

1. First, let us discuss the organization of the battalion's organic medical section. Although composition varies from unit to unit, the basic medical section is composed of about thirty-two officers and men, with three men being ambulance drivers, nine men being company aidmen, and twenty others who, when divided, compose three separate aid stations. One of the three drivers is assigned to each aid station and three aidmen are attached to each rifle company in the battalion. The company aidmen are the first medical personnel to reach a man wounded in battle.

2. For the purposes of reenactment, the process starts when a soldier becomes a casualty. He may take a *hit* voluntarily if he is so obviously exposed to enemy fire that escaping his attacker would be impossible, or, failing to become a casualty voluntarily, he may be designated as hit by a ranking superior or *umpire* and become a casualty. The wounded man will stop firing (*he may not continue to fire once wounded*), fall to the ground, and call for the medic.

3. When the medic arrives, he will retrieve the *Emergency Medical Tag* that the wounded man carries in his first aid pouch (*for this to work every reenactor will be issued a sealed tag upon registration check-in*). When the tag is opened, it will describe the location and the severity of the wound. The medic may dress the wound (*with a reproduction field dressing*), and then, after noting the time on the tag (*this may be discussed at a medic's briefing prior to the start of the tactical*), tie it prominently to the casualty. The medic will then make arrangements to evacuate the man to the aid station.

4. Whether the man is a *walking casualty* or a *stretcher case* depends on the severity of his wounds. On the tag, *LWA-GSW* means *lightly wounded in action – gunshot wound*. All those with light wounds, regardless of their location, will be designated walking casualties. The medic will give the man directions to the aid station, located some 200-500 yards behind the front lines, and send him off.

5. If the Emergency Medical Tag indicates a serious wound has been inflicted, *SWA (seriously wounded in action)*, the casualty will be treated as a stretcher case. The company aidman will dress the fallen man's wound and tag him as he would a walking casualty, but the evacuation of the casualty will be handled differently. NOTE: A seriously wounded man may not walk to the aid station, he must be carried by stretcher or some other means.

6. The medic will notify the company HQ of the seriously wounded man. By radio-telephone, field phone, or messenger, the company HQ will notify the aid station to dispatch *stretcher bearers* and inform the aid station of the location and status of the casualty so as to expedite his evacuation to the aid station. If there are many casualties, the stretcher bearers may require the assistance of additional personnel to effect the evacuation (*at the discretion of the company commander*).

7. Once the wounded man reaches the aid station, the *medical section sergeant* will remove and complete the Emergency Medical Tag while the casualty waits. The wounded man may be required to assist the section sergeant by answering some questions or, perhaps, by providing his *registration documents*.

8. While the casualty receives, perhaps, an infusion in the form of a *cold drink* instead of a plasma transfusion, the tag is turned over to the *battalion surgeon* who checks the accuracy of the information, and completes and signs the bottom of the tag. The tag is maintained in the official event records by the section sergeant to be turned over to the event staff.

Aidman Private First Class Podolinski rushes to the side of Sergeant Field, felled in the fighting around a Norman hamlet sometime after D-Day. Podolinski is one of three Aidmen assigned to E Company, 508th Parachute Infantry Regiment from 2/508th's Battalion Medical Section.

Having been tagged, their wounds noted, two walking casualties are helped from the field. The Emergency Medical Tags listed the severity and location of any wounds, the soldier's name and unit, and most importantly any medications (morphine) that may have been dosed in the field.

Not having the strength to move to the rear under his own power, Sergeant Field is borne from the field to the aid station on a litter by Aidman Podolinski and three of his comrades.

9. The section sergeant issues the wounded man a new, sealed Emergency Medical Tag and with that, the former casualty becomes a new *replacement*. If the S-2 doesn't grab him first to glean fresh information about the enemy, he, the new replacement, will be informed of the general location of his company's CP, and he is free to return to his company (*stragglers will be compelled to do so by the MPs and officers*). The *company first sergeant* may check in at the aid station from time-to-time to gather replacements and return them to their units as well.

10. Upon checking in at the company CP, the replacement will be returned to his former platoon, where, in turn, he will be restored to his former squad where, if not more careful, he may again become a casualty!

11. The whole process will have taken place in little more time than it took you to read this. The effect on the tactical reenactment will be very positive. The overall atmosphere will be greatly enhanced and cooperation between reenactors will be promoted. To further benefit the poor, dumb bastards who were careless enough to get themselves shot, their tags may be placed in a prize pool!

12. The distribution of light, serious, and mortal wounds (*designated: DOW, meaning "died of wounds"*), as well as *KIA*s will be based on the historical evidence at hand. 67% of all wounds in various locations will be classified as light; 3% as serious; 2% mortal; and 28% as killed in action.

13. *DOW* cases and *KIA*s will be evacuated just as the seriously wounded are, except they will be treated as second and third priority, respectively, by aid station personnel and stretcher bearers. If a commanding officer feels that the administering of first aid to, or the evacuation of, any casualty is taking too long, he may undertake to do so himself. However, this is discouraged.

Tag 1

NAME AND ARMY SERIAL NUMBER

DOE, JOHN S. O-132346

GRADE	COMPANY	REGIMENT AND ARM OF SERVICE
CAPT.	E	508TH PIR

DIVISION	CORPS	ARMY	AGE	RACE	NATIV-ITY	SERVICE, YEARS
82D	18TH	9TH	27	W	U.S.	2

STATION WHERE TAGGED:		DATE	HOUR

DIOGNOSIS: IF INJURY, STATE HOW, WHEN, WHERE INCURRED

L W A - G S W

ARM, LEFT

LINE OF DUTY

TREATMENT:

DRESSING AND

SULFADIAZINE 4.0 GM.

ANTITETANIC SERUM: DOSE   TIME

MORPHINE: DOSE 1/2 GR.   TIME

DISPOSITION:	DATE	HOUR

SIGNATURE, WITH RANK AND ORGANIZATION:

Form 52 b - MEDICAL DEPARTMENT, U. S. A.
(Revised October 25, 1940)
16-15434

Tag 2

NAME AND ARMY SERIAL NUMBER

PARKER, WILLIAM A. 23465525

GRADE	COMPANY	REGIMENT AND ARM OF SERVICE
S/SGT	A	504TH PIR

DIVISION	CORPS	ARMY	AGE	RACE	NATIV-ITY	SERVICE, YEARS
82D	18TH	9TH	21	W	U.S.	3

STATION WHERE TAGGED:		DATE	HOUR

DIOGNOSIS: IF INJURY, STATE HOW, WHEN, WHERE INCURRED

S W A - G S W

LEG, RIGHT

LINE OF DUTY

TREATMENT:

DRESSING AND

SULFADIAZINE 4.0 GM.

ANTITETANIC SERUM: DOSE   TIME

MORPHINE: DOSE 1/2 GR.   TIME

DISPOSITION:	DATE	HOUR

SIGNATURE, WITH RANK AND ORGANIZATION:

Form 52 b - MEDICAL DEPARTMENT, U. S. A.
(Revised October 25, 1940)
16-15434

Tag 3

NAME AND ARMY SERIAL NUMBER

SMITH, JOE A. 3025512

GRADE	COMPANY	REGIMENT AND ARM OF SERVICE
PFC	ITEM	505TH PIR

DIVISION	CORPS	ARMY	AGE	RACE	NATIV-ITY	SERVICE, YEARS
82D	18TH	9TH	20	W	U.S.	3

STATION WHERE TAGGED:		DATE	HOUR

DIOGNOSIS: IF INJURY, STATE HOW, WHEN, WHERE INCURRED

D O W - G S W

HEAD

LINE OF DUTY

TREATMENT:

DRESSING AND

SULFADIAZINE 4.0 GM.

ANTITETANIC SERUM: DOSE   TIME

MORPHINE: DOSE 1/2 GR.   TIME

DISPOSITION:	DATE	HOUR

SIGNATURE, WITH RANK AND ORGANIZATION:

Form 52 b - MEDICAL DEPARTMENT, U. S. A.
(Revised October 25, 1940)
16-15434

PART II: COMBAT TACTICS AND TECHNIQUES

"We're Digging In!" Individual Protection.[27]

General. Individual protection will be sought and improved, or excavated whenever troops are halted in a combat zone.

Halts. *a.* When the halt is expected to be brief, troops will take advantage of such natural protection as is afforded by the terrain (for example, ditches or holes in the ground).

b. When the halt is to be for a longer period but less than 6 hours (for example, a halt in an assembly area), individual prone shelters will be constructed. (See fig. 30.) Full advantage will be taken of natural cover and concealment in the construction of these shelters. This type of shelter does not provide as effective protection as the standing type one-man foxhole (see fig. 31-1, 31-2, 31-3), but it permits the man to receive rest and protection simultaneously and can be quickly dug. It furnishes protection from bomb and artillery fragments and small-arms fire but does not furnish full protection against the crushing action of tanks.

c. When the duration of the halt may be more than 6 hours, standing type foxholes will be dug. Men occupy these foxholes only when an attack is in progress or imminent.

During Combat. Under conditions which make it probable that firing from shelters will be required, and when time permits, protection for personnel and weapons will be provided. Suitable types of such protection are indicated below:

a. For individuals. – (1) Standing type one-man foxholes as shown in figure 31-1, 31-2, and 31-3.

(2) Standing type double foxholes or slit trenches as shown in figure 32. This type affords slightly less protection than the one-man foxhole against bomb or shell fragments, but is equally effective against small-arms fire. It furnishes much less protection against the crushing action of tanks. It is more conspicuous to air observers than the one-man type. It tends to increase the combat effect of the troops by providing fighting comradeship. This type is particularly suitable for occupancy by an automatic rifleman and his assistance or for other missions requiring men to act in pairs.

b. *For light machine guns.* – (1) Three standing type one-man foxholes for members of the crew, arranged generally as indicated in figure 33-1 and 33-2. This type permits operation of the weapon and affords the protection of the one-man type foxhole.

(2) An open standing emplacement, constructed approximately as indicated in figure 34. This type furnishes protection against small-arms fire and bomb shell fragments, but affords less protection against the crushing action of tanks, which may destroy the gun platform. If this type is used, crew members should construct one-man type standing foxholes nearby.

c. For 60-mm mortar. – (1) Standing type one-man foxhole for each member of the crew, arranged approximately as shown in figure 35.

(2) A single emplacement for mortar and crew as shown in figure 36-1 and 36-2. It is used to protect against bomb or shell (mortar and artillery) fragments as well as small arms fire. However, it should be supplemented by nearby standing type foxholes for use of the crew in case of a tank attack. The observer's position should be close enough to the mortar to permit him to communicate with the crew by voice. The emplacement is a pit approximately 4 feet wide at ground level, 5 feet long, and 3 1/2 feet deep. The emplacement must be large enough to receive the mortar, the gunner, and his assistant. Also, it must allow room for manipulation of the mortar, provide space for ammunition, and be sufficiently sloped on the forward edge to avoid interference with the sighting and firing. Under favorable conditions, one man using engineer tools can dig this emplacement in medium soil in 4 hours.

Observations Posts. When a defensive position is to be occupied for some time, observation posts, listening posts, or sniper's nests may be developed from foxholes which are widened, deepened, reinforced, and covered with a removable camouflage top. (See figs. 37 and 38.)

Camouflage. Good camouflage matches the surrounding area. Too elaborate camouflage or poor camouflage only serves to attract attention to the fortified area.

Construction Required In Organizing A Rifle Squad Defense Area. Figure 39 shows a bird's-eye view of the disposition of an interior squad in foxholes covering the squad sector between lines 14 and 14a. Foxholes in the rear portion of the squad area are dug to provide all-around defense; they may be either the standing one-man or double type. (See figs. 31, and 32.) Letters enclosed in rectangles are abbreviations to indicate the members of the rifle squad:

Letter	Individual	Weapon
SS	Staff Sergeant, squad leader	M1 rifle
S	Sergeant, assistant squad leader	M1 rifle for antitank rifle grenades
MG	Machine gunner	M1919A4 machine gun, M1A1 carbine (backup weapon)
AMG	Assistant machine gunner	M1 rifle
AB	Ammunition bearer	M1 rifle
R	Rifleman	M1 rifle

OPPOSITE

TOP
Paratrooper of 1/501 uses a shortened version of the M1910 entrenching shovel to scoop out an individual prone shelter or "slit trench" in extremely rocky ground. A pick mattock wrests on the lip of the hole next to his helmet. Whenever troops are halted for any period of time, they will habitually seek cover and concealment, in natural depressions in the earth, or in ditches, etc. If time permits, they dig in. This to protect themselves from flat-trajectory small arms fire, and bomb and shell fragments.

BOTTOM
With dirt excavated from their double foxhole piled around the lip to form a parapet, two men gaze in the direction of the enemy. They dug the hole until they hit solid rock, and could go no further. Then they lined the bottom with straw poached from a local barn. Weapons and grenades are at the ready.

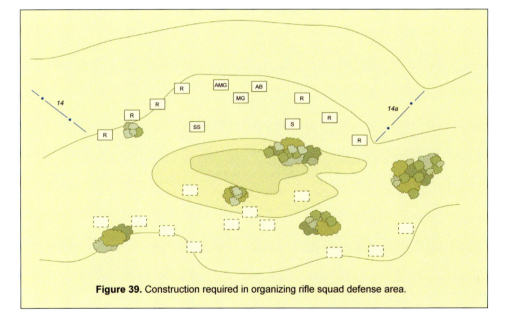

Figure 39. Construction required in organizing rifle squad defense area.

The voice of experience. *"Hasty fortifications, men do not dig foxholes or gun positions deep enough. When not under fire they should be digging. . . . Camouflaging positions should be stressed in training. Some men in shallow holes build their camouflage material too high above the line of the ground, giving the position away." "Defense: Suggest more training in the use of camouflage, the setting of automatic weapons, construction of obstacles and outposting of defensive line, stressing the necessity of changing location of outposts. An outpost known to the enemy has not much value in gaining surprise."*[28]

Figure 30. – Individual prone shelter or slit trench, oblique cross section.
Figure 31-1. – Top view. Standing type one-man foxhole.
Figure 31-2. – Side view. Standing type one-man foxhole.
Figure 31-3. – Rear view. Standing type one-man foxhole. Minimum 2-foot clearance required to protect against tank tracks.

Figure 32. – Standing type double foxhole or slit trench. (See fig. 37 for adaptation as an observation post.)

Note. – The individual prone shelter or slit trench for one man shown in figure 30 when deepened to 4 or 5 feet is large enough for two men and can be used as a standing fire trench. No slit trench should be used for more than two individuals.

Figure 33. – Light machine-gun emplacement with three standing type one-man foxholes. (Spoil thrown up in front of the emplacement provides some protection to the crew from small-arms fire.)

Figure 34. – Light machine-gun emplacement. (The gun platform is approximately 6 inches below ground level. Spoil is used to form a low parapet around the emplacement, or it is scattered; sod is used on top of the parapet.)

Figure 35. – Emplacement for 60-mm mortar with standing type one-man foxholes. (Standing type one-man foxhole for observer is also prepared. His location is within voice range of the mortar emplacement.)

Figure 36. – Emplacement for 60-mm mortar.

Note. – Pit must be long enough to give room for gunner, mortar, and assistant gunner. It must be deep enough to give cover to all three below ground level.

Figure 37. – Observation post in standing type double foxhole

Figure 38. – Observation post utilizing two standing double type one-man foxholes, each with camouflaged removable top.

Occupation and Organization of Firing Positions. *a. Arrival at position.* – Upon arrival at the firing position each light machine gun and mortar is mounted, concealed, and camouflaged in an emergency firing position prepared to open fire at once and to cover its assigned sector of fire.

b. Light machine-gun section. – (1) Work is begun on primary emplacements, clearing fields of fire, and distributing ammunition to the firing positions. The two guns should be placed at least 30 yards apart … When the necessary clearing for the primary position is completed, similar work is commenced on alternate emplacements. Supplementary emplacements are next in priority.

(2) Natural cover, drainage lines, ditches, and other defilade are used for communication and movement to alternate and supplementary positions. Dummy positions are coordinated with those of the rifle units located in the area.

(3) Range cards are prepared by squad leaders for each firing position. Preparations are made to lay the guns and fire on final protective lines both from primary and alternate firing positions …

c. 60-mm mortar section. – (1) As soon as the mortars are mounted in temporary positions, the actual positions are constructed, camouflaged and stocked with ammunition; and the mortars are mounted in these positions. (See figs. 35 and 36.) The primary mortar position and the observation post are first constructed and then shelter for the ammunition bearers. Alternate positions are constructed in a similar manner. The alternate position should be sufficiently far from the primary position to be out of the zone of fire directed at the primary position (usually about 50-100 yards) and have a covered route of movement to it. Supplementary positions are also prepared as necessary …

d. Camouflage. – Camouflage is executed concurrently with the construction of the defensive works. Spoil not used in parapets is disposed of as soon as dug. Parapets are tramped down and sodded as fast as they are finished. The making of new paths ending at installations is avoided.[29]

Challenge, password and reply. a. The challenge, password and reply must be known by a patrol prior to its departure. It must also know of any additional checks to guarantee identification that will be in use when teh patrol returns.

b. A distinctive recognition sign and a reply must be devised for use among patrol members. Natural sounds such as bird calls, may be used when necessary for night patrolling.[30]

Field Fortifications

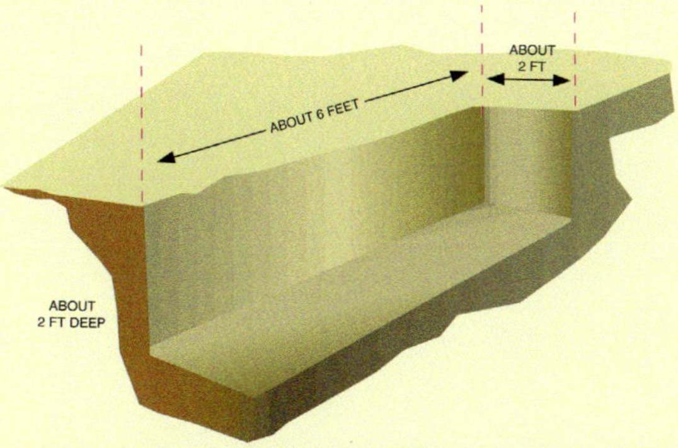

Figure 31. Standing type one-man foxhole.

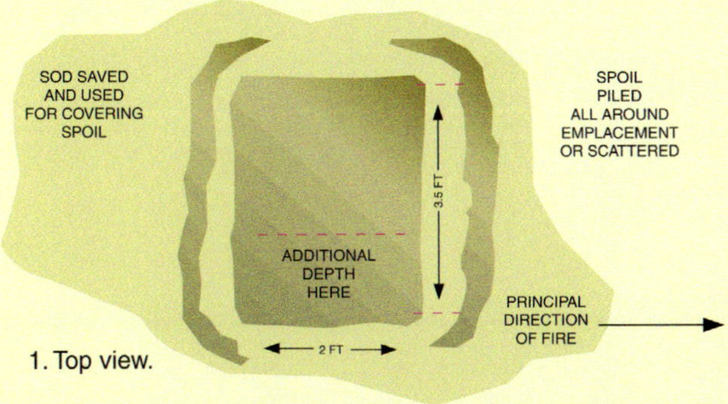

SOD SAVED
AND USED
FOR COVERING
SPOIL

SPOIL
PILED
ALL AROUND
EMPLACEMENT
OR SCATTERED

3.5 FT

ADDITIONAL
DEPTH
HERE

2 FT

PRINCIPAL
DIRECTION
OF FIRE

1. Top view.

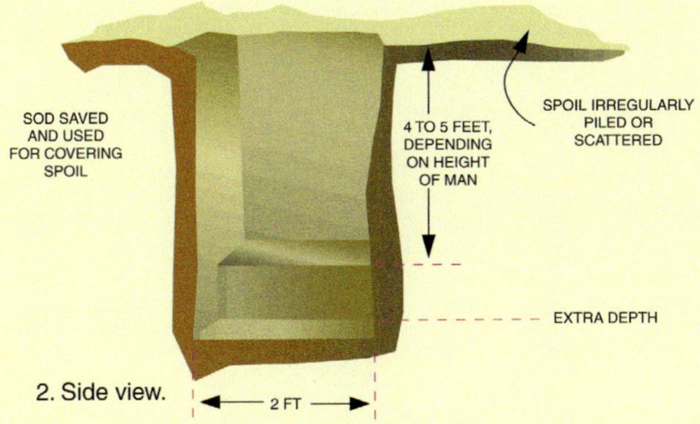

SOD SAVED
AND USED
FOR COVERING
SPOIL

4 TO 5 FEET,
DEPENDING
ON HEIGHT
OF MAN

SPOIL IRREGULARLY
PILED OR
SCATTERED

EXTRA DEPTH

2. Side view.

2 FT

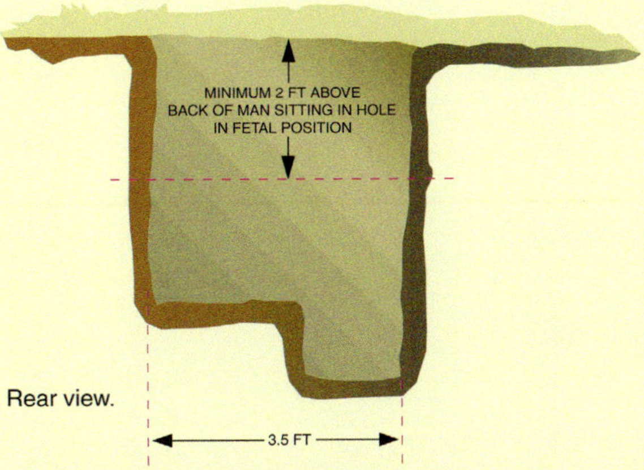

MINIMUM 2 FT ABOVE
BACK OF MAN SITTING IN HOLE
IN FETAL POSITION

3. Rear view.

3.5 FT

Minimum 2-foot clearnace required
to protect against tank tracks.

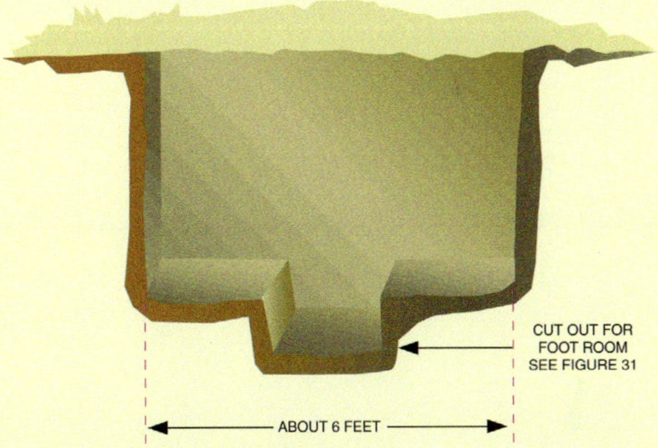

ABOUT
2 FT

ABOUT 6 FEET

ABOUT
2 FT DEEP

Figure 30. Individual prone shelter or slit trench,
oblique cross section.

CUT OUT FOR
FOOT ROOM
SEE FIGURE 31

ABOUT 6 FEET

Figure 32. Standing type double foxhole.
(See fig. 37 for adaptation as an observation post.)

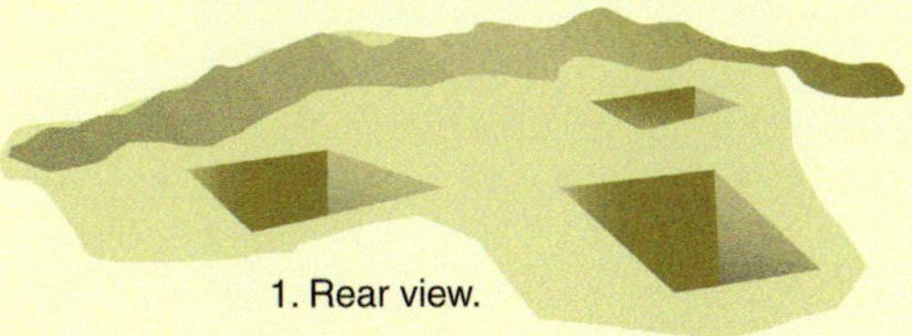

1. Rear view.

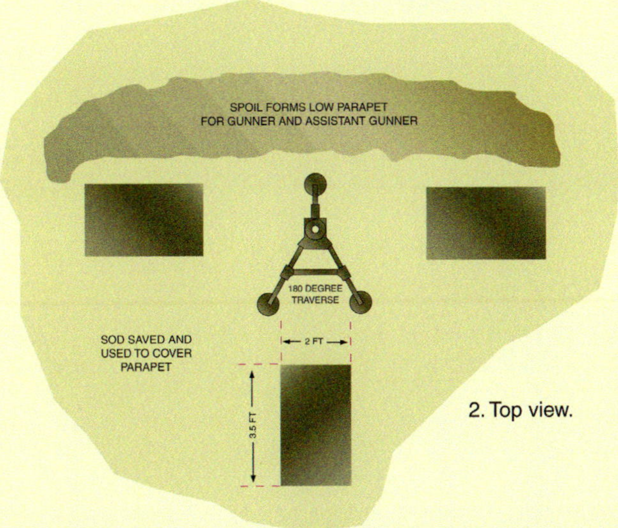

SPOIL FORMS LOW PARAPET
FOR GUNNER AND ASSISTANT GUNNER

180 DEGREE
TRAVERSE

SOD SAVED AND
USED TO COVER
PARAPET

2 FT

3.5 FT

2. Top view.

Figure 33. Light machine gun emplacement with three standing
type one-man foxholes. (Spoil thrown up in front of the emplacement
provides some protection to the crew from small-arms fire.)

Figure 34. Light machine gun emplacement. (The gun platform is approximately 6 inches below ground level. Spoil is used to form a low parapet around the emplacement, or it is scattered; sod is used on top of the parapet.)

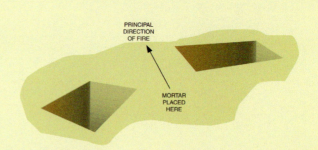

PRINCIPAL DIRECTION OF FIRE

MORTAR PLACED HERE

Figure 35. Emplacement for 60-mm mortar with standing type one-man foxholes. (Standing type one-man foxhole for observer is also prepared. His location within voice range of the mortar emplacement.)

Figure 37. Observation post in standing type double foxhole.

Figure 36. Standing type one-man foxhole.

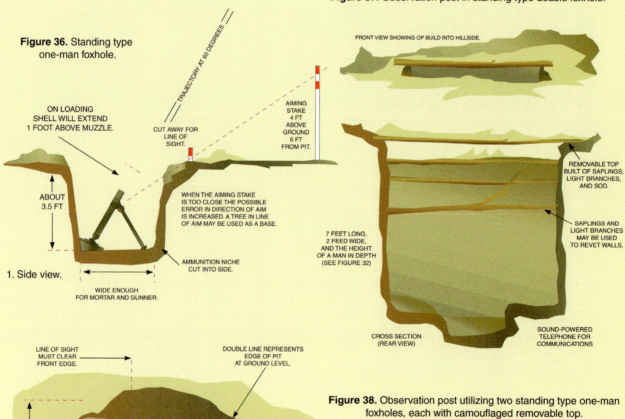

TRAJECTORY AT 60 DEGREES

ON LOADING SHELL WILL EXTEND 1 FOOT ABOVE MUZZLE.

CUT AWAY FOR LINE OF SIGHT.

AIMING STAKE 4 FT ABOVE GROUND 6 FT FROM PIT.

ABOUT 3.5 FT

WHEN THE AIMING STAKE IS TOO CLOSE THE POSSIBLE ERROR IN DIRECTION OF AIM IS INCREASED. A TREE IN LINE OF AIM MAY BE USED AS A BASE.

AMMUNITION NICHE CUT INTO SIDE.

1. Side view.

WIDE ENOUGH FOR MORTAR AND GUNNER.

FRONT VIEW SHOWING OP BUILD INTO HILLSIDE.

REMOVABLE TOP BUILT OF SAPLINGS, LIGHT BRANCHES, AND SOD.

SAPLINGS AND LIGHT BRANCHES MAY BE USED TO REVET WALLS.

7 FEET LONG, 2 FEED WIDE, AND THE HEIGHT OF A MAN IN DEPTH (SEE FIGURE 32)

CROSS SECTION (REAR VIEW)

SOUND-POWERED TELEPHONE FOR COMMUNICATIONS

LINE OF SIGHT MUST CLEAR FRONT EDGE.

DOUBLE LINE REPRESENTS EDGE OF PIT AT GROUND LEVEL.

AMMUNITION NICHE

ABOUT 4 FEET

ABOUT 5 FEET

THE GUNNER   MORTAR   ASS'T GUNNER

2. Top view.

Figure 38. Observation post utilizing two standing type one-man foxholes, each with camouflaged removable top.

SEVERAL YARDS APART BUT CLOSE ENOUGH FOR EASY COMMUNICATION BY VOICE

TANK ATTACK LIKELY

Memorandum: Woods Fighting

Platoon in the attack. The purpose of this section is to acquaint all unit commanders with specific tactics and techniques, developed from actual battle experience, that will greatly improve the overall combat efficiency of their commands, as well as Command and Control, evacuation of casualties and prisoners, lines of communications, re-supply and the integration of infantry, armor, and engineers, in the total combined arms effort.

Specific tactics employed by the enemy in woods fighting will be discussed. Overcoming enemy fortifications as well as obstacles, both natural and manmade, will also be covered.

When the order for the attack is made, the Platoon Commander places connecting groups on his flanks to stay in contact with adjacent units and protect the platoon's flanks.

When the order to attack is given, the assault echelon crosses the line of departure protected by a base of fire from the remainder of the platoon. The attack is made as either a single envelopment or a frontal assault. The assault echelon closes by fire and movement and pushes through the objective. The Platoon Leader presses the attack without pause.

Once the objective is secured, a pursuit by fire is made and all men dig-in in preparation for an enemy counter-attack. The Platoon Leader makes a reconnaissance of the area ahead to scout a route for the advancement of the attack. Ammunition is redistributed. Wounded are sent to the rear.

U.S. Combat Formations. The concentration of strong force on a narrow front is seen as the most effective way of achieving success in woods fighting. Advancing on the enemy, the frontage to be covered by the battalion is roughly 600 yards, the company, 300 yards, platoons, roughly 150 yards, and the squad, 75 yards.

A Tommy-gunner prepares to blast away at enemy soldiers rushing at them through the dense summer foliage. The thick-stone-walled dwellings of the Norman countryside and villages made perfect fortresses against all manner of small arms fire, but it is doubtful that the bricks behind which these two paratroopers are ensconced will stand up for long under and an intense battering of enemy bullets, particularly those of the armor piercing variety that will puncture these bricks with ease.

OPPOSITE

TOP
Looking down the muzzle of an M1919A6 light machine gun wielded by Sergeant Field and 'Trooper Polaszewski.

BOTTOM
The .30 light machine gun was the mainstay of parachute rifle squad firepower. The gun was operated by the machine gunner and the assistant machine gunner and an ammunition bearer. In a pinch, the belts of .30 caliber ammunition could be broken down, and the rounds could be used for the M1 rifle or BAR.

Across the company front, two rifle platoons will be deployed forward with the third rifle platoon deployed immediately to their rear along with the company weapons platoon, under the direct control of the company commander. Forward deployed platoons, constituting the *assault element*, will place two rifle squads forward on the platoon front, each in a *skirmish line* formation and covering 75 yards of the battalion's front. The third rifle squad will be deployed to the immediate rear of the forward squads under the direct control of the platoon commander.

The Assault Element (U.S.). Within the squads that are the "Assault Element," all riflemen act as "scouts." Squad leaders will maintain control of their squads from the center of the formation and maintain the direction of the advance with the aid of a compass. Hand signals should be determined in advance and used to direct the movement of the forward elements. Additionally, to promote further control of the squad, and to decrease the sense of isolation created by woods fighting, squad leaders will call out their soldiers by name and each soldier is to respond. Although this conflicts with the usual policy of exclusively using hand signals in communications, the positive benefit to the morale of the squad overrides any detracting consequences.

Another technique proven to be effective in woods fighting is laying phone wire from the CP by the "Assault Element" as they advance. The wire clearly marks lanes for messengers, resupply teams, and company aidmen and stretcher bearers, expediting their work. Marking the wire at regular intervals (100 yards), is an effective way of determining the progress of the advance.

Security Measures. Squads, in "column" formation, will be deployed by the company commander to protect the flanks of the company during the advance. At night, a reinforced platoon may occupy the forward position while the rest of the company withdraws 400-500 yards to the rear to return just before dawn. This will allow the majority of the company to avoid any evening artillery barrage. And because of the limitations imposed on movement and communications by the forest, night patrols will be effectively abandoned.

Employment of Friendly Armor. When woods fighting, great care should be taken to ensure that armor is deployed effectively. German antitank obstacles are constructed between their MLR and artillery positions and incorporate positions for antitank weapons and machine guns. Germans will usually deploy antitank guns in groups of three, firing enfilade at ranges of 150 to 300 yards supported by various antitank teams. To avoid unnecessary loss of armored vehicles, engineers and infantry must work with armor to successfully overcome these defenses.

All armor must be held from advancing through wooded areas until the infantry have both cleared the woods and secured the flanks to prevent enemy antitank teams from closing in range. Engineers should be prepared to clear any obstacles, such as mines or ditches, and to fight as infantrymen if the situation so determines. Armor may be used to sweep around the enemy's wooded positions to attack from the rear if the terrain offers.

Summary. The above information has been presented to assist company and platoon commanders in overcoming the hazards of woods fighting. As suggested, the concentration and cooperation of all available forces on a narrow front, and the effective and thoughtful use of armor, will offer the greatest opportunity to destroy enemy forces and obstacles encountered.

German Tactics and "Woods Fighting" Techniques. When attacking in forested terrain, German doctrine stresses constant reconnaissance, patrols moving clockwise from their starting positions, to discover the most weakly defended points of our lines. When the Germans advance, they usually do so in a "Wedge" formation, abandoning roads and moving cross-country to effect surprise. When Germans make contact with our forces, they creep forward to close combat range and attempt to storm our positions using grenades, pole charges, etc. Once a breakthrough is achieved, the "Wedge" widens the penetration on both shoulders. The company commander decides to continue the advance or hold for further reinforcements before continuing.

Hastily setup at the base of a small hill, a M1919A4 light machine gun team goes into action spraying enemy positions to shield the advance of the attacking elements as they move toward the crest. The officer at right watches where the tracers are falling and gives orders to adjust the fire as needed.

One observer is detailed per platoon who, armed with an automatic weapon, seeks to eliminate tree top snipers.

When Germans leave a woods to advance across open ground, or to cross a clearing in the woods, all men leave cover simultaneously, advancing at least 100 yards before attempting cover.

On the defensive, German troops will occupy defensive positions in depth. Outpost positions will be the first encountered by advancing Allied forces. Across a German company front of some 600 yards, one platoon will detached for outpost duty. The outpost position is usually some 2000 yards in front of their *main line of resistance* (MLR), and is used to launch small, prepared attacks with limited objectives to harry their enemies attack plans. Outposts are especially active at dusk and dawn as are advanced listening posts.

The Outpost will be located on the edge of woods or hill and take full advantage of fields of fire and camouflage.

The MLR is a series of individual strong points constructed for all around defense that are surrounded by wire and mine belts, contain various support weapons, and that are mutually supportive. Squad strong points are incorporated into platoon, and platoon into company. The entire MLR is usually placed on the enemy side of streams, that are used as tank obstacles, and on reverse slopes.

Again, thorough camouflage is stressed as well as the construction of several alternate positions for support weapons. Earth from the excavation of trenches is piled higher to the rear of their position than in front to avoid silhouetting riflemen. Dugouts are constructed for riflemen and are usually covered with logs and earth. Whenever a position is lost, it is subjected to an immediate counter attack before attackers can consolidate their gains.

Platoon in Defense. The *outpost* or *detached post* is established to protect stream crossings, crossroads, and other valuable terrain features. The platoon digs in for all around defense, and posts observers to cover approaches. The platoon also establishes road blocks within small arms range (200-400 yards) of the outpost and keeps them under constant observation. If a road or road block is mined, a guard is placed at this area to prevent damage to friendly vehicles. Terrain should be utilized to provide protection from mechanized attack. Patrolling, for platoon security, will be undertaken using half-squads.

Summary. The successful accomplishment of military assignments require that individuals, and small units, do their jobs quickly and efficiently, ignoring peripheral distractions. One veteran 17th Airborne Division mortarman said that he had to learn how to tune out all distractions around him and focus on leveling the 60mm mortar to which he was assigned. "It was useless [the gun]," he said, unless it was leveled. So, regardless of what was going on around him, he had to focus on doing his job so that he could support the team. The most important job that each reenactor has is to obey the orders of his squad leader or platoon leader. This will help the team and ultimately make the reenactment smoother and, all things being equal, more fun.

Reciting quotes from the manual might be enlightening and interesting but in these few pages it is impossible to cover all the little details. The major points about which the reader should have some understanding after a glance at this pamphlet are: the organization of the platoon, the basic function of its members, and the platoon organization's most rudimentary function in combat. Real combat wasn't found in the book and, just as in real combat common sense decisions for changing situations were more important than the book's doctrine, so too will this be found best in reenacting World War II combat.

The most important objectives that we should be 'attacking toward' are the further incorporation of all members into the group, the accurate portrayal of World War II paratroopers, and safely having fun. These rudimentary tactics, provided herein, are a base on which individuals and units may, in the future, build and practice more sophisticated tactics; but more importantly they provide the means to reach the above listed objectives.[31]

PART III: ADVANCED SUBJECTS

Basic Communications (messenger, wire, radio, and signal).

Get the message? Just as did far flung groups of American combat troops in the field during World War II, disparate groups of World War II reenactors engaged in tactical battle simulations must rely on numerous methods to effectively communicate. Modes of communication may be categorized as either visual or audible. Well known is the fact that while the U.S. Army of World War II fielded the best radio equipment of its day, this technology was, nevertheless, extremely unreliable in combat. When possible, radiotelephones may be used. Wire communication, especially in static positions, may also prove effective.

In the absence of the two former modes of signal communication, more often than not the job of conveying 'the word' will fall to company and platoon messengers carrying hand-written messages. Though we live in the age of cell phones, these, save in the case of emergencies, have no place in World War II reenactments. Finally, hand and arm signals may be used by infantry in the field, such as reconnaissance patrols stalking the enemy at close quarters, when other, less stealthy means of communication prove impractical. And the shrill blast of whistle signals may be heard over the den of small arms fire in order to warn the fighting unit against the approach of enemy armored vehicles.[32]

Within the reenacting company, personnel designated as first sergeant, communication sergeant, bugler, orderly, and messengers have duties pertaining to signal communication. For duties of personnel, see preceding section: *The Company Headquarters and the Platoon Members and Their Functions*. Messengers are assigned to company headquarters, and to each rifle platoon. The bugler is included in communication personnel because of his employment in the air-antitank warning system.

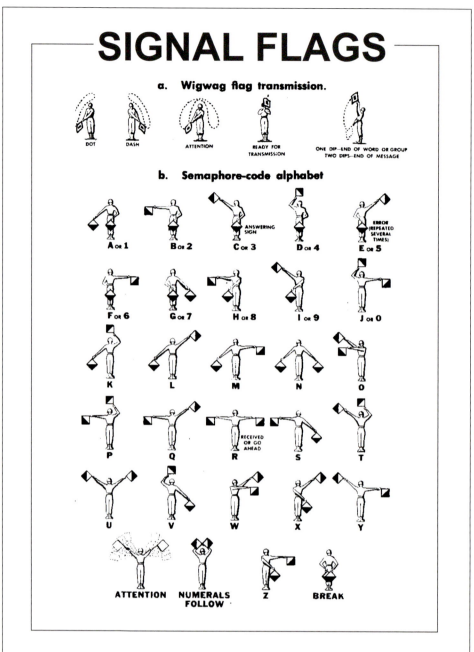

Lieutenant Soltis speaks into the handset of an EE-8 field telephone. Wire and Reel equipment was organic to the company-level organization, but the phones themselves were provided to the company by the parent battalion headquarters' communications section.

The following equipment, typically furnished to late World War II-era rifle companies, is recommended for communication purposes for reenactment:

(1) Wire – sets of reel equipment CE-11 (EE-8B battery-powered field telephone set).
(2) Ground signal projectors (and very pistols).
(3) Flag sets. (Orange-colored flags mounted on staffs.)
(4) Flashlights.
(5) Marking panels, black and white.
(6) Whistles.
(7) SCR536 Radio-telephone.
(8) SCR300 Radio-telephone.

For historically correct allotments of these items, individuals should refer to the Table of Basic Allowances and Tables of Organization which apply to the unit that is to be reenacted.

Early-war wire communication equipment is designated as reel equipment CE-11. One set of reel equipment CE-11 consists of one sound-powered telephone handset and one breast reel containing 1/2 mile of light wire. In order to establish communication between two points it is necessary to use two sets of reel equipment CE-11. As much wire as is needed, using either or both reels, is installed between the two points and a telephone handset is clipped on each end of the line. Thus two sets are required to provide one channel of communication over a maximum distance of 1/2 mile. A set of tool equipment TE-33 is a companion set for use with reel equipment CE-11. During 1944-1945, EE-8B battery-powered field telephone sets, which are employed in much the same way as sound-powered telephones, are also used. The electrically powered signal of the EE-8B sets allow for wire communication over greater distances, at the cost of greater weight.

Two basic types of wire are used for both the sound- and battery-powered sets: assault wire, and field wire. Assault wire is lightweight, double-strand wire, itself of two types: W130 (30lb/mile), and WD1/TT (48lb/mile). The talking range of assault wire is up to 5 and 14 miles respectively. Field wire, W110B and W143 (about 130lb/mile) has a talking range of from up to 20 and 27 miles respectively.[33]

Employment of Means of Signal Communications. Two field telephone sets may be employed to provide communication between:

(1) The company and battalion command posts, when directed by the battalion commander.
(2) The company command and observation posts.
(3) The company commander and –
    (a) A platoon leader.
    (b) The light machine gun section.
    (c) A close-in reconnaissance or security detachment.
    (d) The company transport (if available).
(4) Any two elements of the company

Messengers are used for communications within the company and with the headquarters of battalion and other units when a more rapid means is not available. One messenger is sent to the battalion command post by the company command post when the company takes up a deployed formation. These messengers should be relieved frequently by others in order that the messenger on duty may be familiar with the location of his unit. Messengers should be trained to take brief notes when receiving oral messages and to deliver them promptly and correctly. Ordinarily only one simple oral message should be given to a messenger at one time. The standard *Book, message, Signal Corps, M210A*, should also be used when available.

The principal means of visual signaling in the rifle company are arm-and-hand signals. These are employed as described in *FM 22-5, Infantry Drill Regulations, 4 August 1941* (see below).

Flashlights, flags, (and pyrotechnics) are used to send only the simplest kinds of prearranged messages. During World War II, pyrotechnics, fired by ground signal projectors and Very pistols, are used in accordance with the instructions of the battalion commander which in tern are based on signal operation instruction of higher headquarters. The principal use of pyrotechnic signals by front-line units (platoons or companies) is to call for prearranged supporting fires, to signal for these fires to cease or shift, or to signal arrival at a certain point. They are also valuable to give warning of enemy approach.

During World War II, marking panels, issued to rifle squads, are displayed by front-line units on signal from the infantry liaison airplane in order that the progress and location of leading infantry units may be reported to higher headquarters. Marking panels are most readily visible to aircraft when moved or waved during display. The white panels are normally used; the black panels are used when snow is on the ground.

This lieutenant gives a shrill blast on his thunderer whistle. Carried by every officer and NCO at or above the rank of sergeant, the whistle was used to fix the attention of their units preparatory to giving orders, or signals, and to warn against air, mechanized, or gas attacks.

Sound signals are employed primarily to give warning of hostile (air or) mechanized attack. They are also employed to give gas alarms. The whistle is used by leaders to fix the attention of their units preparatory to giving commands or signals.

Orders Relative to Signal Communication. Each field order issued by the company commander contains instructions for signal communication. Frequently such instructions consist only of the location of the commander or his command post. Other instructions relative to signal communication may be issued in fragmentary form and may include the use of pyrotechnic signals (in conformity with instructions of higher headquarters) or the allotment or use of any of the signal communication means available to the company.

Relation of Battalion Communication System (when applicable). In attack, communication between the battalion command post and the rifle companies is by messenger. When sufficient means are available the battalion commander may allot field telephone equipment or portable radio-telephones (SCR-536 or SCR-300) to front-line companies for communication with the battalion command post. These are to supplement the parachute rifle company's six organic SCR-536 "Handie-Talkie" radio sets, and its two backup SCR-536s.

In the defense whenever practicable telephone communication is established between the battalion command post and rifle companies.

When the rifle company or elements thereof are employed on distant security or reconnaissance missions (e. g., patrols, outposts, and flank detachments) light, portable radio-telephones are employed, when practicable, for communication between such detachment and the commander who sends it out. Radio equipment for units on these missions is, historically speaking, provided by the battalion communications section.

Signals. Signals are for the purpose of transmitting essential commands under conditions rendering verbal commands inadequate. Signals may be audible or visible as prescribed herein.

a. Subordinate commanders repeat signals or give appropriate orders to their units whenever necessary to insure prompt and correct execution.

b. Standard signal for use by ground troops to warn of mechanized danger. – The following signals will be used by observers in transmitting warning of the approach or presence of mechanized vehicles: Three long blasts of a whistle, repeated several times; or three equally spaced shots with a rifle or pistol; or three short bursts from a machine gun or submachine gun. In daylight, the individual giving the signal points in the direction of the impending danger; at night, the alarm signal will be supplemented by voice warning to indicate the direction of the danger.

Hand and arm signals. If a movement is to be executed by a particular subordinate unit or units of a command, a signal designating the unit or units will be given before the signal for movement.

Forward; To Right (Left); To Rear. – Face and move in the desired direction of march; at the same time extend the hand vertically to the full extent of the arm, palm to the front, and lower the arm and hand in the direction of movement until horizontal.

Down; or, Take Cover. – Turn toward the unit or group and raise the hand, palm down, in front of the elbow, forearm horizontal; thrust the hand downward and back to this position.

Double Time; or, Rush. – Carry the hand to the shoulder, fist closed; rapidly thrust the fist upward vertically to the full extent of the arm and back to the shoulder several times. This signal is also used to *increase* gate or speed.

Quick Time (Walk). – Raise the elbow to a position above and to the right (left) of the shoulder and extend the forearm to the left (right), hand above the head, palm to the front. This signal is also used to *decrease* gait or speed.

Change Direction. – Carry the hand that is on the side toward the new direction across the body to the opposite shoulder and, with the palm down and the forearm horizontal, swing the forearm in a horizontal plane, extending the arm and hand to point in the new direction.

Enemy in Sight. – Hold the rifle horizontally above the head with arm or arms extended as if guarding the head.

As Skirmishers. – Raise both arms laterally until horizontal, arms and hands extended, palms down. If it is necessary to indicate direction of march, signal *Forward* , moving at the same time in the desired direction.

As Skirmishers, Right (Left). – Raise both arms laterally until horizontal, arms and hands extended, palms down; swing the arm and hand on the side toward which the deployment is to be made, upward until vertical and back immediately to the horizontal position; repeat swinging movement several times; hold the other arm and hand steadily in the horizontal position until the signal is completed.

Assemble. – Raise the hand vertically to the full extent of the arm, fingers extended and joined, and describe large horizontal circles with the arm and hand.

Are You Ready? – Extend the arm toward the leader for whom the signal is intended, hand raised, fingers extended and joined, palm toward the leader.

I Am Ready. – Execute the signal *Are You Ready*.

Commence Firing. – Extend the arm and hand horizontally in front of the body to their full extent, palm of the hand down; move them several times through a wide horizontal arc.

Fire Faster. – Execute rapidly the signal *Commence Firing*. For machine guns, a change to the next higher rate of fire is required.

Fire Slower. – Execute slowly the signal *Commence Firing*. For machine guns, a change to the next lower rate of fire is required.

Cease Firing. – Raise the hand in front of the forehead, palm to the front, and swing it up and down several times in front of the face.

Sergeant Domitrovich (l), receives orders for a fire mission over his **SCR-536** radio-telephone. The "Handie-Talkie" was organic to the airborne rifle company, but was limited in its capability, having a range of little more than a mile under the best of conditions. "As usual the 536 wasn't any good when we needed it the most ..." Captain J.E. Adams, Jr., A/508.

Hand and Arm Signals
FM 22-5 Infantry Drill Regulations, 1941

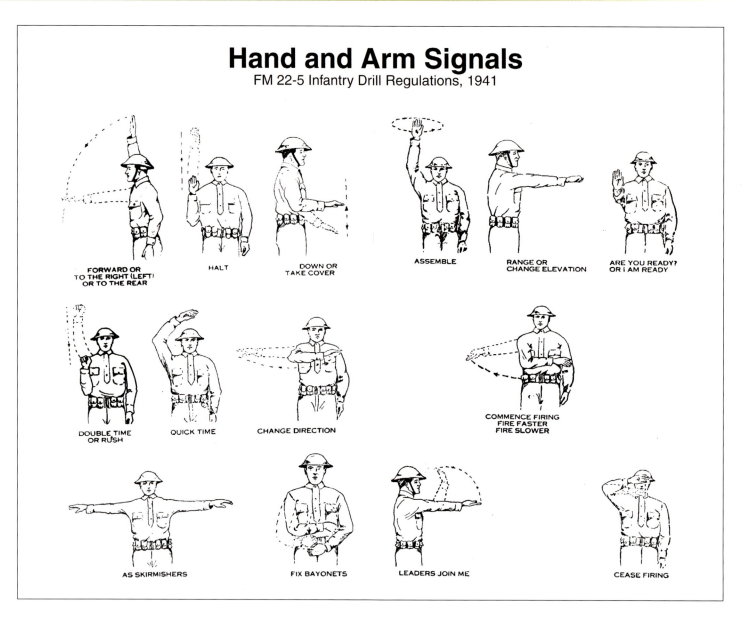

Fix Bayonets. – Simulate the movement of the right hand in fixing a bayonet on rifle.

Leaders Join Me. – Extend one arm toward the leaders and beckon the leaders to you.

Squad. – Extend one arm toward the squad leader, palm of the hand down; distinctly move the hand up and down several times, holding the arm steady.

Section. – Extend one arm toward the section leader, palm of the hand down and describe large vertical circles

Platoon. – Extend both arms toward the platoon leader, palm of the hands down and describe large vertical circles.

Wedge Formation. Raise both arms vertical overhead, palms inward and in contact with each other.

Author's note: Generally speaking, additional wartime hand and arm signals were prearranged between individuals and groups and were of the most basic type. In several of the more recent Hollywood movies, elaborate hand signals have been used as a means to increase the dramatic effect of certain combat scenes; again, proving the adage, "never let the truth get in the way of telling a good story."[34]

Platoon leader, Lieutenant Soltis, r, gives the hand and arm signal for "Are you ready?" to one of his squad leaders. FM 22-5 Infantry Drill Regulations proscribed the Army's basic hand and arm signals. Beyond these, patrols and other combat formations worked out simple signals on their own on an ad hoc basis.

Whistle signals. Whistle signals will be made with the whistle prescribed for the leader of commander concerned and will be confined to ATTENTION TO ORDERS, CEASE FIRING, and TANK WARNING.

Attention to Orders. – Sound a short blast of the whistle. The signal is used to fix the attention of troops, or of their commanders and leaders preparatory to giving commands, orders, or other signals.

Cease Firing. – Sound a long blast of the whistle. This signal will be verified at once by an arm and hand signal or by other means.

Tank Warning. – Three long blasts, repeated several times.[35]

Map Reading & Land Navigation

"Maps are a primary fighting instrument of the commander of any unit from an army to a squad." — Map and Aerial Photograph Reading: Complete.

Land navigation. During tactical recreations, just as during World War II, maps will play an important part in every operation. With his map in hand, a rifle company commander scrutinizes the area over which he and his men will soon be crossing on the way to their assigned objective. Placing an onion skin overlay over his map, the commander marks the positions of friendly troops units, as well as those enemy positions the Battalion Intelligence staff have been able to fix. From the map, the commander is also able to discern favorable terrain features that will aid his approach, and also some unfavorable features which may pose serious or even fatal obstacles to his advance. After settling upon the route his men will take to the objective, the commander marks his map. Then, he issues orders which describe in detail the movement he has plotted on his map to his subordinates.

Military grid coordinates. "Because of their military importance, such features as hills and road junctions are carefully identified on military maps, usually by numbers which not only identify them, but frequently indicate their elevation." The locations of other features, such as woods or buildings, for example, are usually expressed in *military grid coordinates*.

Normandy, France. In preparation for moving on their next objective, a company commander and his executive officer use a lensatic compass to orient their tactical map. The lensatic compass and its OD#7 water resistant pouch were issued to all officers and NCOs of the airborne rifle company at or above the rank of sergeant.

"Military grid coordinates is a system of evenly spaced, numbered vertical (north and south) and horizontal (east and west) lines printed on a map. The east-west lines, called the x coordinates, are numbered serially from west to east, and the north-south lines, called the y coordinates, are numbered serially from south to north … Grids are always read from *west* to *east* and from *south* to *north*, that is, from x to y."[36]

"American military grids are usually spaced 1,000 yards apart on maps of [1:25,000] scale … Any object on a grid square map may be indicated by giving the numbers of the two grid lines that form the beginning (west edge and south edge) of the square." A specific point within a grid square, may be expressed using fractions. When identifying any specific point on a map, always remember to measure its location from beginning of the square; in other words, right from the west edge, and then up from the south edge. An easy way to remember this rule is to memorize the expression: READ RIGHT UP. Always remember to "enclose coordinates in parenthesis and separate them by a dash."[37]

To make identifying specific points on your map easier, you should construct a simple grid card using "the corner of any card, envelope, paper, message blank or corner of the map itself. On two corners of the card, tick off 100-yard divisions corresponding with those represented by the maps graphic scale. It's that simple.[38]

Contour lines on maps. Form lines, or *contours* "represent the variations of the earth's surface caused by hills, ridges, and valley, and the like. The exact shape and condition of the ground has a great influence on all military operations. The map, therefore, must give the person who uses it a clear picture of the shape of the ground. Since the map is flat, special conventional signs are necessary to show these different shapes. A contour line represents an imaginary line on the ground. Every part of which is at the same height above sea level. If you walk along a contour line you neither go uphill nor downhill, but always stay on a level."[39]

Determining distance. The distance between two points on a map may be easily measured using the *graphic scale* printed on the map. The graphic scale is "a line divided into equal divisions, each division marked with the distance it represents on the ground." To measure the straight distance between two points on a map, line up the edge of a strip of paper along the two points and mark the points with *ticks*. Then, simply line up these ticks along the graphic scale to determine the ground distance. To measure an irregular line, merely divide "the irregular line into straight sections and" measure each. By adding these sections together, you'll get your total.[40]

Converting distance to march time. A map is a valuable tool for planning the amount of time required to move troop units from one point to another. When planning the movement of troop units using a map, it is useful to remember that foot soldiers typically march at a daytime road speed of 2 1/2 miles per hour. Bear in mind when planning your route of advance that when traversing more difficult terrain, such as forest or steep grades, the speed of marching troops may be substantially diminished. Over these types of terrain, the march speed may be reduced to as little as 1 1/2 miles per hour or less. Moreover, practically speaking, most reenactors are not as young or in the same physical condition as their historical counterparts, and a commander must take this in to account also. In any case, "the distance to be marched, divided by the rate of march, will give you the time required for the movement."[41]

Example: An infantry rifle company is ordered to march from their line of departure (point A) to a new assembly area (point B). The distance between point A and point B by road is measured and determined to be 1½ miles. Since the average road speed of infantry is 2½ miles per hour, the march time problem may be expressed as the following equation: 1.5 miles ÷ 2.5 mph = 0.6 hours (or about 36 minutes). Therefore, it will take about 36 minutes to march from point A to point B.

Azimuth. The terms "azimuth" and "direction" are interchangeable, save that azimuth is a statement of direction in degrees, as in degrees determined by a compass. When using a map, determining direction is just as important as determining distance. By using a

The liquid-filled wrist compass was issued to all men in the parachute rifle companies at or below the rank of corporal.

compass and a map, one should be able to determine the direction and distance to one's objective, and find one's own position on the map.

Scale. The scale of a map is usually shown in one of three ways. (1) It may be shown by a single or double line, divided into parts. Each part is marked with the distance which it represents on the ground and may be expressed in feet, yards or miles. (2) The scale may be stated in words or figures, as "3 inches = 1 mile." Therefore 3 inches on the map equals one mine on the ground. If the map is divided into grids, another way that scale could be measured could be "1 grid equals 1 kilometer." (3) The scale may be expressed as a "representative fraction" (called *RF*), which is merely a fraction in which the numerator (the number above the line) is a certain distance on the map, and the denominator (the number below the line) is the corresponding distance on the ground. Example 1/12,000 Scale, or 1:12,000 Scale.

Orientation by map inspection or compass. One's map is considered "oriented" when the north pointing arrow on the map points north on the ground. This makes all the lines on the map parallel to the corresponding lines on the ground. One's map should always be oriented whenever one uses it. If one does not have a compass with which to orient his map, he may still orient his map, by lining it up with two or more recognizable terrain features that he can also locate on the map. If one has a compass he needs only to find north, then turn the map so that the north-facing arrow on the map lines up with the north-facing needle of the compass.

One is said the be "oriented" when he can find his own position on the map. Suppose you have been proceeding on a mission over unfamiliar ground and you are not now sure of our location on the map. Orient your map. Select a feature of the terrain, such as a hill, and from that feature draw a line on the map toward yourself. Now do the same with reference to another terrain feature. The point where these lines cross or intersect will be your location on the map.[42]

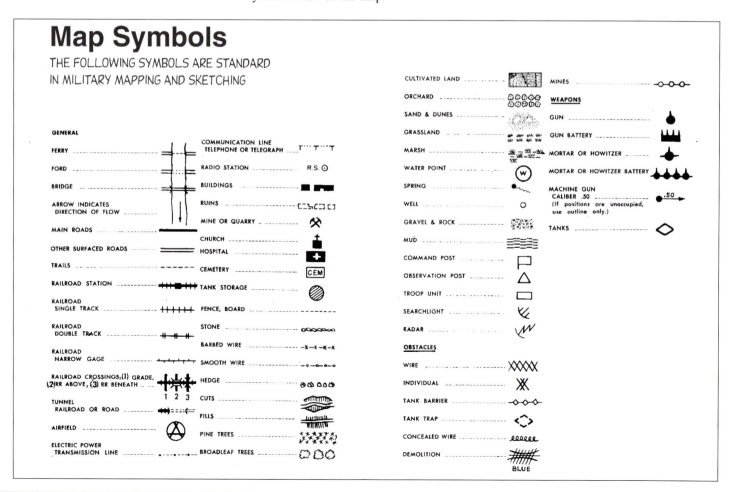

Color Coded

Battalion "colors" as expressed by tactical markings on the helmet.

Battalion and Company Designations for the Parachute Infantry Regiment

Regimental Headquarters - "Yellow"
Headquarters and Band
Headquarters Company
Service Company

1st Battalion - "Red"
Headquarters and Headquarters Company
"A" or Able Company
"B" or Baker Company
"C" or Charlie Company

2nd Battalion - "White"
Headquarters and Headquarters Company
"D" or Dog Company
"E" or Easy Company
"F" or Fox Company

3rd Battalion - "Blue"
Headquarters and Headquarters Company
"G" or George Company
"H" or How Company
"I" or Item Company

International Morse Code

A · —	N — ·	1 · — — — —
B — · · ·	O — — —	2 · · — — —
C — · — ·	P · — — ·	3 · · · — —
D — · ·	Q — — · —	4 · · · · —
E ·	R · — ·	5 · · · · ·
F · · — ·	S · · ·	6 — · · · ·
G — — ·	T —	7 — — · · ·
H · · · ·	U · · —	8 — — — · ·
I · ·	V · · · —	9 — — — — ·
J · — — —	W · — —	0 — — — — —
K — · —	X — · · —	
L · — · ·	Y — · — —	
M — —	Z — — · ·	

Symbols Describing Military Units

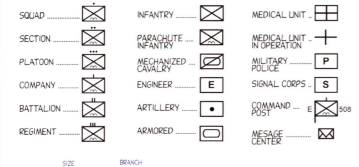

SQUAD	INFANTRY	MEDICAL UNIT
SECTION	PARACHUTE INFANTRY	MEDICAL UNIT IN OPERATION
PLATOON	MECHANIZED CAVALRY	MILITARY POLICE [P]
COMPANY	ENGINEER [E]	SIGNAL CORPS [S]
BATTALION	ARTILLERY [·]	COMMAND POST [E] 508
REGIMENT	ARMORED	MESAGE CENTER

SIZE   BRANCH

SMALLER UNIT
COMPANY
PLATOON
BATTERY
2D [ ] **506**
SUPERIOR UNIT
DIVISION
BRIGADE
REGIMENT
BATTALION

AREA OCCUPIED BY COMPANY E, 508TH PARACHUTE INFANTRY

2ND PLATOON, COMPANY D, 506TH PARACHUTE INFANTRY (RGT)

Phonetic Alphabet And Numerals

SPEAK ONLY THE WORD REPRESENTING THE LETTER, AS **LOVE**, **ZEBRA**. <u>DO NOT</u> SAY **L** AS IN LOVE, OR L FOR LOVE.

A - ABLE	N - NAN	1 - WUN
B - BAKER	O - OBOE	2 - TOO
C - CHARLIE	P - PETER	3 - THUH-REE
D - DOG	Q - QUEEN	4 - FO-WER
E - EASY	R - ROGER	5 - FI-YIV
F - FOX	S - SUGAR	6 - SIX
G - GEORGE	T - TARE	7 - SEVEN
H - HOW	U - UNCLE	8 - ATE
I - ITEM	V - VICTOR	9 - NINER
J - JIG	W - WILLIAM	0 - ZERO
K - KING	X - XRAY	
L - LOVE	Y - YOKE	
M - MIKE	Z - ZEBRA	

BULLET POINT: FIELD RATIONS

The "A-B-Cs" of U.S. Army Rations In World War II. By Army definition, a 'ration' is the allocation of food for an individual soldier for one day. During World War Two, the United States Army developed numerous and distinct types of rations. Seven of these, those most relevant to reenacting, are described below.

Quoted directly from The Officer's Guide, (The Military Service Publishing Company, Harrisburg, Pennsylvania, 1944), pp. 250-252.

Garrison Ration. The garrison ration is that prescribed in time of peace for all persons entitled to a ration, except under specific conditions for which other rations are prescribed, and consists of the following:

Meat: Bacon; fresh beef; fresh pork; fresh chicken.

Eggs.

Dry vegetables and cereals: Beans; rice; rolled oats.

Fresh and canned vegetables: Beans, string and canned; canned corn; onions, canned peas; potatoes; canned tomatoes.

Fruit: Canned apples; jam or preserves; canned peaches; canned pineapple; canned prunes.

Beverages: Coffee, roasted or roasted and ground; cocoa; tea.

Milk, evaporated and fresh.

Lard; or lard substitute.

Butter; wheat flour; baking powder; macaroni; cheese; sugar; cinnamon; flavoring extract; black pepper; cucumber pickles; salt; syrup; vinegar.

The garrison ration is issued in the form of a sash allowance. Each month the total value of the rations due an organization for that period is placed to its credit with the Quartermaster. The unit purchases selected articles of the ration in the amounts desired and obtains a settlement of its account at the end of the month. Any savings accrued are paid in cash. This is called ration savings and may be used to pay for food items only. This procedure is known as the ration savings privilege. It permits the serving of a wide variety of food.

Field Ration – "A". This ration corresponds a nearly as practicable to the components of the garrison ration. It includes fresh meat, fresh fruits and vegetables, and other items which are highly perishable. The approximate weight of this ration is five to six pounds. It is extremely bulky and difficult to handle because of the perishable items involved. This type of field ration is issued in the zone of the interior at fixed posts, camps and stations equipped with adequate refrigeration facilities to preserve the perishable components.

Field Ration – "B". This ration is similar to the "A" ration except that processed, canned, or other non-perishable products replace the perishable components of the "A" ration. Components of the "B" ration will not deteriorate quickly. The components of this ration will vary depending on the climatic conditions of the region in which they are to be used and the length of time they are to be stored. The weight of this ration is approximately five pounds. It is the standard combat zone ration and is used, normally, wherever organized cooking facilities are to be found.

Field Ration – "C". This individual combat ration consist of three cans of "M" unit and three cans of "B" unit.

"B" unit cans contain biscuits, confections, cigarettes, and a beverage. The meat components in the "M" units are more acceptable when heated but they may be consumed cold if the situation so warrants.

Unit commanders are well advised to insist upon heating this ration whenever possible. Otherwise many men tire of the ration and tend to develop nausea. Beverages may be prepared without difficulty in either hot or cold water. The lemon powder should be consumed each day as it is the most important source of Vitamin C in the ration.

DESCRIPTION OF THE "C" RATION. *Breakfast "B" Unit* : Biscuits; confection; sugar; coffee, soluble; cigarettes (3). *Dinner "B" Unit* : Biscuits; confection; sugar; lemon powder, syn.; cigarettes (3). *Supper "B"*

Sergeant Domitrovich and Lieutenant Soltis hoist canned field rations from the back of a regimental service company Peep. Note the reflective disk affixed to the back of the helmet wresting atop the ration case in the Peep. These disks were affixed to individual's clothing, helmets, and equipment bundles as a simple means of nighttime recognition.

Crowded on the front porch of a shell-shattered building, paratroopers pass around a variety of field rations, including C, K, and D. It was often the case that after subsisting on the emergency K-rations for long periods in combat, when soldiers were able to enjoy even C-rations, their stomachs would revolt.

Unit : Biscuits; confection; cocoa beverage. *"M" Units* (Any combination of three of these issued with each ration): Type I – Meat and beans, 12 oz.; Type II – Meat and vegetable hash, 12 oz.; Type III – Meat and vegetable stew, 12 oz.; Type IV – Ground meat and spaghetti, 12 oz.; Type I – English-style stew, 12 oz.

Field Ration – "**D**". The "D" ration is used by troops under emergency conditions when the supply of other rations fails. Sometimes it is issued as an addition to other rations, filling the purpose of ordinary candy. It consists of three four-ounce chocolate bars each wrapped in cellophane and overwrapped in a wax-dipped carton. These bars are made of chocolate, sugar, oat flour, cocoa fat, skim milk powder, artificial flavoring, and are fortified with thiamin hydrochloride (Vitamin B-1). The bars have a high melting point, approximately 120° F., a characteristic which tends to make them desirable as an extreme emergency ration for storage over long periods of time under extreme atmospheric conditions. It is anticipated that this product will be limited to two days use. Ration (three bars) contains 1800 calories.

Field Ration – "**K**". The "K" ration, like the "C" ration, is for the soldier on combat duty. It consists of three packages labeled "Breakfast Unit," "Dinner Unit," and "Supper Unit," and is issued to the individual soldier for consumption either heated or cold. It differs from the "C" ration in that it is lighter in weight and more compact because the majority of the components are packaged in materials other than tin. The soldier, therefore, can carry his food supply more easily.

DESCRIPTION OF THE "K" RATION. *Breakfast Unit* : K-1 biscuits; K-2 biscuits; meat and egg product; fruit bar; coffee product, soluble; sugar cubes (4 each); cigarettes (4 each); chewing gum (1 stick); key, can (1 each). *Dinner Unit* : K-1 biscuits; K-2 biscuits; cheese product; confection; lemon juice powder, syn.; sugar cubes (4 each); Chewing gum (1 stick); cigarettes (4 each); matches (1 book of 10); key, can (1 each). *Supper Unit* : K-1 biscuits; K-2 biscuits; meat product; chocolate bar (Field Ration D); bouillon powder; cigarettes (4 each); chewing gum (1 stick); tissue, toilet (12 sheets); key, can (1 each).

The "10-in-1" Ration. The "10-in-1" represents the solution to the problem of finding a well balanced, compactly packed, easily handled method of issuing rations. It is based on actual experience gained the present war and is being enthusiastically received throughout the Army. As its name implies, the "10-in-1" is ten rations packed in a single scientifically designed container. It may be issued to ration ten men for one day or five men for two days. Through an ingenious packing method, the contents are broken down into two units of five rations each.

Five different menus are available for issue and, through rotation of menus, it is possible for soldiers to subsist on this type of ration over long periods of time. The "10-in-1" is composed entirely of canned, evaporated, and dehydrated foods and it will keep indefinitely.

Preparation of meals from the "10-in-1" is relatively easy. By utilizing an abbreviated "K" ration unit (which can be carried in the soldier's pocket) for the noon meal, it is not necessary to light a fire to prepare this meal.

A TYPICAL "10-IN-1" MENU. *Breakfast* : Cereal; bacon and eggs; biscuits and jam; coffee and milk. *Dinner* : 1 "K" ration unit per man (abbreviated); 1 can "K" ration egg product per man. *Supper* : Corned beef hash; lima beans; biscuits and butter; chocolate bar; grape drink.

Note: Halazone tablets are included to purify water for drinking. Toilet paper, paper towels, all-purpose soap, individual can opener, cigarettes and matches are also included with each menu.

BULLET POINT: FORAGING

Living off the land is something in which soldiers throughout the ages have engaged. Some armies actually planned that foraging would be a means to supplement issued rations. In the context of reenacting it makes very compelling theater to encourage participants to bring their own 'foraged' food to events to prepare and imbibe either in bivouac or in the field. The setting of the event would dictate what would be reasonable. Necessary equipment might include a spare M1 helmet that had been scoured out to bare metal or, more useful still, a 'field requisitioned' cast iron skillet and cooking utensils.

What follows is a simplified, "one pot," regional European dish, with chicken as the featured ingredient, that soldiers may attempt. Chicken was chosen because of its universal nature and because it is relatively cheap. The additional ingredients for this dish were chosen with respect to both the geography of the campaign in which it is rooted, and the time of year in which that campaign occurred, thusly affecting which ingredients may be available. Making food taste appetizing in the field was more an art than a science. Those who had a knack for both scrounging up victuals, and for being able to make them palatable were lucky indeed.

Example: Norman-French Farmstead Fair for the Field: There are a good many reenactment events that center around the Invasion of Normandy and the subsequent campaign. There are a number of food stuffs that would be wonderful to incorporate into a 'foraged' meal to be prepared and served during such an event. Some staples of Norman-French countryside fair include apples, Calvados, cider, butter (*Beurre de Baratte*), cream, and cheeses including *Pont L'Éveque*, *Livarot*, and *Camembert*. The following is a recipe is a Norman classic.

Having pocketed it until a lull in the fighting, Corporal Dautrich chews an apple plucked from a Dutch orchard nearby Teufels Berg, Holland, 19 September 1944. The chevrons sewed to the sleeves of his M1943 field jacket are regulation khaki cotton embroidered on dark blue cotton.

Patrol of the 508th Parachute Infantry moves down a lane in Holland under a dense autumn canopy of foliage.

Volaille au Vinaigre de Cidre (Chicken with Cider Vinegar)

INGREDIENTS:
- 1 chicken cut into 8 serving pieces
- 4 Tablespoons clarified unsalted butter (may substitute 4 Tablespoons plain salted butter)
- 4 shallots, finely chopped (may substitute 1 onion)
- 1 cup cider vinegar
- 1 cup chicken stock (may substitute 1 cup water)
- 1 Tablespoon unsalted butter, cold and cut into pieces (may substitute 1 Tablespoon plain salted butter)
- salt and freshly ground black pepper

PREPARATION:
1. In a sauté pan, large enough to hold the chicken pieces in a single layer, heat the clarified butter.
2. Sprinkle the chicken with some salt. Working in batches, add the chicken to the pan, skin side down. Sauté until lightly browned on all sides, about 10 minutes.
3. Set the chicken pieces aside and add the shallots to the pan.
4. Sauté the shallots for a couple of minutes, then stir in the vinegar, scraping the bottom of the pan to loosen all the brown bits.
5. Simmer until the vinegar is reduced by half, then pour in the chicken stock and return the chicken to the pan.
6. Bring the liquid to a boil, cover the pan, reduce the heat to low and cook for 20 to 30 minutes, until it is tender.
7. Remove the chicken to a warm serving dish and simmer the cooking liquid until it coats a spoon.
8. Strain the liquid into a small saucepan. Place the saucepan over low heat and whisk in the tablespoon of the butter piece by piece. Taste and season with salt and pepper.

TO SERVE:
Pour the finished sauce over the chicken and serve.

For a nice Norman accompaniment, serve with a some sautéed apple slices, crusty bread, and a hunk of ripe *fromage*, all 'pinched' from a local farm.

"SNAFU: Situation Normal, All Fucked Up!" — Anonymous

A clear objective. In order to conduct a successful and worthwhile tactical battle recreation, one must fully understand the authentic tactics employed by the United States Army parachute infantry formations during World War II – both in terms of doctrine and the actual combat experience – as well as those of its enemies (in this case the German *Wehrmacht* and *Luftwaffe* field forces, and the *Waffen-SS*). One must intelligently modify real doctrine and tactics in order to create as realistic a setting as possible. This will allow for the event to flow smoothly, and for participants to enjoy it fully.

Lines of battle. During an attack, *Phase Lines* (lines represented on maps by connecting two or more grid coordinates) were employed by the Army as necessitated by the need to keep units of men moving forward on a solid front in order to leave no open flanks. An important point that reenactors should bear in mind is that objectives such as fuel dumps and ammunition dumps were, in terms of the overall Allied strategy for the conduct of the war in Europe, not historically important. The Army's doctrine of the time stressed maintaining contact with the enemy in order to kill his troops in the field as rapidly as possible in order to reduce his ability to fight.[1] The *Line of Departure*, is another such line; an imaginary line on a map that represents the place from which soldiers will begin their advance upon commencement of an attack. There are also the enemy's and one's own MLR (*Main Line of Resistance*) and OPL (*Outpost Line*).

Does size *really* matter? Yes. *"Once the soldier moved inland, he entered an arena eerily empty of the enemy. One observer described the battlefield as small groups of men apparently out on a hike; occasionally one would gesticulate and fall."*[2] In tactical battle recreations, reenactors and event creators should strive to use the available terrain in a manner as historically *correct to scale* as the hobby will allow. Too often, tactical battles attempt to take in the scope of entire historical clashes which often covered tens or hundreds of square miles. Remember, as has been previously stated, the battalion front was normally about 600 yards; the company front 300 yards; the platoon front 150 yards; and the squad front some 75 yards.

Why not recreate just one small facet of a battle? It may be about a place or a town that no one has ever heard of, or that the history books give only brief mention. But we all must remember, these are the places where most of our men fought and died. They are every bit as important as those places known to all, just for this reason.

Also to consider is the fact that it is hard to maintain cohesion between individuals and reenacting units that have an already pre-established "chain of command" or system of control in place. So why then does it so often happen that this difficulty to maintain control is further exacerbated by overcrowding the battlefield. Too often is the case that without the means to effect command on the battlefield, the would-be World War II "tactical battle recreation" devolves quickly into something more like a Civil War clash with each side in ranks firing into the other at close range. A waste of time.

Simulating a respect for the fire power of small arms.

"Weaver could hear the German officer shouting the commands, but the cadence was interrupted as Sergeant Vannett sprayed them with machine-gun fire. The exercising Germans had stacked their rifles. When the bullets began decimating them, Weaver saw them running for their weapons. The machine gunners on the tanks following Weaver's also delivered withering fire. The Germans were falling as though some giant had pulled the parade ground from under them. In another of the light tanks, Donald Yoerk's gunner, Technician 5th Grade George Wyatt from Rosie, Arkansas, also raked the parade ground. As the bullets dug into the blacktop, they reminded Yoerk of hailstones hitting Lake Aurora."[3]

World War II-era infantry weapons rained death and destruction upon an enemy in a volume and with a power unsurpassed to that point. Small trees and shrubbery were certainly not sufficient to protect soldiers from enemy bullets when fired within their range of effectiveness (up to a half a mile!). What this means in terms of battle recreation is that just because an enemy cannot see you hiding in a clump of bushes, this doesn't mean that he cannot deliver fire (albeit blanc fire) into that clump of foliage and render you just as "dead." Significant fortifications and/or excavation is required to provide adequate shelter from flat trajectory small arms.

Plotting a good story. A bit of theater may be what this hobby is sorely lacking! Consider that a tactical battle recreation seeks to tell the *story* of a particular battle, or facet of a battle. One component of a story is the "main character." We may consider reenactors as the main characters of a tactical battle. Another vitally important component of a story is the plot. Lesser characters (*non-player characters*) and well-timed events (*modular scenarios*) are introduced into the story by the author as a means of propelling the action or *plot* along, and nudging the main characters in the right direction. Umpires also serve to keep the plot on track, and exert control over the main characters. The inclusion of non-player characters, umpires, and semi-scripted modular scenarios, are all effective ways to bring history to life more fully, and to create a more enjoyable experience for participants.

Modular Scenarios As Part of the Tactical Event. These so-called "modular scenarios" are examples of pre-arranged events, triggered by event organizers that can a much color and excitement to a tactical battle recreation.

Fox and Hounds. A French FFI fighter brings word to U.S. troops that a U.S. pilot has been forced to parachute from his crippled fighter and has landed somewhere in no-man's land. As German patrols are very active, there is no time to waste in mounting a search for, and recovery of, the downed pilot. As he may be wounded or otherwise unable to walk, a medic and two litter bearers will have to accompany any patrol. A jettisoned parachute or other clues may serve to lead the rescuers to their target, or the Germans to their quarry.

Ach, du Leiber! A German dispatch rider on bicycle unwittingly approaches the U.S. lines from the east, down a road crowded by tall fir trees. Around a bend in the road, he runs headlong into a U.S. roadblock. Suddenly discovering the error of his way, the German attempts to flee. But the alert GIs will undoubtedly gun him down. After the German is subdued, the GIs cautiously advance to search his dispatch case for useful intelligence, and personal belongings, too. They then send a runner back to headquarters to report the exchange, and to deliver what documents have been discovered.

Bump In the Night. Blacken your faces and hands with burnt cork! Reconnaissance patrols should be mounted at night by friendly and enemy soldiers. It will be the job of these patrols to obtain such items of information about the opposing force as the locations of his outposts, and the exact location of his command post. **No firing of weapons after sunset, and no hand-to-hand contact, is to be allowed.** As such, patrol members will be counted as captured if, at close quarters, they are discovered by members of the opposing force who signal by shouting "Patrol!." Those 'captured' should freely give themselves up until which time their parole can be arranged. Each patrol should be instructed to take its time and do its job well. Friendly forces should be alerted to the departure of their own patrols, and at which time and place said patrols plans to re-enter their own lines. Should a friendly patrol be mistaken for that of the opposing side, and the signal "Patrol!" be shouted, then it is to be considered that nervous sentries have fired on, and wiped out, a friendly patrol. Knowledge of the password and countersign may serve to avoid this. Troops of both sides should be instructed to post sentries, and to camouflage their positions against discovery by enemy patrols.

The Combat Photographer. Joining our gallant paratroopers at an event will be a combat photographer (acting as a member of an Army Signal Photo Company). His photographs may appear in an *After Action Report* that may be posted on the internet.

Captured in the fighting on D+2 in Holland, this **SS** infantry soldier is kept under close guard by his paratroop captor. This Nazi former-Superman is lucky to be a prisoner; the fluid state of combat and lack of facility often precluded the taking of prisoners.

With weapons in hand, a combat patrol prepares to depart. Prior to the commencement of any patrol, objectives are clearly defined. All members of the patrol are briefed on the group's mission as well as their individual roles. The time and place that the patrol is to leave and is expected to return is reported to friendly troops, and a system of signal communication is organized. And the patrol members are informed of the challenge and reply.

OPPOSITE
Mecklenburg Plain, Germany, May 1945. The news of the German 21st Army's surrender brings a smile to the faces of Private Podlaszewski and Private Feige behind the wheel of the borrowed ¼ ton command reconnaissance vehicle, as this Jeep patrol led by Captain Baumann returns to the fold.

The Doughnut Dugout. A makeshift Red Cross doughnut stand with glazed doughnuts, coffee, cokes, and Red Cross volunteers.

The Expatriate. A German soldier waving an Allied propaganda/'Safe Conduct' leaflet checks over his shoulder as he moves west along a line of trees. The fleeing deserter should be searched, questioned for useful military information, and then turned over to the MPs for transfer to the PW pen. The German will be relieved of his weapon and equipment which will be turned over to the custody of the MPs, until which time the prisoner can be paroled.

The Old Man. The commanding general of your sector decides to drop in for a visit in his jeep. He moves around the front lines very conspicuously, becoming a juicy target for a sniper that has worked his way up to within range of your lines.

The Trojan Horse. Within observation from Allied lines, out of stand of pines and into the open steps a German officer. He holds before him an 'Safe Conduct' leaflet or a conspicuous white flag. He cautiously peers about the clearing, seemingly as much to make sure that his actions are not observed by his countrymen, as to take care that he is not shot before he can give himself up. He will advance a few more paces, and then hunker down next to a tree for a rest. A GI patrol will be dispatched to reel in the German. However, this time, the German is a decoy, and the GIs are being led into a trap. As the GIs close in, a wave from the decoy signals the start of an ambush. From the pines will come forth a hail of fire from an unseen number of enemy soldiers. The GI commander will quickly send re-enforcements to the aid of his patrol, and as they enter the fray, the Germans will fade back to their own lines ending the fire fight.

The DP. Pushing his belongings along in front of him in a crudely fashioned cart, an French (Belgian, Dutch, German) displaced person (DP) wearily approaches the GIs from

the east. The GIs may attempt to question him for useful information by using their issue language manual. The US Soldiers may attempt to barter with the DP for his goods and food, or purchase items from him with their 'invasion currency'. The DP's belongings might include Lucky Strike cigarettes, a chicken, miscellaneous vegetables, bottles or vin rouge (n/a), water, sausages, cheese wrapped in cheese cloth, et cetera. If this is a German spy masquerading as a refugee, he may be hiding a weapon, and even, possibly, a picture of *Der Fuhrer* amongst his belongings, and as such, would, upon its discovery, be detained by the soldiers and remanded to the custody of the MPs.

"Venez avec moi, soldats!" A French (Belgian, Dutch) partisan startles a US foot patrol from the bushes along the roadside. The Maquis member then approaches, and proceeds to – in his native tongue – tell the GIs how he has shot a German soldier and that he can lead the patrol to the place where the German now lies badly wounded but alive. The German soldier has a gunshot wound, inflicted by the partisan, and cannot walk. The platoon will gather what information they can from the partisan, and the wounded German, and then usher them towards the rear. US medics will need to be called forward in order to retrieve the wounded German. Better keep your GI issue European language guides handy!

Cat and Mouse. A lone German sniper holds up the advance of a Allied patrol until which time the GIs can deploy and eliminate him. If casualties should be taken by the GIs, care and time must be taken to remove them from the field to safety.

Mail Call! Yanks should expect mail call: a V····-Mail letter from their folks, new socks, mom's cookies, or maybe nothing at all. 'Troopers may also get some 'mail' from the enemy in the form of German propaganda leaflets. Likewise, German reenactors might receive packages from their relatives back in the 'Fatherland'. They may also receive 'mail' post marked from the Yanks, too, in the form of *Safe Conduct* leaflets calling for their surrender. NOTE: Mail parcels will be prepared and addressed in advance, and be distributed to individuals at a pre-designated hour.

Examples of other letters, including comic letters, are as follows:
• A classic 'Dear John' letter.
• Mail referencing the recipient as "4-F."
• A roll of toilet paper.
• A War Department telegram addressed to a doggie announcing, erroneously, his recent demise. "The War Department regrets to inform you …"
• A letter to a Yank from home, in Germantown, with all sorts of references to a deeply German family and ancestry, a brother, Fritz who is serving in the German Army on the Eastern front, all German-named relatives, and a can of the doggie's favorite fare: sauerkraut. A picture of the doggie's brother, in German uniform might be included, too. The letter may also go on to say that since the House Committee on Un-American Activities started mixing in, the German-American Bund has "temporarily" shut down, and papa has a lot of free time on his hands now. "Who knows what sort of mischief he'll get into?" Idle hands and all. All comically calling into question this GI's loyalties.
• Maybe a newspaper from home … simple.
• An absolutely smashed cake … what a shame.
• Something good to eat … what a pleasure.
• An empty box with only a packing list … what an insult! (pilfered by some rear echelon garritroopers!).

Set dressing. Borrowing the term from a task associated more often with stage plays, such garnishing of the *setting*, the battle area, might include simulated mine fields, propaganda leaflets "fired" to and from the enemy, European-style road signs, various military signs, road blocks and emplacements, properly fashioned "military" maps of the tactical area, even more elaborate props such as burned out (or burning-smoking) vehicles, smoke over the battle area, wire entanglements, pillboxes, et cetera. Set dressing may also include a list of popular songs and music of the era and mock radio traffic, and indeed *non-player characters*: other reenactors working alongside event organizers in order to add "color" to the event.

Examples of Further Airborne Event Titles and Subjects.

    Palm Trees In the Snow. *An Ardennes Campaign Tactical Battle Scenario based on the operations of the 551st Parachute Infantry Battalion, in the attack, in the vicinity of Trois Ponts, Belgium, 2-7 January 1945.*

    Duel On A Dutch Levee. *A Rhineland Campaign Tactical Battle Scenario based on the airborne assault on Holland, Operation Market-Garden, 17 September 1944.*

    Across the Rhine! *A Central Europe Campaign Tactical Battle Scenario based on the U.S. 17th Airborne Division's air assault across the Rhine River, Operation VARSITY-PLUNDER, in the vicinity of Wesel, Germany, 23 March 1945.*

    Dug-In and Holdin' Out! *A 'One-Sided' Tactical Battle For the Public, This scenario places a platoon of Paratroops along a hedgerow in Normandy, where they have dug in, and emplaced their weapons. The public is free to stroll just behind the lines to view the soldier's improving their foxholes, to watch patrols come and go, to listen as orders are given and received from the company CO.*

    Tennessee Maneuvers. *U.S. Reenactors only … Red Army vs. Blue Army.*

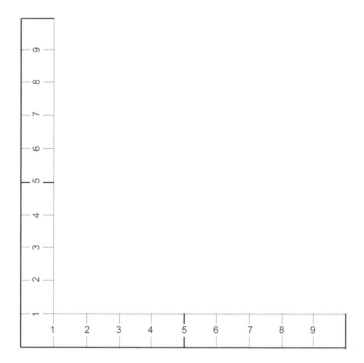

Map square.

Signs of Recent Fighting

DANGER
MINES NOT
CLEARED BEYOND
THIS POINT

*The Siegfried Line
Hurtgen Forest, Germany
February 1945*

SAINT-MARCOUF 2ᴷ
BARFLEUR   26ᴷ

*Vic. St.-Marcouf,
Normandy, France
D-Day
June 1944*

6ᴷ BASTOGNE   LA ROCHE 22ᴷ

BASTOGNE

*Bastogne, Belgium
December 1944*

Périers -16 Km

Cherbourg

*Carentan, France, D+6
June 1944*

*Crossroads vic.
Champs, Belgium
December 1944*

MSG. CTR

CHALLENGE

BLUE
C.P.

CHAMPION
C.P.

THIS TOWN
OFF LIMITS
TO ALL MILITARY
PERSONNEL

*Posted
Outside of
Carentan, France
June 1944*

*Headquarters 3/505th PIR,
Normandy, France
June 1944*

*82nd Airborne Division
Command Post
Holland, September 1944*

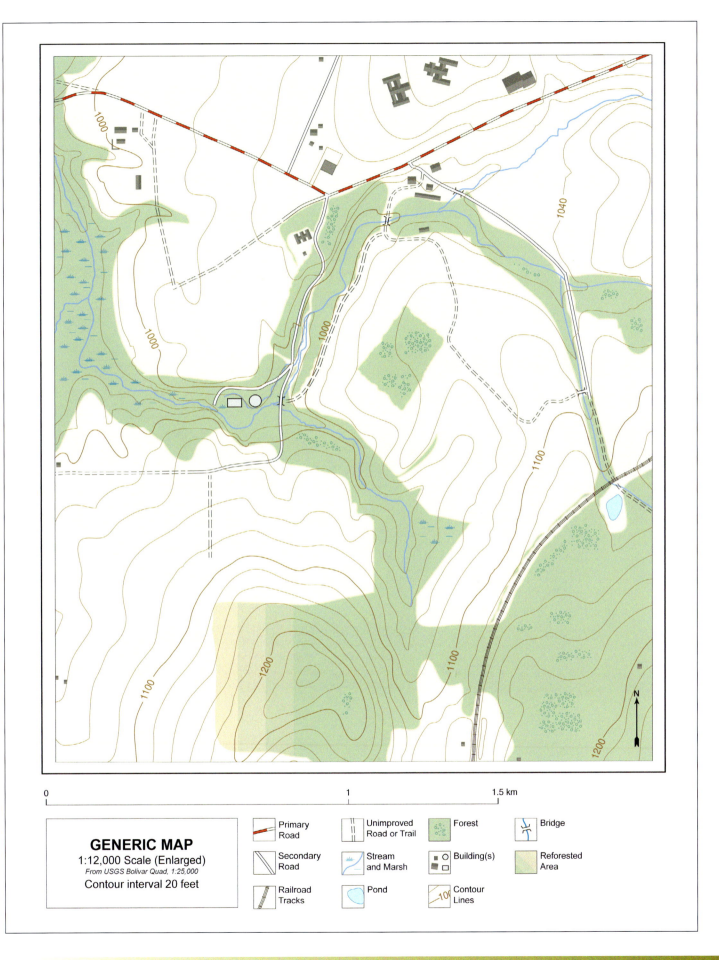

SAFE CONDUCT

The German soldier who carries this safe conduct is using it as a sign of his genuine wish to give himself up. He is to be disarmed, to be well looked after, to receive food and medical attention as required, and is to be removed from the danger zone as soon as possible.

PASSIERSCHEIN

An die britischen und amerikanischin Vorposien: Der deutsche Soldat, der diesen Passierschein vorzeigt, benutzt ihn als Zeichen seines ehrlichen Willens, sich zu ergeben. Er ist zu entwaffnen. Er muss gut behandelt werden. Er hat Anspruch auf Verpflegung und, wenn nötig, ärztliche Behundlung. Er wird so bald wie möglich aus der Gefahrenzone entfernt.

A War of Words

Recreations of German and U.S. propaganda leaflets, and organizational newspaper headers.

Top: DEVIL'S DIGEST, 508th Parachute Infantry Regiment Newspaper, Header for the 2nd Battalion, "Conquest from the Clouds" news. This header shows 2/508's helmet marking, the 'double lightning bolts'.

Above: DEVIL'S DIGEST, 508th Parachute Infantry Regiment Newspaper, Header for the 1st Battalion, "Fighting First" news. This header shows 1/508's helmet marking.

IMPORTANT NOTICE

In case you are taken prisoner, you will very likely wish to have your relatives informed with as little delay as possible that you are alive and out of danger.

JERRY'S FRONT RADIO

has arranged to announce the names and addresses of prisoners of war and their serial numbers. The announcements will be made three times daily.

You will understand how **valuable** this service is when you consider that your relateives are spared the dreadful feeling of anxious suspense concerning your fate.

Be prepared and fill in this blank. it will be useful to you if you should be captured.

A1-042-2-44

FILL IN THIS BLANC AND KEEP IT

USE BLOCK LETTERS
TO BE TRANSMITTED BY JERRY'S FRONT RADIO:

Name: _____

Rank: _____

Serial Number: _____

Street Address: _____

Town: _____

Country: _____

In this panel write a short message of not more than 15 words which will be transmitted by radio

Above left: U.S. First Army Safe Conduct leaflet inviting German soldiers in both English and German to surrender with the promise of good treatment. When the enemy did surrender his fate, however, was not always clearcut. Battlefield expedients sometimes meant that a prisoner's treatment consisted of being herded to the nearest ditch and being shot.

Far left: Obverse of German propaganda leaflet inviting GIs to be prepared in the event of their capture. Leaflets such as these were meant to plant seeds of doubt in a soldier's mind as to his fate.

Left: Reverse of the same German propaganda leaflet with blanks to be filled in with a GI's personal information. Practically all U.S. troops disregarded these leaflets. Some GIs took to collecting these as one would collect stamps as a means of passing the time.

Sample Event 1
Objective: Normandy
Tactical Battle Scenario Recreating the U.S. Army's Airborne Assault on Normandy France,
Principally by elements of the 505th, 507th, and 508th Parachute Infantry Regiments,
Vicinity Chef-du-Pont, Picauville, La Fiere, 6 June 1944.

Real World Information.
Date: –
Place: –
H-hour, D-day: –

The Historical Setting.
In 1944, the land immediately behind what became known as UTAH Beach in Normandy was not the pastoral scene that comes to mind when one envisions the countryside of France. Rather, in June 1944, it was swamp-like, with flooded fields, marshes, and canals and rivers intersecting the landscape, with few shallow hills, bridges and a meager road network rising above the water to connect the hamlets and villages. But it was this high ground, these roads and these clusters of buildings that would have to be captured if an invading force was to gain a foothold. Having occupied France since 1940, German troops garrisoned the towns and had turned the thick-walled stone Norman dwellings into fortified strong points. Enemy patrols traverse the roads and paths and his outposts guard his lines of communication. With thousands of Allied troops scheduled to land by sea on the beaches of Normandy at dawn on June 6, it will be Allied paratroops who will air assault during the night preceding the seaborne elements to capture and hold the strategic routes inland. Without these avenues off the beaches, the invading forces risk being hurled back into the sea.

This tactical battle scenario recreates the setting described above, D-Day in Normandy. It begins in the hedgerows and fields of the Cotentin Peninsula, near the Merderet River where scattered and disorganized Allied paratroopers will, aided by Pathfinder elements, attempt to make their way to designated assembly areas during the hours of darkness, and then move upon their objectives. In the midst of this confusion, German troops, alerted by the clamor of engines, will try to assay the intentions of the Anglo-American forces, and dispatch patrols to learn the extent of the crisis. Just before dawn, the first Allied gliders will descend on landing zones. And at daybreak the German command will learn that Allied amphibious forces have breached the Atlantic wall and are moving west, inland from the beaches, intent on a linkup with the airborne spearhead.

Wary of snipers, a combat patrol of the 82nd Airborne Division enters a Norman hamlet on the morning of D-Day, 6 June 1944.

S E C R E T

H.Q., 508TH PARACHUTE INF. REGT.
SALTBY, ENGLAND,
26 MAY 1944

S E C R E T

By Auth: CO, 508th PIR
27 May 1944 _____

FIELD ORDER 19.

Map (presented as map and overlay): OPERATIONS MAP, VIC. CHEF-DU-PONT, FRANCE, 1:12,000 SCALE (ENLARGED)

1. ENEMY FORCES. German infantry and motorized forces garrison hamlets in the PICAUVILLE—CHEF-DU-PONT area. The enemy has established outposts to guard the road-bridges in the vicinity of these hamlets. Enemy forces maintain contact patrols between these garrisons, and outposts. These forces are believed to be elements of the 91ST INFANTRY DIVISION.

2. FRIENDLY FORCES, PHASE 1—LANDING. E/508th Parachute Infantry Regiment, will, on H-hour, D-day, and preceded by Pathfinder elements, air assault the PICAUVILLE—CHEF-DU-PONT area (see accompanying Operations Map) and establish an airhead. The battalion will consolidate and prepare for offensive operations.

    a. Composition of forces.

        (1) FORCE "A" shall consist of 1E/508(-) less 2/1E/508.

        (2) FORCE "B" shall consist of 2E/508.

        (3) FORCE "C" shall consist of 3E/508(+) reinforced by 2/1E/508.

        (4) FORCE "D" shall consist of E/508 Company Headquarters, Enlisted Cadre, and attached medical personnel.

    b. FORCE "A" will land at DZ "N-1" (311944) and move to capture BRIDGE 1 (313946). There, FORCE "A" will establish a strong defensive position, roadblock and outpost, and deny the enemy this avenue of advance into the airhead. Road bed will be mined to deny its use by enemy vehicles. All approaches to BRIDGE 1 will be covered by fire.

    c. (1) FORCE "B" will land at DZ "N-2" (319950) and establish a strong defensive position facing northwest and northeast along the line (316947-318949-319948).

        (2) One squad will be detached to establish a ROAD BLOCK at ROAD JUNCTION (317952) and BRIDGE 2 (317953). The road bed will be mined to deny its use by enemy vehicles. These mines will be covered by fire.

        (3) 1E/508(-) CP will be placed at (316947).

    d. (1) FORCE "C" will land on DZ "N-3" (321946) and move to establish a strong defensive position facing southwest and southeast along the line (319948-317946-316947).

        (2) 2/1E/508 will move to occupy HILL 323, and be disposed so as to deliver grazing fire across its front northwest to east.

        (3) 3E/508(+) CP will be placed at (317946).

    e. FORCE "D" will land at DZ "N-3" (321946) and move to establish a Command Post, and the Medical Aid Station at (317947). All precautions of shelter and cover will be taken.

    f. 1st PATHFINDERS (DETACHMENT) will land at DZ "N-3" (321946) at H(-30) and prepare to receive the arrival serials.

-1-

S E C R E T

3. COMMUNICATION.

     a. Radio, radio telephone, and written communication will be established and maintained by all units as per Signal Plan published separately.

4. MINEFIELDS.

     a. On orders from Company CO, mines will be laid on roads and on road verges to deny enemy troops and vehicles the use of these as an approach to our main line of resistance.

     b. The exact locations of all friendly mine fields will be reported in written form, including map coordinates, without delay to Company CO at Company CP.

5. D-DAY and H-HOUR will be announced.

           By Order of ROY E. LINDQUIST
           COLONEL, 508th Parachute Infantry Regiment
           Commanding.

OFFICIAL:

_____

       Captain, E/508th Parachute Infantry Regiment
       Commanding.

ANNEXES:

No. 1. Intelligence Annex
No. 2. S-2 Report
No. 3. Administrative Annex
No. 4. Operations Memorandum
No. 5. Operations Map
No. 6. Signal Plan
No. 7. Medical Plan
No. 8. Serial Order

DISTRIBUTION:

Copy No.	Officers or Units
1	CO, E Company, 508th PIR
2	XO, E Company, 508th PIR
3	S-2, 2/508th PIR
4-5	1st Platoon, E Company, 508th PIR
6-7	2nd Platoon, E Company, 508th PIR

<u>S E C R E T</u>

H.Q., 508TH PARACHUTE INF. REGT.
SALTBY, ENGLAND,
26 MAY 1944

INTELLIGENCE ANNEX
To FIELD ORDER. 19.

1. <u>SUMMARY OF ENEMY SITUATION</u>.

    See Intelligence Report for details.

2. <u>ESSENTIAL ELEMENTS OF INFORMATION</u>.

    a. Will the enemy attack?

    b. If so, when, from what direction, and with what forces?

3. <u>RECONNAISSANCE AND OBSERVATION MISSIONS</u>.

    Until specific reconnaissance or combat missions are assigned, individuals and units will maintain their defensive positions only.

4. <u>MEASURES FOR HANDLING PRISONERS AND CAPTURED DOCUMENTS</u>.

    a. PWs will be delivered to the custody of Company HQ personnel who will process and arrange for movement of prisoners.

    b. Individual weapons and all papers will be taken from prisoners (upon re-enactor PW's consent) and sent to the acting 2/508 S-2 at the Company CP with the guard delivering prisoners.

    c. Captured or found documents will be sent to the Company CP without delay, and brought to the attention of the acting 2/508 S-2.

5. <u>COUNTER INTELLIGENCE</u>.

    a. Security Practice.

        (1) Troops will be reminded to give only name, rank, and serial number, and nothing more in event of capture.

        (2) Elements possessing confidential and secret documents will bury or conceal documents in case of imminent capture.

    b. Challenges and Answers. Change at 2400 hours daily on date indicated:

DATE	CHALLENGE	ANSWER
5 June	LIMEHOUSE	COCKNEY
6 June	FLASH	THUNDER
Emergency No. 1	CORNWALL	SMUGGLER
Emergency No. 2	ARKANSAS	TRAVELER

    c. Civilian Control.

        (1) Civilians (re-enactors portraying civilians) entering the lines from enemy territory, attempting to move into enemy territory through our lines, or suspected of espionage will be arrested and turned over to Company HQ personnel at Company CP. A statement of the circumstances will be made as soon as practicable in each instance. Immediately upon arrest they will be searched (upon consent of re-enactor civilian) for weapons and documents.

        (2) All re-enactors will take separate precautions to see that their private property is secured from theft or tampering by bona fide civilians who may enter the tactical area. Suspicious individuals should be reported at once to the Company CO who may contact local Law Enforcement.

    d. Security of Bivouac and Command Post.

        (1) Re-enactor-civilians will be excluded, and all bona fide civilians and unfamiliar military personnel will be made to identify

-3-

<u>S E C R E T</u>

themselves before being allowed freedom of movement.

      (2) Blackout. Strict blackout discipline will be observed.

      (3) Camouflage and Concealment.

          (a) Bivouacs, CPs and parked vehicles, singularly or in groups, will be placed as much as possible under natural cover. In the absence of cover, camouflage nets will, if available, be used and vehicles will be well dispersed.

          (b) Ration cans and other bright objects will not be left exposed.

          (c) Groups will not assemble unnecessarily in the open.

                                 _____

                                 Captain, E/508th Parachute Infantry
                                 Commanding.

OFFICIAL:

_____ _____

First Lieutenant,
2/508th Parachute Infantry Regiment,
S-2.

S E C R E T

H.Q., 508TH PARACHUTE INF. REGT.
SALTBY, ENGLAND,
26 MAY 1944

S-2 REPORT
(Source, 82nd Airborne Division G-2 Report No. 7)

1. WEATHER.

a. The average high temperature of the Tactical Area during the month of April is 61 degrees; the low 37 degrees; the average mean temperature being 49 degrees.

b. Average precipitation for the month of April is 4.19-inches.

c. The 7 Day forecast for the Tactical Area including conditions of wind, cloudiness and moisture, and visibility is as follows: TBD

d. Astrological Conditions: DST, W79.223/N40.417.

```
        (1)        SUNRISE  SUNSET   MOONRISE   MOONSET
        June 5     0634     2000     1838       0549 on following day
        Phase of the Moon: Waxing gibbous with 97% of the Moon's visible
disk illuminated.

        June 6     0632     2002     1940       0612 on following day
        Phase of the Moon: Waxing gibbous with 99% of the Moon's visible
disk illuminated.

        June 7     0631     2003     2043       0638 on following day
        Phase of the Moon: Full Moon.
```

Note: Information herein obtained from aa.usno.navy.mil (U.S. Naval Observatory, Astronomical Applications Department).

DISTRIBUTION: Same as Field Order 19.

-5-

<u>S E C R E T</u>

H.Q., 508TH PARACHUTE INF. REGT.
SALTBY, ENGLAND,
26 MAY 1944

ADMINISTRATIVE ANNEX
To FIELD ORDER. 19.

1. <u>SUPPLY</u>.

    a. <u>Rations</u>:

        (1) Individuals will make separate arrangements to secure ample personal supply of rations and water prior to commencement of event. Rations enough for three (3) meals will be required of each individual.

        (2) Personal water supply is to be at the rate of 1/2 gallon per man per day.

        (3) Rations and water, constituting one day's supply, will be carried by each individual.

        (4) Each individual's supply of rations and water not carried on his person, and therefore constituting resupply, will be tagged to show name, and stored at the Company CP.

2. <u>AMMUNITION</u>.

    a. Initial load of ammunition, consisting of that carried on the back plus one (1) day of resupply, will be issued prior to embarkation. [H-hour, D-day. drawn (secured) and brought forward prior to commencement of the tactical event]. Ammunition carried as initial load and that consisting of resupply:

| | Allowance Per Weapon | |
| Type of Weapon | Initial Load | D+1 Resupply |

    As per <u>PARACHUTE RIFLE COMPANY</u> SOP.

    b. Each re-enactor will make separate arrangements for securing his personal supply of blank ammunition in accordance with this annex.

    c. Individual loads of ammunition may be procured from _____

_____

3. <u>MINES</u>.

    As per <u>PARACHUTE RIFLE COMPANY</u> SOP.

4. <u>RATIONS</u>.

    As per <u>PARACHUTE RIFLE COMPANY</u> SOP.

5. <u>BEDROLLS</u>.

    As per <u>PARACHUTE RIFLE COMPANY</u> SOP.

6. <u>EVACUATION</u>.

    a. <u>Casualties</u>:

        (1) All casualties, both friendly and captured enemy, will be evacuated to the battalion aid station. (See The Aid Station and the Battalion Medical Section, <u>PARACHUTE RIFLE COMPANY</u>, for procedures and flow.)

        (2) Replacements and sick and wounded returned from aid station will be "re-equipped" at company command post, and held pending further instructions from officiating officer.

<u>S E C R E T</u>

H.Q., 508TH PARACHUTE INF. REGT.
SALTBY, ENGLAND,
26 MAY 1944

OPERATIONS MEMORANDUM
To FIELD ORDER. 19.

1. The information published herein has been extracted from Fifth Army directives designed to coordinate certain operational activities and is published herewith for the information and guidance of all officers and enlisted men. Company and detachment commanders will carefully instruct their officers and men in the information contained herein.

2. TIME SYSTEM.

    As per <u>PARACHUTE RIFLE COMPANY</u> SOP.

3. THE PHONETIC ALPHABET. The phonetic alphabet herein reproduced will be used throughout this organization:

    As per <u>PARACHUTE RIFLE COMPANY</u> SOP.

    Examples:

    A, b, c, d, etc., will be spoken "Able, Baker, Charlie, Dog." Difficult words will be spoken as in the following example: "Catenary - I spell: "Charlie, Able, Tare, Easy, Nan, Able, Roger, Yoke - Catenary."

4. PRONUNCIATION OF NUMERALS.

    As per <u>PARACHUTE RIFLE COMPANY</u> SOP.

5. STANDARD CODE NAMES.

    a. The following code names will be used in all written and radio-telephone conversations and messages:

DESIGNATION	CODE NAME
E/508 CO	DIABLO SIX (6)
E/508 XO	DIABLO FIVE (5)
1st Platoon, E/508	DIABLO ONE (1)
2d Platoon, E/508	DIABLO TWO (2)
3d Platoon, E/508	DIABLO THREE (3)

    b. Security will rely on the consistent use of code names.

-7-

SECRET

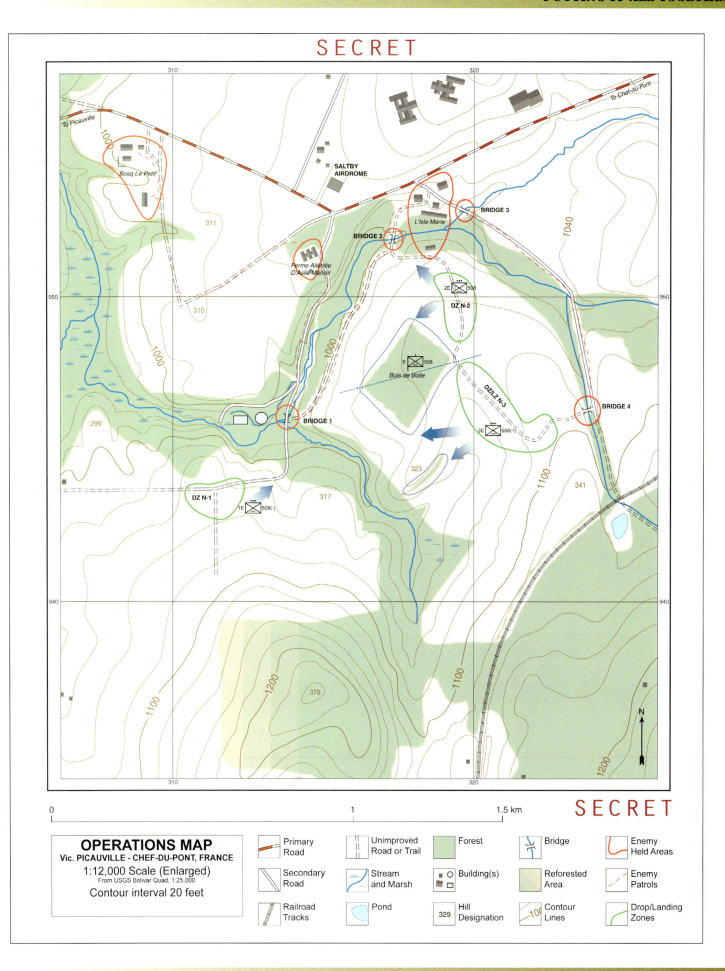

SECRET

OPERATIONS MAP
Vic. PICAUVILLE - CHEF-DU-PONT, FRANCE
1:12,000 Scale (Enlarged)
From USGS Bolivar Quad, 1:25,000
Contour interval 20 feet

Primary Road	Unimproved Road or Trail	Forest
Secondary Road	Stream and Marsh	Building(s)
Railroad Tracks	Pond	Hill Designation

Bridge	Enemy Held Areas
Reforested Area	Enemy Patrols
Contour Lines	Drop/Landing Zones

Sample Event 2
There Will Be No Withdrawal
A Tactical Battle Scenario Recreating the Defense of the Salm River Line
By "A" Company, 508th Parachute Infantry Regiment, 82nd Airborne Division,
Vic. Rencheux, Belgium, December 23-24, 1944

Real World Information.
Date: –
Place: –
H-hour, D-day: –

The Historical Setting.
On December 16, 1944, began the largest land battle on the Western Front during World War II, which came to be known as the Battle of the Bulge. Pouring westward out of the *Schnee Eifel* and through the inhospitable terrain of the *Ardennes* Forest came a massive German counteroffensive, a 250,000-man-strong tide that washed over the 85 mile-long Allied lines held by some 83,000 unsuspecting American troops.

In the vicinity of Saint-Vith, Belgium, the line was held by green troops of the newly arrived U.S. 106th Infantry Division. By nightfall of the first day, two regiments of the division were in the process of being encircled and cut off, while the third was fighting its way back to the Our River and beyond. By the morning of December 18, elements of Brigadier General Robert W. Hasbrouck's U.S. 7th Armored Division were hustled south, then east, to take up a crescent-shaped blocking position around Saint-Vith, denying this crucial crossroads to the enemy. Hasbrouck's team was further buttressed by the U.S. 112th Infantry on December 19, increasing the number of defenders to nearly 22,000.

For more than five days Hasbrouck's command fought off incessant attacks hurled at his so-called "Fortified Goose Egg." But, after more than 6,000 casualties, at 0600 on December 23, the 7th Armored and attached elements were ordered to break off and withdraw west behind a new line that had been established by the U.S. 82nd Airborne Division at the Salm River, hotly pursued by elements of the German 9th SS Panzer Division.

The enemy's timetable has been disrupted, his plans injured, and his tide slowed. But will it be enough to turn the tide of battle?

Withdrawing from bivouac, and with little more than fifteen hour's notice, the U.S. 82nd Airborne Division was entrucked and moving toward the front, a distant 150 miles east. Prior to departure, units gathered what weapons, ammunition and equipment they could, and hastily assimilated new replacements. Each man was issued one 'K' ration.

At dawn on the morning of December 21, 1/508 began to occupy its new positions, with A Company west of the Salm River. B Company was on A Company's left, and elements of 3/112 occupied positions on A Company's right. The company commander of A Company was told that "this is where the 82nd Airborne Division will make its stand, there will be no withdrawal."

Dug in in defensive positions in the vicinity of Rencheux, Belgium, Second Lieutenant Soltis and First Sergeant Weaver wait for the onrushing tide of enemy forces. Orders have come down. The situation is desperate. They will stand or die where they are.

S E C R E T

508TH PARACHUTE INF. REGT.
IN THE FIELD, BELGIUM,
17 DECEMBER 1944

S E C R E T

By Auth: CO, 508th PIR
17 December 1944 _____

FIELD ORDER 25.

Map (presented as map and overlay): OPERATIONS MAP, RENCHEUX, BELGIUM,
1:12,000 SCALE (ENLARGED)

1. ENEMY FORCES. Strong German infantry and mechanized forces are attacking
WEST from SAINT-VITH on a line following roughly the 830 Northing. These
forces are believed to be KAMPFGRUPPE KRAG, an element of the 9th SS PANZER
DIVISION.

2. FRIENDLY FORCES. 1st Battalion, 508th Parachute Infantry Regiment, will
organized its sector with its MLR facing EAST along a roughly NORTH-SOUTH line
(595830-593826), and will, by establishing strong defensive positions,
roadblocks and outposts, and by carrying out aggressive patrolling and raids
forward of this position, prevent the enemy from crossing the SALM RIVER.

    a. 1/508 Command Post (CP), Assembly Area, and the Battalion Aid Station
will be located at the hamlet of LE SABLON (588834). All precautions of
shelter and cover will be taken.

    b. B/508 will establish a defensive position along the NORTH-SOUTH line
(594828-595830), digging in along the crest of the THIER-DU-MONT RIDGE, in a
position to cover the road to its front by fire.

       (1) A ROAD BLOCK will be established at ROAD JUNCTION (595830).
The road bed will be mined to deny its use by enemy vehicles. These mines will
be covered by fire.

       (2) Outpost(s) will be placed to warn against approach of enemy
and to cover prepared obstacles by fire.

    c. A/508 will organize its defense facing EAST with its right flank
anchored on and incorporating the BRIDGE (594826), in a line following the
road (595830-594825).

       (1) 1A/508 will wire the bridge at (594826) for demolition and dig
in in a blocking position WEST of the road (594825-594826).

       (2) 2A/508 will dig in in a blocking position WEST of the road
(594826-592828).

       (3) 3A/508 as Company Reserve will be located behind the MLR
NORTHWEST of (592828).

       (4) A/508 Company CP will be located NORTHEAST of (590826).

       (5) Outpost(s) will be placed to warn against approach of enemy
and to cover prepared obstacles by fire.

    d. c/508 will constitute the Battalion Reserve and will place itself at
(590829). All precautions of shelter and cover will be taken.

    e. ADJACENT UNITS.

       (1) 2/508 will tie in on the left flank of 1/508.

       (2) 3/112 will tie in on the right flank of 1/508.

3. MOVEMENT.

    a. All movements from assembly area will be made with secrecy and/or
under cover of darkness.
    b. All troops occupying front line positions must exercise extreme
caution particularly during daylight to not reveal their presence to the

-1-

<u>S E C R E T</u>

enemy.

4. Communication.

    a. Radio, radio telephone, and written communication will be established and maintained by all units as per Signal Plan published separately.

    a. On orders from Company CO, mines will be laid on roads and on road verges to deny enemy troops and vehicles the use of these as an approach to our main line of resistance.

    b. The exact locations of all friendly mine fields will be reported in written form, including map coordinates, without delay to Company CO at Company CP.

6. D-DAY and H-HOUR will be announced.

                    By Order of ROY E. LINDQUIST
                    COLONEL, 508th Parachute Infantry Regiment
                    Commanding.

OFFICIAL:
                    _____
                    Captain, 508th Parachute Infantry Regiment.
                    S-3

ANNEXES:

No. 1. Intelligence Annex
No. 2. S-2 Report
No. 3. Administrative Annex
No. 4. Operations Memorandum
No. 5. Operations Map
No. 6. Signal Plan
No. 7. Medical Plan

DISTRIBUTION:

Copy No.	Officers or Units
1	CO, 1/508th PIR
2	XO, 1/508th PIR
3	S-2, 1/508th PIR
4-9	A Company, 508th PIR
10-14	B Company, 508th PIR
15-19	C Company, 508th PIR

S E C R E T

508TH PARACHUTE INF. REGT.
IN THE FIELD, BELGIUM,
17 DECEMBER 1944

INTELLIGENCE ANNEX
To FIELD ORDER. 25.

1. SUMMARY OF ENEMY SITUATION.

       See Intelligence Report for details.

2. ESSENTIAL ELEMENTS OF INFORMATION.

       a. Will the enemy attack?

       b. If so, when, from what direction, and with what forces?

3. RECONNAISSANCE AND OBSERVATION MISSIONS.

       Until specific reconnaissance or combat missions are assigned, individuals and units will maintain their defensive positions only.

4. MEASURES FOR HANDLING PRISONERS AND CAPTURED DOCUMENTS.

       a. PWs will be delivered to the custody of Battalion HQ personnel who will process and arrange for movement of prisoners.

       b. Individual weapons and all papers will be taken from prisoners (upon re-enactor PW's consent) and sent to the acting 2/508 S-2 at the Company CP with the guard delivering prisoners.

       c. Captured or found documents will be sent to the Company CP without delay, and brought to the attention of the acting 2/508 S-2.

5. COUNTER INTELLIGENCE.

       a. Security Practice.

           (1) Troops will be reminded to give only name, rank, and serial number, and nothing more in event of capture.

           (2) Elements possessing confidential and secret documents will bury or conceal documents in case of imminent capture.

       b. Challenges and Answers. Change at 2400 hours daily on date indicated:

DATE	CHALLENGE	ANSWER
23 December	ARKANSAS	TRAVELER
24 December	CORNWALL	SMUGGLER
Emergency No. 1	RENO	DIVORCE
Emergency No. 2	LIMEHOUSE	COCKNEY

       c. Civilian Control.

           (1) Civilians (re-enactors portraying civilians) entering the lines from enemy territory, attempting to move into enemy territory through our lines, or suspected of espionage will be arrested and turned over to Battalion HQ personnel at Battalion CP. A statement of the circumstances will be made as soon as practicable in each instance. Immediately upon arrest they will be searched (upon consent of re-enactor civilian) for weapons and documents.

           (2) All re-enactors will take separate precautions to see that their private property is secured from theft or tampering by bona fide civilians who may enter the tactical area. Suspicious individuals should be reported at once to the Battalion or Company CO who may contact local Law Enforcement.

-3-

S E C R E T

   d. Security of Bivouac and Command Post.

       (1) Re-enactor-civilians will be excluded, and all bona fide civilians and unfamiliar military personnel will be made to identify themselves before being allowed freedom of movement.

       (2) Blackout. Strict blackout discipline will be observed.

       (3) Camouflage and Concealment.

           (a) Bivouacs, CPs and parked vehicles, singularly or in groups, will be placed as much as possible under natural cover. In the absence of cover, camouflage nets will, if available, be used and vehicles will be well dispersed.

           (b) New paths and roads will not be made.

           (c) Ration cans and other bright objects will not be left exposed.

           (d) Groups will not assemble unnecessarily in the open.

                                              _____
                                              Captain, 508th Parachute Infantry
                                              S-2

OFFICIAL:

       _____
       First Lieutenant,
       508th Parachute Infantry Regiment,
       Assistant S-2.

S E C R E T

508TH PARACHUTE INF. REGT.
IN THE FIELD, BELGIUM,
17 DECEMBER 1944

S-2 REPORT
(Source, XVIII Corps G-2 Report No. 15)

1. WEATHER.

        a. The average high temperature of the Tactical Area during the month of December is 40 degrees, the low 25 degrees, the average mean temperature being 33 degrees.

    b. Average precipitation for the month of November is 3.41-inches.

    d. The 7 Day forecast for the Tactical Area including conditions of wind, cloudiness and moisture, and visibility is as follows: TBD

    e. Astrological Conditions: W79.3/N40.4.

(1)	SUNRISE	SUNSET	MOONRISE	MOONSET
December 22	0706	1658	1710	1004 on following day

Phase of the Moon: Waning gibbous with 97% of the Moon's visible disk illuminated.

December 23	0707	1657	1753	1058 on following day

Phase of the Moon: Waning gibbous with 92% of the Moon's visible disk illuminated.

December 24	0708	1657	1845	1141 on following day

Phase of the Moon: Waning gibbous with 86% of the Moon's visible disk illuminated.

    Note: Information herein obtained from aa.usno.navy.mil (U.S. Naval Observatory, Astronomical Applications Department).

DISTRIBUTION: Same as Field Order 25.

-5-

S E C R E T

508TH PARACHUTE INF. REGT.
IN THE FIELD, BELGIUM,
17 DECEMBER 1944

ADMINISTRATIVE ANNEX
To FIELD ORDER. 25.

1. SUPPLY.

a. Rations:

(1) Individuals will make separate arrangements to secure ample personal supply of rations and water prior to commencement of event. Rations enough for three (3) meals will be required of each individual.

(2) Personal water supply is to be at the rate of 1/2 gallon per man per day.

(3) Rations and water, constituting one day's supply, will be carried by each individual.

(4) Each individual's supply of rations and water not carried on his person, and therefore constituting resupply, will be tagged to show name, and stored at the Company CP.

2. AMMUNITION.

a. Initial load of ammunition, consisting of that carried on the back plus one (1) day of resupply, will be issued prior to embarkation. [H-hour, D-day. drawn (secured) and brought forward prior to commencement of the tactical event]. Ammunition carried as initial load and that consisting of resupply:

	Allowance Per Weapon	
Type of Weapon	Initial Load	D+1 Resupply

As per PARACHUTE RIFLE COMPANY S.O.P.

b. Each re-enactor will make separate arrangements for securing his personal supply of blank ammunition in accordance with this annex.

3. MINES.

As per PARACHUTE RIFLE COMPANY S.O.P.

4. RATIONS.

As per PARACHUTE RIFLE COMPANY S.O.P.

5. BEDROLLS.

As per PARACHUTE RIFLE COMPANY S.O.P. Each man will bring his bedroll forward with him.

6. EVACUATION.

a. Casualties:

(1) All casualties, both friendly and captured enemy, will be evacuated to the battalion aid station. (See PARACHUTE RIFLE COMPANY S.O.P., for procedures and flow.)

(2) Replacements and sick and wounded returned from aid station will be "re-equipped" at company command post, and held pending further instructions from officiating officer.

<pre>
                        S E C R E T

                              508TH PARACHUTE INF. REGT.
                              IN THE FIELD, BELGIUM,
                              17 DECEMBER 1944

OPERATIONS MEMORANDUM
To FIELD ORDER. 25.

1. The information published herein has been extracted from Fifth Army
directives designed to coordinate certain operational activities and is
published herewith for the information and guidance of all officers and
enlisted men. Company and detachment commanders will carefully instruct their
officers and men in the information contained herein.

2. TIME SYSTEM.

     a. "A" time will be used in future operations.

3. THE PHONETIC ALPHABET. The phonetic alphabet herein reproduced will be used
throughout this organization:

     As per PARACHUTE RIFLE COMPANY S.O.P.

          Examples:

          A, b, c, d, etc., will be spoken "Able, Baker, Charlie, Dog."
Difficult words will be spoken as in the following example: "Catenary - I
spell: "Charlie, Able, Tare, Easy, Nan, Able, Roger, Yoke - Catenary."

4. PRONUNCIATION OF NUMERALS. The following rules will be observed in the
pronunciation of numerals:

     As per PARACHUTE RIFLE COMPANY S.O.P.

5. STANDARD CODE NAMES.

     a. The following code names will be used in all written and radio-
telephone conversations and messages:

          DESIGNATION   CODE NAME

          1/508 CO   DIABLO RED SIX (6)
          1/508 XO   DIABLO RED FIVE (5)
          A/508 CO   DIABLO ABLE SIX (6)
          A/508 XO   DIABLO ABLE FIVE (5)
          1A/508 CO   DIABLO ABLE ONE-SIX (1-6)
          1A/508 XO   DIABLO ABLE ONE-FIVE (1-5)
          2A/508 CO   DIABLO ABLE TWO-SIX (2-6)
          2A/508 CO   DIABLO ABLE TWO-FIVE (2-5)
          3A/508 CO   DIABLO ABLE THREE-SIX (3-6)
          3A/508 CO   DIABLO ABLE THREE-FIVE (3-5)
          B/508 CO   DIABLO BAKER SIX (6)
          B/508 XO   DIABLO BAKER FIVE (5)
          1B/508 CO   DIABLO BAKER ONE-SIX (1-6)
          1B/508 XO   DIABLO BAKER ONE-FIVE (1-5)
          2B/508 CO   DIABLO BAKER TWO-SIX (2-6)
          2B/508 CO   DIABLO BAKER TWO-FIVE (2-5)
          3B/508 CO   DIABLO BAKER THREE-SIX (3-6)
          3B/508 CO   DIABLO BAKER THREE-FIVE (3-5)
          C/508 CO   DIABLO CHARLIE SIX (6)
          C/508 XO   DIABLO CHARLIE FIVE (5)
          1C/508 CO   DIABLO CHARLIE ONE-SIX (1-6)
          1C/508 XO   DIABLO CHARLIE ONE-FIVE (1-5)
          2C/508 CO   DIABLO CHARLIE TWO-SIX (2-6)
          2C/508 CO   DIABLO CHARLIE TWO-FIVE (2-5)
          3C/508 CO   DIABLO CHARLIE THREE-SIX (3-6)
          3C/508 CO   DIABLO CHARLIE THREE-FIVE (3-5)

     b. Security will rely on the consistent use of code names.

                              -7-
</pre>

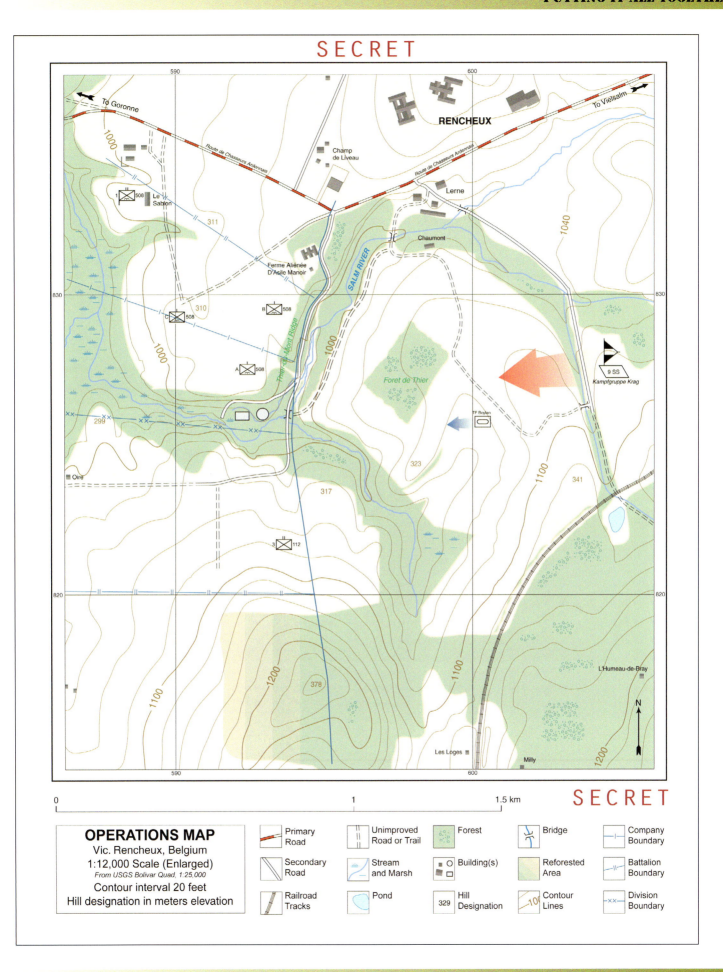

0   1   1.5 km

OPERATIONS MAP
Vic. Rencheux, Belgium
1:12,000 Scale (Enlarged)
From USGS Bolivar Quad, 1:25,000
Contour interval 20 feet
Hill designation in meters elevation

Primary Road	Unimproved Road or Trail	Forest
Secondary Road	Stream and Marsh	Building(s)
Railroad Tracks	Pond	329 Hill Designation
Bridge	Reforested Area	100 Contour Lines
Company Boundary	Battalion Boundary	Division Boundary

GLOSSARY OF COMMON ABBREVIATIONS

AP .... Armor Piercing
AT .... Antitank
Atchd (unit) . Attached Unit
Bn .... Battalion
CG .... Commanding General
CO .... Commanding Officer
COP .... Combat Outpost
CP .... Command Post
CR .... Crossroads
D Day .... Day of an attack
Det .... Detachment
EM .... Enlisted Man
ETO .... European Theatre of Operations
Ex .... Executive (Officer)
FM .... Field Manual
FO .... Field Order
GI .... Government Issue
H Hour .... Zero Hour
HQ .... Headquarters
Incl .... Inclusive
Inf .... Infantry
IP .... Initial Point
LD .... Line of Departure
LP .... Listening Post
LM .... Land Mine
Mbl .... Mobile
MC .... Medical Corps
MLR .... Main Line of Resistance
MP .... Military Police(man)
Msg (Cen) ... Message (Center)
NCO .... Non-Commissioned Officer
O .... Officer
OP .... Observation Post
OPL .... Outpost Line
Pt .... Point
Prcht .... Parachute
PW .... Prisoner(s) of War
RB .... Road Bend
Rcn .... Reconnaissance
RCT .... Regimental Combat Team
Rd .... Road
RJ .... Road Junction
RR .... Railroad
Rr Gd........... Rear Guard
RRL............. Regimental Reserve Line
Sig .... Signal
SOP .... Standard Operating Procedure
Sup Pt .... Supply Point
S-1 .... Personnel Officer, and sometimes Adjutant, as well.
S-2 .... Intelligence Officer
S-3 .... Operations (Plans) and Training Officer.
S-4 .... Supply Officer
TBA............. Table of Basic Allowance
Tk .... Tank
T/O .... Table of Organization
T/O & E....... Table of Organization and Equipment
W Sup......... Water Supply
XO .... Executive Officer

LIST OF FIELD MANUALS AND TECHNICAL MANUALS

Field Manuals

FM 5-20A Camouflage of Individuals and Infantry Weapons (February 1944).

FM 5-20C Camouflage of Bivouacs, Command Posts, Supply Points, and Medical Installations (May 1944).

FM 5-25 Explosives and Demolitions (29 February 1944).

FM 5-30 Obstacle Technique (30 June 1943).

FM 5-31 Land Mines and Booby Traps (1 November 1943).

FM 5-34 Engineer Field Data (1947).

FM 5-35 Reference Data (24 March 1944).

FM 7-10 Rifle Company, Rifle Regiment (2 June 1942).

FM 7-20 Infantry Battalion (1 October 1944).

FM 17-40 Armored Infantry Company (November 1944).

FM 21-6 Basic Field Manual. List of Publications for Training (1 February 1944) (Change 7) (1 September 1944).

FM 21-13 Army Life (10 August 1944).

FM 21-20 Physical Training (March 1941). or FM 21-20 Physical Training (January 1946).

FM 21-25 Elementary Map and Aerial Photograph Reading (15 August 1944).

FM 21-75 Scouting, Patrolling, and Sniping (6 February 1944).

FM 21-100 Basic Field Manual. Soldier's Handbook (23 July 1941).

FM 22-5 Infantry Drill Regulations (4 August 1941).

FM 23- Basic Weapons (an extensive list of field manuals pertaining to individual weapons under this heading).

FM 24-5 Signal Communication (19 October 1942) (+Changes 1-7).

FM 24-18 Radio Communication (January 1944).

FM 24-75 Telephone Switchboard Operating Procedure (November 1944).

FM 27-10 Rules of Land Warfare (1940).

FM 31-30 Tactics and Techniques of Airborne Troops (1942).

FM 105-5 Umpire Manual (10 March 1944).

Technical Manuals

TM 5-325 Enemy Land Mines and Booby Traps (April 1945).

TM 9- Ordnance (an extensive list of technical manuals pertaining to individual weapons under this heading).

TM 11-227 Signal Communications Equipment Directory. Radio Communications Equipment (20 April 1944).

TM 11-235 Radio Sets SCR-536-A, -B, -C, -D, -E, and -F (May 1945).

TM 11-242 Radio Set SCR-300-A (15 June 1943) (+Supplements 1-3).

TM 11-333 Telephones EE-8, EE-8-A and EE-8-B (March 1945).

TM 11-454 The Radio Operator (12 May 1943).

TM 11-462 Signal Corps Reference Data (25 September 1944).

TM 12-260 Personnel Classification Tests (31 December 1942).

TM 12-407 Officer Classification – Commissioned and Warrant: Military Classification and Coding. Field Operations (30 October 1943).

TM 12-427 Military Occupational Classification of Enlisted Personnel (12 July 1944).

TM 27-251 Treaties Governing Land Warfare (7 January 1944).

TME 30-451 Handbook on German Military Forces (March 1945).

Table of Basic Allowances No. 7
Table of Basic Allowances No. 21
Table of Organization 7-31 and **Table of Organization 7-31T***
Parachute Infantry Regiment
- 17 February 1942
- 16 December 1944 (with changes C1-C2)

Table of Organization 7-32 and **Table of Organization 7-32T***
Parachute Infantry Regiment, Infantry Headquarters & Headquarters Company,
- 17 February 1942
- 1 August 1944
- 16 December 1944 (with changes C1-C2)

Table of Organization 7-35 and **Table of Organization 7-35T***
Parachute Infantry Battalion,
- 17 (or 7?) February 1942
- 24 February 1944*
- 1 August 1944
- 16 December 1944 (with Changes C1-C2)*

Table of Organization 7-36 and **Table of Organization 7-36T***
Parachute Infantry Battalion, Headquarters & Headquarters Company,
- 1 July 1941
- 17 February 1942
- 1 August 1944
- 16 December 1944 (with changes C1-C2)*

Table of Organization 7-37 and **Table of Organization 7-36T***
Parachute Infantry Battalion, Parachute Infantry Company
- 1 July 1941
- 17 February 1942
- 1 August 1944
- 16 December 1944 (with changes C1-C2)*

Table of Organization 2-77T
Reconnaissance Platoon, Airborne Division
- 16 December 1944

ENDNOTES

Prologue

1. Paraphrased from Ross, Kirk, B., *Airborne All the Way!, Reenacting the All Americans of World War II*, published in Living History, Summer 1997, p. 42.

Introduction

1. Paraphrased from McCullough, David, *John Adams*, Simon & Schuster Audioworks, 2001. A March 25, 1826, letter from Thomas Jefferson discussing Jefferson's grandson's intent to visit John Adams.

2. Adams, Michael C.C., *The Best War Ever, America and World War II*, The Johns Hopkins University Press, Baltimore, 1994; Marshall, S.L.A., *Men Against Fire, The Problem of Battle Command*, University of Oklahoma Press, Norman, 2000.

3. Adams, Michael C.C., *The Best War Ever, America and World War II*, The Johns Hopkins University Press, Baltimore, 1994, p. 90.

Chapter 1, Historical Reconnaissance

1. Ross, Kirk B., The Sky Men, Schiffer Publishing, Ltd., Atglen, 2000, used with permission by the author.

2. Goolrick, William K., Editor, *The Home Front: U.S.A.*, Time-Life Books, Chicago, 1978, pp. 42-45, 47, and quoted from p. 44.

3. Ibid., pp. 44-45, and quoted from p. 45.

4. Ibid., p. 47.

5. Ibid., quoted from p. 49.

6. Ibid., p. 52.

7. Ibid., quoted from p. 55.

8. Ibid., pp. 30-39.

9. Craik, Dinah Mulock, 1826-1887.

10. D'Este, Carlo, *Fatal Decision, Anzio and the Battle for Rome*, HarperCollins Publishers, New York, 1991, p. 319.

11. Ross, Robert T., *The Supercommandos, First Special Service Force 1942-1944, An Illustrated History*, Schiffer Publishing Ltd., Atglen, 2000; Adelman, Robert H., and Walton, Col. George, *The Devil's Brigade*, Chilton Books, New York, 1966; Burhans, Robert D., *The First Special Service Force, A War History of the North Americans 1942-1944*, The Battery Press, Nashville, 1996; D'Este, Carlo, *Fatal Decision, Anzio and the Battle for Rome*, HarperCollins Publishers, New York, 1991.

12. D'Este, Carlo, *Fatal Decision, Anzio and the Battle for Rome*, HarperCollins Publishers, New York, 1991, p. 323.

13. Hyams, Jay, *War Movies*, W.H. Smith Publishers, Inc., New York, 1984, pp. 6-9, 98-100, 114.

Bullet Point: Dog Tags

1. *The Officer's Guide*, 9th Edition, July 1942; Army Regulations AR 600-35, Section VI, 31 March 1944; AR 600-40, Section III, 31 March 1944; FM 10-63 Graves Registration, 15 January 1945; War Department Pamphlet 21-13 Army Life, 10 August 1944; TM 12-250 Administration, February 10, 1942; Army Service Forces Catalog MED 3, 1 March 1944; Quartermaster Supply Catalog QM 3-4, 1945.

Bullet Point: Chronology of the War

1. Eisenhower, Dwight D., *Crusade In Europe*, Doubleday and Company, Inc., Garden City, 1948, paraphrased and also quoted from pp. 518-522; Kemp, Anthony, *D-Day and the Invasion of Normandy*, Harry N. Abrahams, Inc., Publishers, 1994, pp. 182-183; *History of the War*, New York Journal American, August 25, 1945.

U.S. Army Airborne Unit Combat Chronicles

1. Stanton, Shelby L., World War II Order of Battle, Galahad Books, New York, 1984, quoted there from; The Center of Military History, Airborne Division Combat Chronicles, http://www.history.army.mil/html/forcestruc/cbtchron/abndiv.html.

Chapter 2, Looking the Part

1. *The Officer's Guide, 10th Edition*, The Military Service Publishing Co., Harrisburg, 1944, pp. 115, 117, 125-139.

2. Ibid., p. 128.

3. Ibid., pp. 115-116.

4-14. Ibid., quoted and/or copied verbatim or nearly verbatim, pp. 141-145.

15. War Department, *FM 21-100, Basic Field Manual, Soldier's Handbook*, U.S. Government Printing Office, Washington, 1941, p. 18.

16. Katcher, Philip, *The American Soldier: U.S. Armies In Uniform, 1755 To the Present, Osprey Publishing, Ltd.*, New York, 1990, p. 172.

17.-18. *The Officer's Guide, 10th Edition*, The Military Service Publishing Co., Harrisburg, 1944, quoted and/or copied verbatim or nearly verbatim, p. 146.

19. Ibid., pp. 158-161.

20. Ibid., pp. 162-163.

21. Ibid., pp. 158-162.

Chapter 3, Tools of A Grim Trade

1. Adams, Michael C.C., *The Best War Ever, America and World War II*, The Johns Hopkins University Press, Baltimore, 1994, p. 102.

Parts I-IV. Ross, Robert T., *The Supercommandos, First Special Service Force 1942-1944, An Illustrated History*, Schiffer Publishing Ltd., Atglen, 2000, pp. 258-271.

2. War Department, *Technical Manual TM9-1940, Land Mines, July 14, 1943*.

3.-10. Quoted and/or paraphrased from War Department, *Field Manual FM 5-30, Obstacle Technique*, pp. 1-2, 23-26.

11.-14. Quoted and/or paraphrased from War Department, *Field Manual FM 5-31 Land Mines and Booby Traps, 1 November 1943*.

15. (from FM 5-30, Obstacle Technique, pp. 48-49)

16. Quoted and/or paraphrased from War Department, *Field Manual FM 5-31 Land Mines and Booby Traps, 1 November 1943*; War Department, *Field Manual FM 5-30, Obstacle Technique*, pp. 63-69.

17. Quoted and/or paraphrased from War Department, *Field Manual FM 5-30, Obstacle Technique*, pp. 65-67.

18.-23. Quoted and/or paraphrased from War Department, *FM 5-25 Explosives and Demolitions, 29 February 1944*, pp. 1-30.

Chapter 4, Soldiering Skills

1.-3. 17. *Quoted nearly verbatim and paraphrased from wartime pamphlet, The Information Hand Book for the Soldier*.

4. Quoted from, *The Officer's Guide, 10th Edition*, The Military Service Publishing Co., Harrisburg, 1944, quoted and/or copied verbatim or nearly verbatim, p. 322.

5.-6. 10., 12.-14., 18. War Department, *FM 21-100, Basic Field Manual, Soldier's Handbook*, U.S. Government Printing Office, Washington, 1941.

7.-9. 11., 15.-16. Quoted and paraphrased from, *The Officer's Guide, 10th Edition*, The Military Service Publishing Co., Harrisburg, 1944, quoted and/or copied verbatim or nearly verbatim, pp. 319, 321-324.

19. Eisenhower, Dwight D., *Crusade In Europe*, Doubleday & Company, Inc., Garden City, New York, 1948, p. 158.

20.-25. Quoted directly from: *FM 7-10, Infantry Field Manual, Rifle Company, Rifle Regiment*, War Department, June 2, 1942, pp. 7-11.

26. Ibid., pp. 186-187.

27. Ibid., pp. 120, 202-213.

28. Excerpts from: *First Special Service Force, Lessons Learned from the Italian Campaign*.

29. Quoted directly from: *FM 7-10, Infantry Field Manual, Rifle Company, Rifle Regiment*, War Department, June 2, 1942, pp. 179-180.

30. Quoted directly from: *FM-21-75, Scouting, Patrolling, and Sniping*, War Department, 6 February 1944, p. 105.

31. Quoted directly from Ross, Kirk B., *EM 1-01 The Field Guide, Operations Memorandum Number 1: "Notes On Woods Fighting,"* pp. 21-42, and based on U.S. War Department, *Handbook on German Military Forces*, Louisiana State University Press, Baton Rouge, 1990; Wilson, George, *If You Survive: From Normandy to the Battle of the Bulge to the End of World War II - One American Officer's Riveting True Story*, Ivy Books, New York, 1987; and Doubler, LtCol. Michael D., *Closing with the Enemy: How GIs Fought the War in Europe, 1944-1945*, University of Kansas Press, Lawrence, 1994.

32. Quoted directly from: *FM 7-10, Infantry Field Manual, Rifle Company, Rifle Regiment*, War Department, June 2, 1942, pp. 199-201.

33. Forty, George, *U.S. Army Handbook, 1939-1945*, Alan Sutton Publishing, Ltd., Phoenix Mill, 1995, p. 172.

34-35. Quoted directly from: *FM 22-5, Basic Field Manual, Infantry Drill Regulations*, Government Printing Office, Washington, 1941, pp. 186-194.

36.-38. Quoted directly and/or paraphrased from FM 21-25, Elementary Map and Aerial Photograph Reading, 15August 1944, pp. 19, 21-23.

39. War Department, *FM 21-100, Basic Field Manual, Soldier's Handbook*, U.S. Government Printing Office, Washington, 1941, p. 163.

40. Quoted directly and/or paraphrased from FM 21-25, Elementary Map and Aerial Photograph Reading, 15August 1944, pp. 29-30.

41. Ibid., p. 35.

41. War Department, *FM 21-100, Basic Field Manual, Soldier's Handbook*, U.S. Government Printing Office, Washington, 1941, pp. 155-159.

Bullet Point: Sound Off

1. WordOrigins.org.

Bullet Point: Form for Field Orders

1. 32. Forty, George, *U.S. Army Handbook, 1939-1945*, Alan Sutton Publishing, Ltd., Phoenix Mill, 1995, pp. 204-205.

Chapter 5, Putting It All Together

1. Doubler, LtCol. Michael D., *Closing with the Enemy: How GIs Fought the War in Europe, 1944-1945*, University of Kansas Press, Lawrence, 1994; Adams, Michael C.C., *The Best War Ever, America and World War II*, The Johns Hopkins University Press, Baltimore, 1994.

2. Adams, Michael C.C., *The Best War Ever, America and World War II*, The Johns Hopkins University Press, Baltimore, 1994, p. 101.

3. Baron, Richard, Major Abe Baum and Richard Goldhurst, *Raid!, The Untold Story of Patton's Secret Mission*. G.P. Putnam's Sons, New York, 1981.

SUGGESTED READING

Adams, Michael C.C., *The Best War Ever, America and World War II*, The Johns Hopkins University Press, Baltimore, 1994.

Ambrose, Stephen E., *Band of Brothers, E Company, 506th Regiment, 101st Airborne From Normandy to Hitler's Eagle's Nest*, Touchstone Simon and Schuster, New York, 1992.

Andrews, John C., *Airborne Album Volume One: Parachute Test Platoon To Normandy*, Phhillips Publications, Williamstown, 1982.

– , *Airborne Album 1943-1945: Normandy To Victory*, Phillips Publications, Williamsburg.

Autrey, Jerry, *William C. Lee Father of the Airborne, "Just Plain Bill,"* Airborne Press, Raleigh, 1995.

Bando, Mark, *The 101st Airborne at Normandy*, Motorbooks International, Osceola, 1994.

– , *The 101st Airborne From Holland To Hitler's Eagle's Nest*, Motorbooks International, Osceola, 1995.

– , *The 101st Airborne: The Screaming Eagles At Normandy*, Motorbooks International, Osceola, 2000.

Baron, Richard, Major Abe Baum and Richard Goldhurst, *Raid!, The Untold Story of Patton's Secret Mission*. G.P. Putnam's Sons, New York, 1981.

Blair, Clay, *Ridgway's Paratroopers, The American Airborne in World War II*, Dail Press, New York, 1985.

Breuer, William B., *Drop Zone Sicily*, Presidio Press, Novato, 1983.

– , *Geronimo! American Paratroopers in World War II*, St. Martin's Press, New York, 1989.

– , *Operation Dragoon, The Allied Invasion of the South of France*, Presidio Press, Novato, 1987.

Burgett, Donald R., *Curahee: A Screaming Eagle At Normandy*, Houghton Mifflin, New York, 1967.

– , *The Road To Arnhem, A Screaming Eagle In Holland*, Presidio Press, Novato, 1999.

– , *Seven Roads To Hell: A Screaming Eagle At Bastogne*, Presidio Press, Novato, 1999.

– , *Beyond the Rhine: A Screaming Eagle In Germany*, Presidio Press, Novato, 2001.

Carter, Ross, *Those Devils In Baggy Pants*, Signet Books, New York, 1951.

Crookenden, Napier, *Dropzone Normandy*, Charles Scribner's Sons, New York, 1976.

Davis, Brian L., *Key Uniform Guides 6; US Airborne Forces Of World War Two*, Lionel Leventhal Limited, London, 1974.

D'Este, Carlo, *Fatal Decision, Anzio and the Battle for Rome*, HarperCollins Publishers, New York, 1991.

De Trez, Michel, *American Warriors, Pictorial History of the American Paratroopers Prior To Normandy*, D-Day Publishing, Wezembeek-Oppem, Belgium, 1994.

– , *At the Point of No Return, Pictorial History of the American Paratroopers In the Invasion of Normandy*, D-Day Publishing, Wezembeek-Oppem, Belgium, 1994.

– , *Saint-Mere-Eglise: Photographs of D-Day, 6 June 1944*, D-Day Publishing, Wezembeek-Oppem, Belgium, 2005.

Devlin, Gerard M. (1979): *Paratrooper!, The Saga Of The U.S. Army and Marine Parachute Troops During World War II*, St. Martin's Press Inc., New York, 1979.

Doubler, LtCol. Michael D., *Closing with the Enemy: How GIs Fought the War in Europe, 1944-1945*, University of Kansas Press, Lawrence, 1994.

Egger, Bruce E., and Otts, Lee MacMillan, *G Company's War, Two Personal Accounts of the Campaigns in Europe, 1944-1945*, The University of Alabama Press, Tuscaloosa, 1992.

Eisenhower, Dwight D., *Crusade In Europe*, Doubleday & Company, Inc., Garden City, New York, 1948.

Foley, Jr., William A., *Visions From a Foxhole, A Rifleman In Patton's Ghost Corps*, Ballantine Books, New York, 2003.

Forty, George, *U.S. Army Handbook, 1939-1945*, Alan Sutton Publishing, Ltd., Phoenix Mill, 1995.

Gabel, Kurt, *The Making Of A Paratrooper; Airborne Training and Combat In World War II*, University Press Of Kansas, Lawrence, 1990.

Gavin, James M., *Airborne Warfare*, Infantry Journal Press, Washington D.C., 1947.

– , *On To Berlin*, The Viking Press, New York, 1978.

Gawne, Jonathan, *Spearheading D-Day*, Histoire & Collections, Paris, 1998.

Goldman, William, *William Goldman's Story Of A Bridge Too Far*, Dell Publishing, New York, 1977.

Howard, Gary, *America's Finest, US Airborne Uniforms, Equipment, and Insignia Of World War Two*, Greenhill Books, London, 1994.

Hoyt, Edwin P., *Airborne, The History Of The American Parachute Forces*, M.C.N. Press, Tulsa, 1978.

Hunter, D.P., *U.S. Army Infantry Rifle Squad and Platoon Organization and Tactics, 1944*.

Hyams, Jay, *War Movies*, W.H. Smith Publishers, Inc., New York, 1984.

Kemp, Anthony, *D-Day and the Invasion of Normandy*, Harry N. Abrams, Inc., Publishers, 1994.

Langdon, Allen L., Ready, *A World War II History Of The 505th Parachute Infantry Regiment*, 82nd Airborne Division Association Educational Fund Inc., Western Newspaper Publishing Co. Inc., Indianapolis, 1986.

Lassen, Don & Schrader, K., *Pride Of America, An Illustrated History Of The U.S. Army Airborne Forces*, Pictorial Histories Publishing Inc. Missoula, 1991.

Laughlin, Cameron P., *Uniforms Illustrated No. 18, US Airborne Forces Of World War Two*, Arms And Armor Press, London, 1987.

Leinbaugh, Harold P., and Campbell, John D., *The Men of Company K, The Autobiography of a World War II Rifle Company*, William Morrow and Company, Inc., New York, 1985.

MacDonald, Charles B., *Company Commander*, Infantry Journal Press, Washington, DC, 1947.

– , *A Time for Trumpets, The Untold Story of the Battle of the Bulge*, William Morrow & Company, New York, 1985.

MacKenzie, Fred, *The Men Of Bastogne*, David McKay Co. Inc., 1986.

Marshall, S. L. A., *Night Drop, The American Airborne Invasion Of Normandy*, Little Brown & Company Inc. New York, 1962.

Mauldin, Bill, *Up Front*, Henry Holt and Company, New York, 1944.

Mitchell, Ralph B., *The 101st Airborne Division's Defense Of Bastogne*, Combat Studies Institute, Fort Leavenworth, Kansas, 1986.

Orfalea, Gregory, *Messengers of the Lost Battalion, The Heroic 551st and the Turning of the Tide at the Battle of the Bulge*, The Free Press, New York, 1997.

Ospital, John, *We Wore Jump Boots And Baggy Pants*, Willow House, 1977.

Pyle, Ernie, *Brave Men*, Henry Holt and Company, New York, 1944.

Rathbone, A. D., *He's In The Paratroops Now*, Robert M. McBride & Company, New York, 1943.

Rentz, Bill, *Gernimo, U.S. Airborne Uniforms, Insignia, And Equipment In World War II*, Schiffer Military History Atglen, PA, 1999.

Ridgeway, Matthew B., as told to Harold H. Martin, *Soldier: The Memoirs of Matthew B. Ridgeway*, Harper & Row Publishers, Inc., New York, 1956.

Ross, Kirk B., *The Sky Men, A Parachute Rifle Company's Story of the Battle of Bulge and the Jump Across the Rhine*, Schiffer Publishing, Ltd., Atglen, 2000.

Ross, Robert T., *The Supercommandos, First Special Service Force, 1942-1944, An Illustrated History*, Schiffer Publishing, Ltd, Atglen, 2000.

– , *U.S. Army Rangers and Special Forces of World War II, Their War in Photographs*, Schiffer Publishing, Ltd., Atglen, 2002.

Rottman, Gordon, *US Army Airborne 1940-1990*, Osprey Publishing LTD, London, 1990.

Rush, Robert S., *US Infantryman in World War II (2), Mediterranean Theater of Operations 1942-45*, Oprey Publishing, Oxford, England, 2002.

– , *US Infantryman in World War II (3), European Theater of Operations 1944-45*, Oprey Publishing, Oxford, England, 2002.

Ryan, Cornelius, *The Longest Day*, Simon And Schuster, New York, 1959.

– , *A Bridge Too Far*, Simon And Schuster, New York, 1974.

Smith, Carl, & Chappell, Mike, *US Paratrooper 1941-45*, Osprey Publishing LTD, London, 2000.

Standifer, Leon C., *Not In Vain, A Rifleman Remembers World War II*, Louisiana State University Press, Baton Rouge, 1992.

Thompson, Leroy, *Uniforms Illustrated No. 1; US Special Forces of World War Two*, Arms And Armour Press, Lionel Leventhatl Limited, London, 1984.

– , *The All Americans, The 82nd Airborne*, David and Charles, Devon, England, 1988.

Tucker, William H., *The 82nd Airborne in World War II, From North Africa To Italy and D-Day Through the Battle of the Bulge*, Airborne Books, Harwichport.

– , *Rendezvous at Rochelinval The Battle of the Bulge*, Airborne Books, Harwichport.

– , *Parachute Soldier, A Memoir of World War II Experiences As An 82nd Airborne Paratrooper*, (Second Revised Edition), Airborne Books, Harwichport, 1995.

U.S. War Department, *Handbook on German Military Forces*, Louisiana State University Press, Baton Rouge, 1990.

Webster, David, K., *Parachute Infantry, An American Paratrooper's Memoir of D-Day and the Fall of the Third Reich*, Louisiana State University Press, 1994.

Weeks, John, *Assault From The Sky; A History Of Airborne Warfare*, G. P. Putnam's Sons, New York, 1978.

– , *The Airborne Soldier*, Blandford Press LTD, Dorset, England, 1982.

Weller, George, *The Story of the Paratroopers*, Random House Inc., New York 1958.

Whiting, Charles, *48 Hours To Hammelburg, Patton's Secret Mission*, Ballantine, New York, 1970.

Wilson, George, *If You Survive: From Normandy to the Battle of the Bulge to the End of World War II - One American Officer's Riveting True Story*, Ivy Books, New York, 1987.

NOTES

NOTES

NOTES

NOTES

NOTES

THANKS ...

The author wishes to thank the members of Company E, 508th Parachute Infantry Regiment, 82nd Airborne Division (Living History) for portraying so well Parachute Infantrymen. Pictured are, standing l to r, Brian Domitrovich, Thomas Soltis, Steven Feige, Robert Podolinski, Robert Field, Joseph P. Soltis, Ron Allen, Daniel Benfer, Ken Podlaszewski, Ron Weaver; and kneeling l to r, Morgen Dautrich, Joshua Allen, Neil Baughman, Andrew Soltis, Jordan Rhodes, Chris Domitrovich, Matt Podlaszewski, and not pictured, Steve Soltis. (www.508pir.com).